Hollywood

IN VINTAGE POSTCARDS

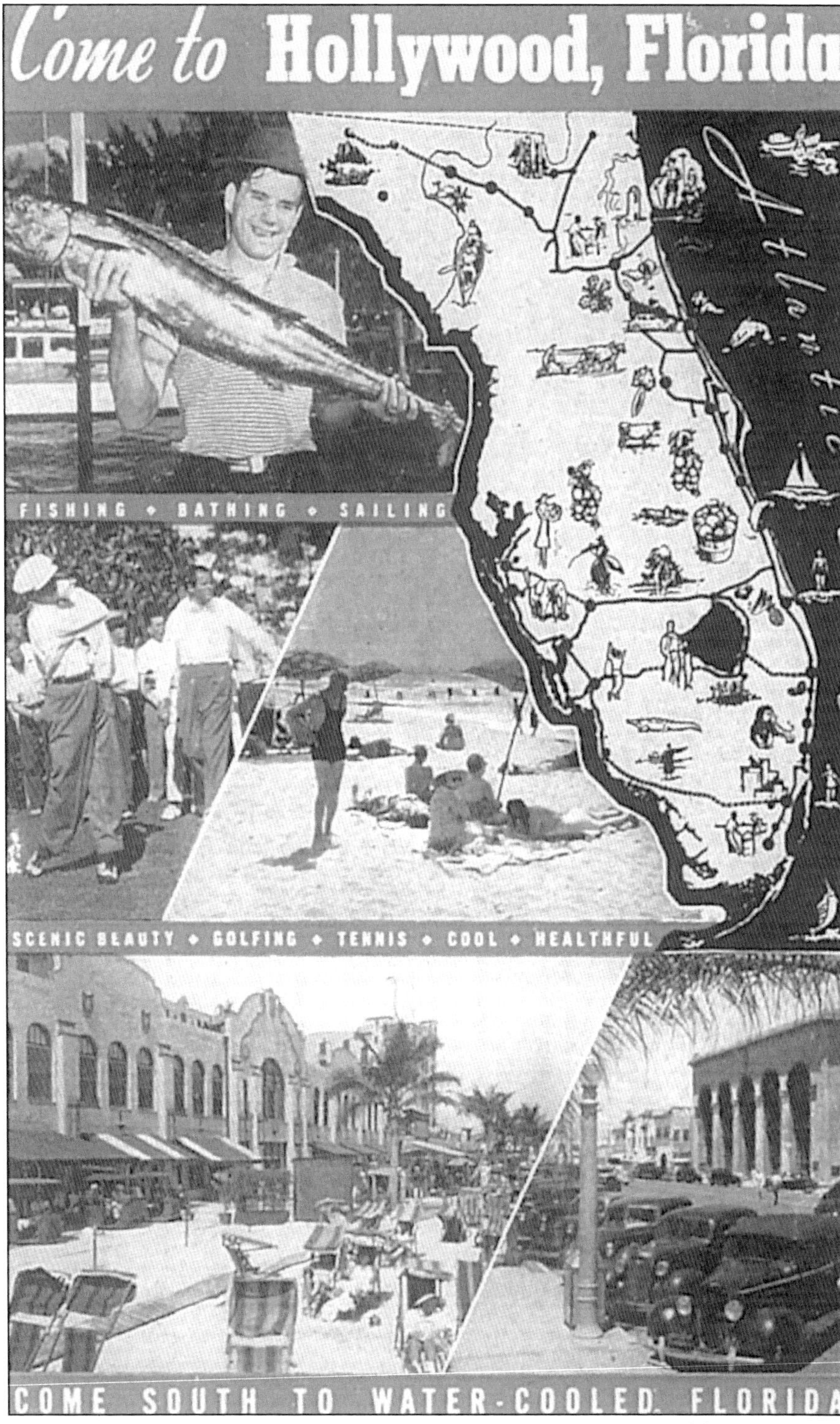

Come along on this visit through the history of Hollywood, Florida, as told by its postcards.

Hollywood

IN VINTAGE POSTCARDS

Bonnie Wilpon

ARCADIA
PUBLISHING

ISBN 978-0-7385-0218-2

Published by Arcadia Publishing
Charleston, South Carolina

Printed in the United States of America

Library of Congress Control Number: 99-65368

For all general information contact Arcadia Publishing at:
Telephone 843-853-2070
Fax 843-853-0044
E-mail sales@arcadiapublishing.com
For customer service and orders:
Toll-Free 1-888-313-2665

Visit us on the Internet at www.arcadiapublishing.com

Contents

Acknowledgments 6

Introduction 7

1. The Dream and the Destruction 9

2. Changing Landmarks 27

3. Homes and Hotels 43

4. Community Life 67

5. Shopping and Restaurants 87

6. Recreation and Tourism 109

ACKNOWLEDGMENTS

I am grateful to my family, Al and Evelyn Wilpon, Amy and Bruce Weinberg, and Todd and Julie Wilpon, for sharing their Hollywood experiences. Many thanks to Dana and Sue Sanborn for allowing several of the postcards from their collection to be used in this book. This book is dedicated to my nieces and nephews, Alexis, Evan, Francie and Trevor, to help them know and appreciate both their history and their future.

Introduction

Hollywood-by-the-Sea was a dream that began in the mind of one man and became a reality through his strength, charisma, investment, and intensely hard work. Joseph Young, to some just the name of the park in the downtown circle, turned his vision into a thriving city.

The story of Hollywood is one of the most inspirational in Florida's history. It's the saga of a dream that, just when it was almost realized, was crushed—quite literally—by the forces of nature. It's the tale of a town made up of a conglomeration of people from all over the United States and Canada, whose residents banded together to rebuild their lives, their hopes, and their city.

In 1896 Henry Flagler's trains first began running between Fort Lauderdale and Miami. The railroad created cities from land Flagler donated in exchange for the railroad project and the dredging on the Intracoastal Waterway, which was done by his Florida Coast Line Canal & Transportation Company. Representatives of Flagler's Model Land Company established Modello (later called Dania) and Hallandale in 1898. Around 1915 a group of settlers who had worked on the Panama Canal founded Zona, which later became Davie, the first settlement on land reclaimed through drainage. No settlement, however, had developed in the coastal swamp between Modello and Hallandale; the area remained occupied by only a few farmers. The site intrigued Joseph Wesley Young and it would later become the community he saw so clearly in his imagination.

Born on August 4, 1882, in Gig Harbor, Washington, Joseph was the son of a boat captain. He went to sea at age 14 and later adventured to the Yukon for the great gold rush. In 1905 he was part of a new real estate investment company in California. Its partners had a brainstorm that would revolutionize home sales. Rather than just selling lots or individual houses, they would plan and develop whole communities including streets, public buildings, parks, and commercial areas.

Young traveled to Miami in 1920 to sell acreage to raise money for the city he had already built in his mind's eye. He outlined the design that still makes Hollywood a beautiful city. "There will be a wide boulevard extending from the ocean westward to the edge of the Everglades. We'll create 2 lakes, each with a turning basin for yachts. Centrally located on the plat will be the business section. This will be a city for everyone—from the opulent at the top of the industrial and social ladders to the most humble of working people."

During the next few years swampland became a city through Joseph Young's Hollywood Land and Water Company. There was a land boom in the 1920s along with Young's tremendous efforts to attract people to the area. By 1925 Hollywood, which didn't even exist at the beginning of the decade, boasted 20,000 residents, thriving businesses, and luxury beach hotels.

On September 17, 1926, Joseph Young's vision, along with the plans of Hollywood's new residents, was destroyed by a huge hurricane. Buildings fell like houses of cards as winds reached 140 miles per hour. Federal Highway was flooded with 18 inches of salt water and sand buried the ground floor of the elegant Hollywood Beach Hotel. The storm killed 400 people, caused property damage totaling millions of dollars, and created headlines that frightened away potential residents and effectively brought an end to the area's land boom.

Worst of all, most people, being new to living in the area, had never experienced a major hurricane and had no idea how to prepare or what to expect. Many frightened people abandoned their new homes, fleeing back to the states from which they came. But many more stayed. "We will rebuild," said Young, but he had overextended himself and his company. He had conveyed many buildings and other assets to the new city of Hollywood and couldn't meet his loan payments to the Highway Construction Company, which had installed streets and sidewalks in the new Hollywood Hills development.

That company, headed by Samuel Horvitz, bought 24,000 of Young's homesite lots for $35,000 at sheriff's sale and later became Hollywood Inc., completing much of the development envisioned by Young. Dania and Hallandale, which had asked to be annexed to Hollywood at the height of the boom in 1925, quickly de-annexed in 1927 to escape liability for the city's debts.

Hollywood's remaining residents were determined to rebuild their city, and they did. Hollywood Boulevard is still 90 feet from curb to curb (120 feet with the swales) and is filled with elegant royal palm trees. The business district is still centered between Young and Administrative Circles.

Today the city of Hollywood has a population exceeding 122,000 and is well known as a resort and residential city with the lovely Broadwalk along its Atlantic Ocean beachfront.

Although I was born in Florida, my early youth was spent in New York. My family's return to Florida in 1966 turned out to be a genuine homecoming for me. I have lived in many places since, but I've always returned to Florida's sandy shores, and the Sunshine State is truly my home.

As a teenager in Hollywood I was proud to be part of the Class of '69, the very first graduating class of Hollywood Hills High School. Hollywood honored me by presenting me with a Key to the City, as one of its top teens. It was my high school French teacher who presented the opportunity for me to study in France during the summer of 1968, and that experience kindled a love of travel that has been a major force in my life.

The city of Hollywood has opened many doors for me, and I hope this book will return the favor by opening its history to visitors, residents, and friends.

–Bonnie Wilpon
June 1999

One

The Dream and the Destruction

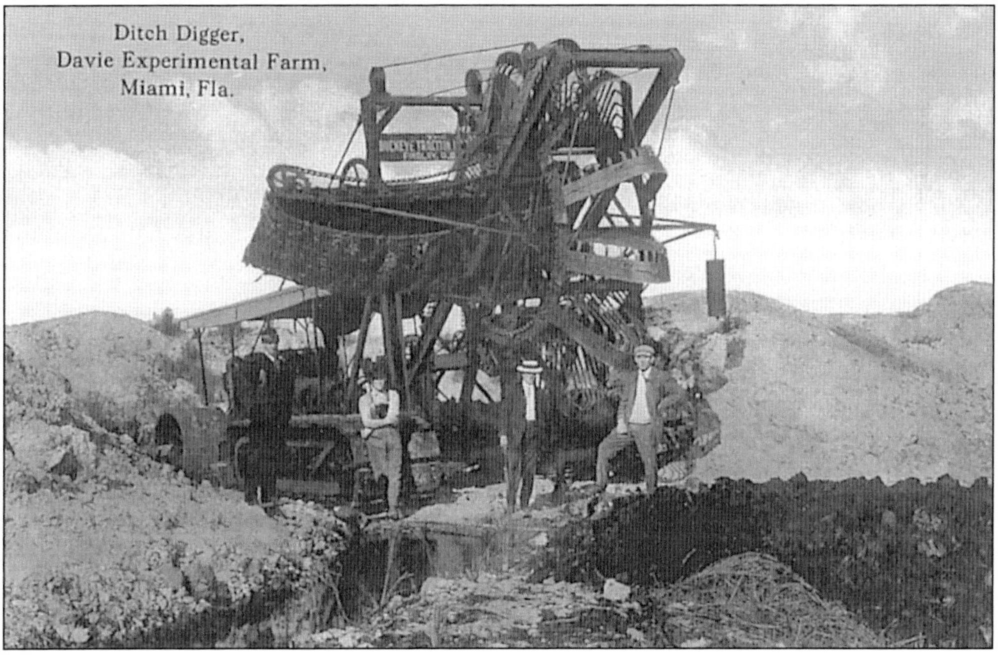

Floridians had always believed they could drain the swampy Everglades by cutting channels through its coral ridge, allowing the land to be used for farms, houses, and orange groves. In fact, Governor Broward's campaign slogan was "Water will run downhill." In 1905, during Governor Broward's administration, the digging of the first drainage canal was approved. Zona, which was later renamed Davie, was the first area to be settled on reclaimed land. But by the 1920s, it was painfully clear that the canal system would never drain the Everglades. And all that dredging created another problem—a cycle of fires and drought that continues today. Salt water eventually forced its way up the canals and into the fields, killing the orange trees in the groves that had been planted on drained Everglades acreage.

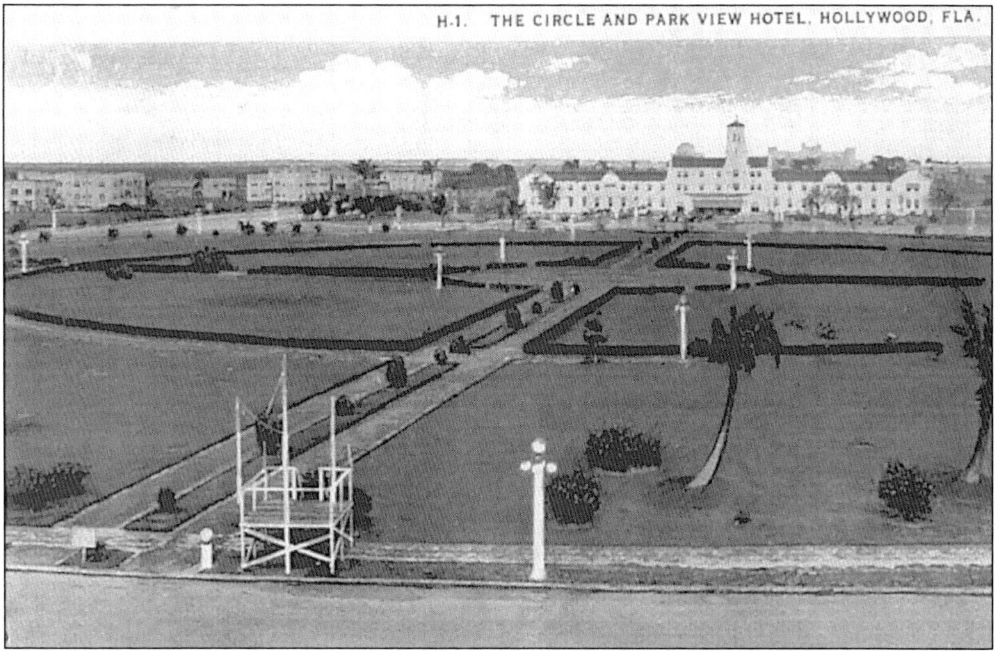

Because of the terrain and his clear mental image of Hollywood-by-the-Sea, Joseph Young leveled the entire area and built his dream city from the ground up. He began with three circles, designed to force cars to slow down and look around. The easternmost circle, later named Young Circle, has always been the heart of the city.

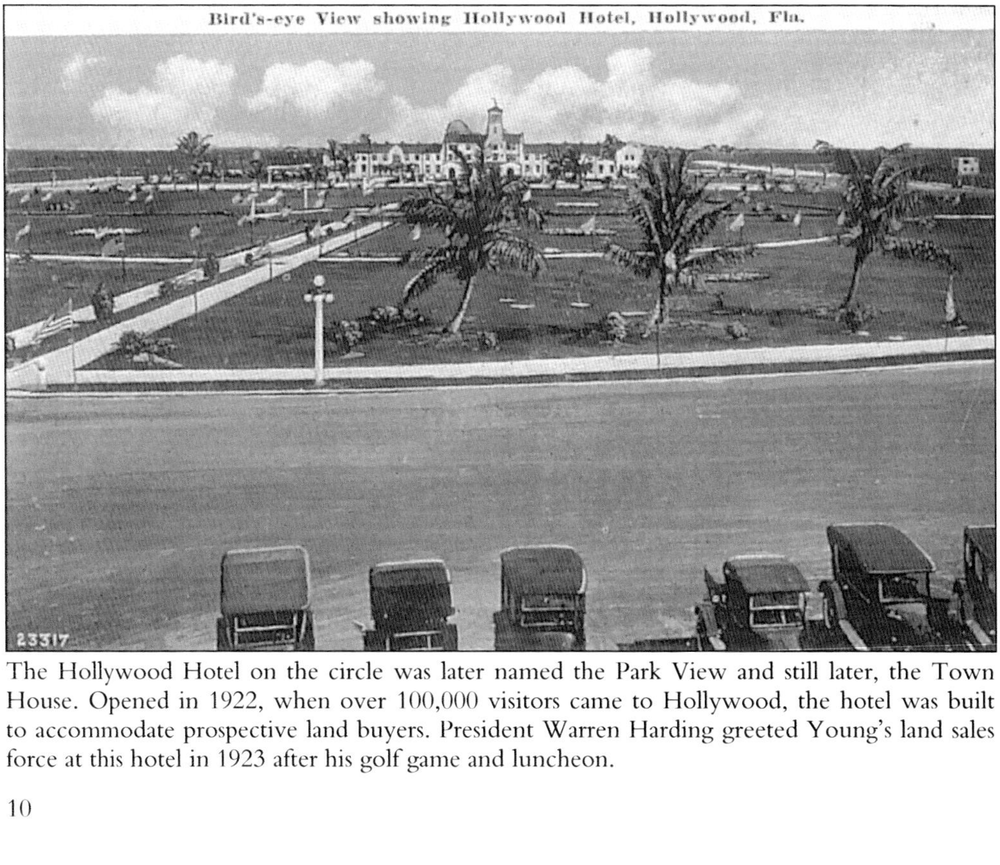

The Hollywood Hotel on the circle was later named the Park View and still later, the Town House. Opened in 1922, when over 100,000 visitors came to Hollywood, the hotel was built to accommodate prospective land buyers. President Warren Harding greeted Young's land sales force at this hotel in 1923 after his golf game and luncheon.

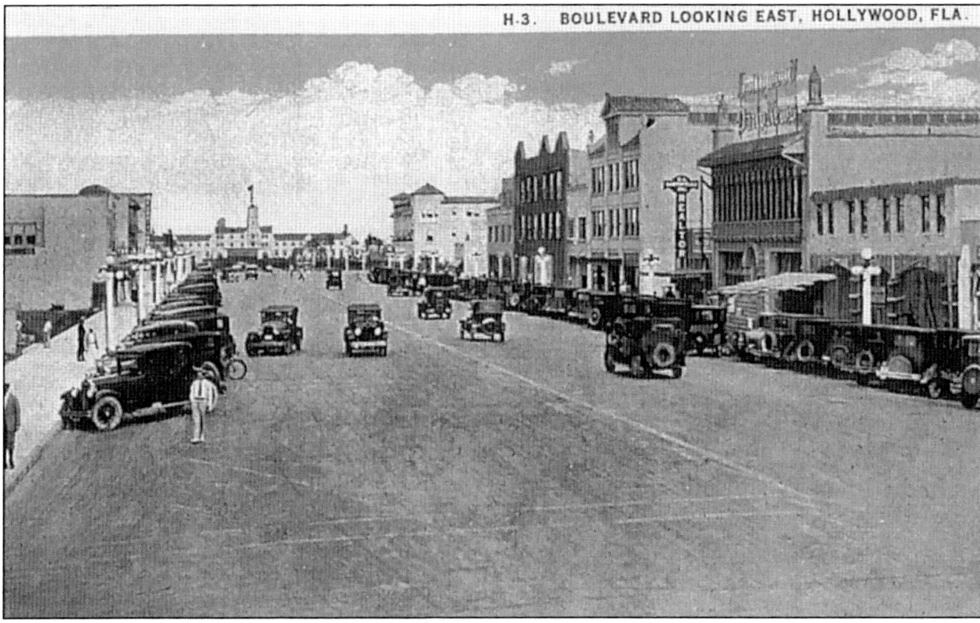

Businesses developed along Hollywood Boulevard, which connected the circles. By 1923 Hollywood was on the road to prosperity, mainly due to the boom in real estate and land development. The most prominent sign on the right side of this postcard was the realtor's.

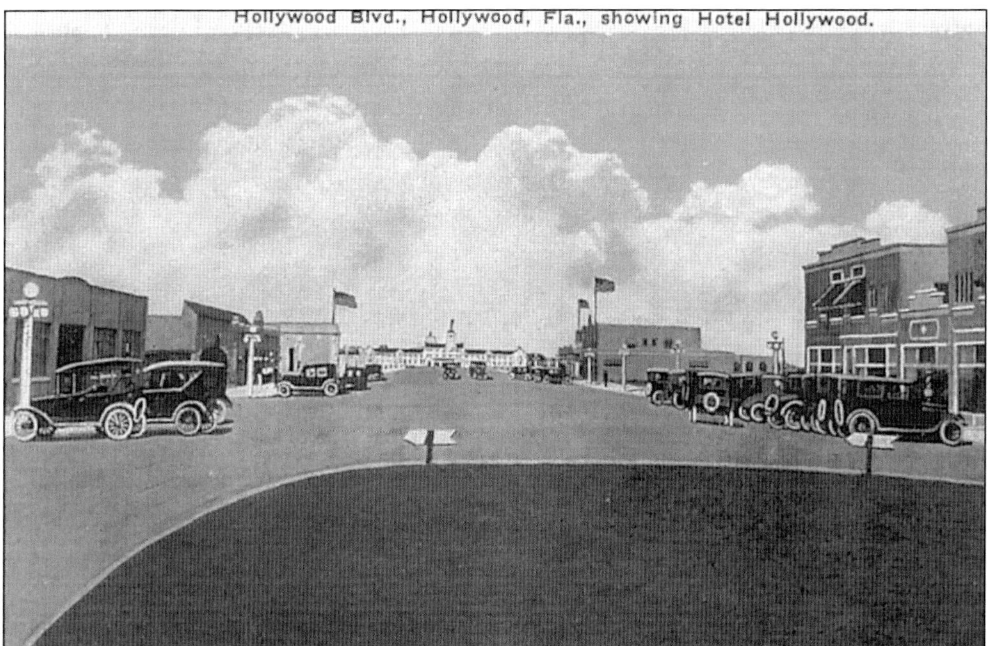

The downtown shopping and business area spread westward from the downtown circle. On November 25, 1925, Hollywood was incorporated and elected Joseph Young as its first mayor. Young resigned after two months to devote all of his time to his Hollywood Land and Water Company.

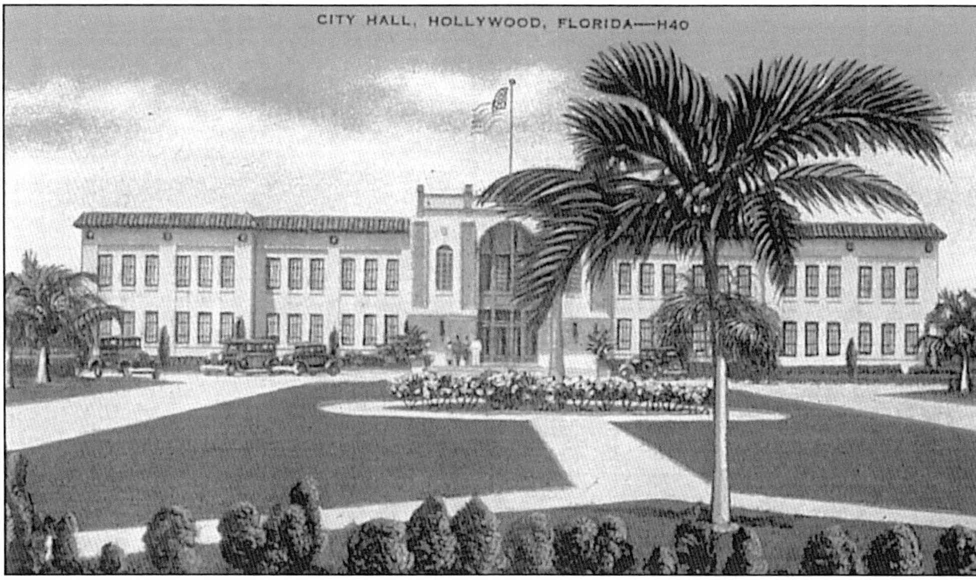

To the west, the next circle was Administrative Circle, also called City Hall Circle. Hollywood's original city hall was built there. Today the new city hall stands on this spot, and the Hollywood Public Library is right next door.

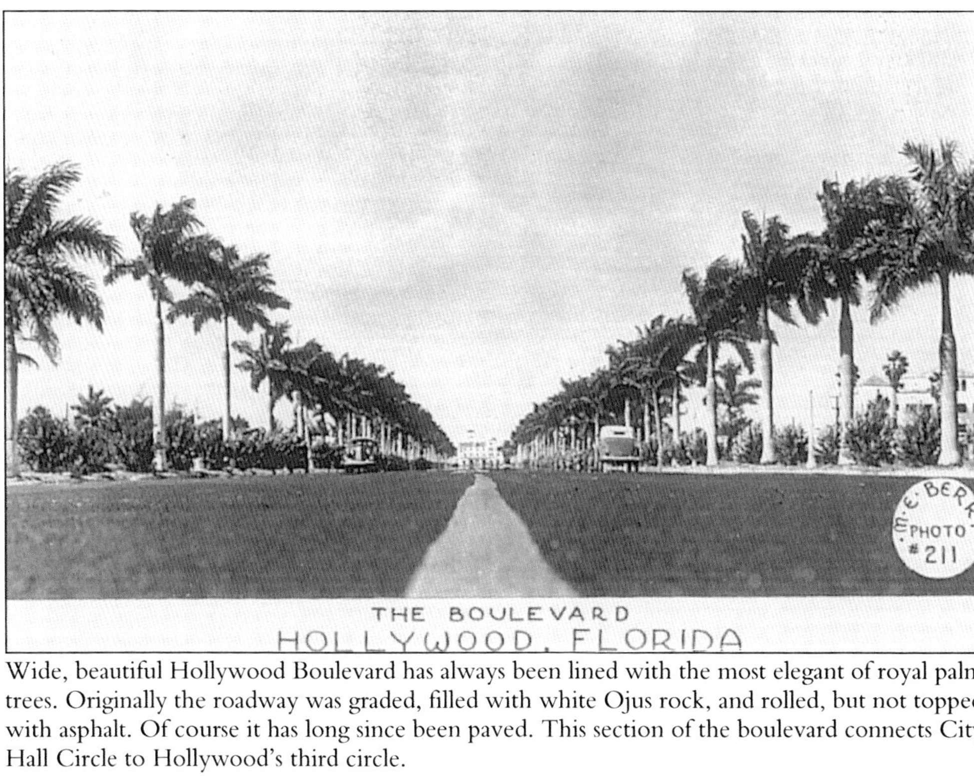

Wide, beautiful Hollywood Boulevard has always been lined with the most elegant of royal palm trees. Originally the roadway was graded, filled with white Ojus rock, and rolled, but not topped with asphalt. Of course it has long since been paved. This section of the boulevard connects City Hall Circle to Hollywood's third circle.

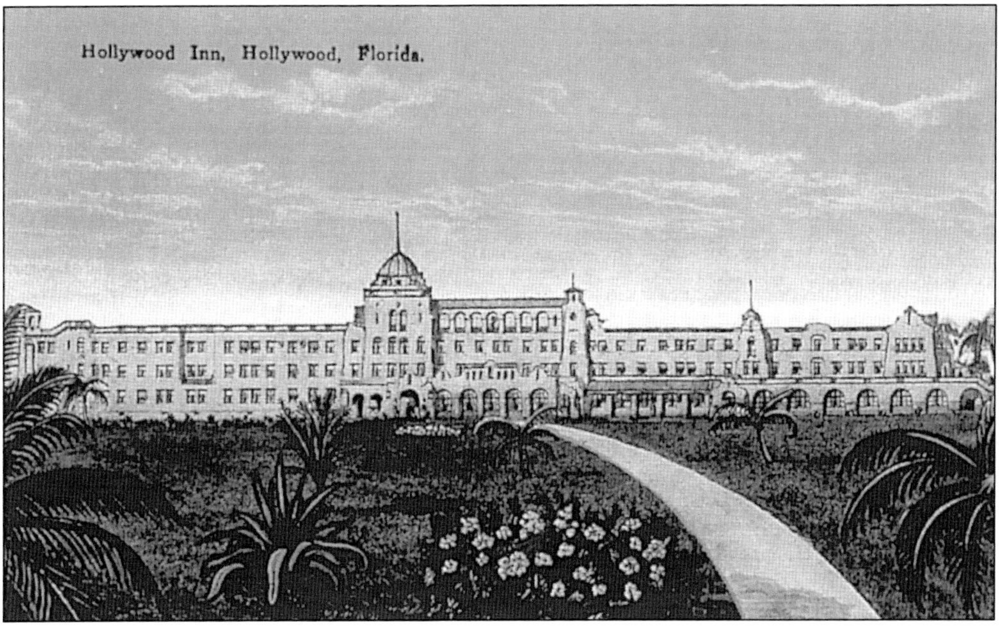

Hollywood Inn, on the westernmost circle in Hollywood Hills, could host 500 and was the last hotel built by Young. Open for only one season (1925), it was filled with people the salesmen had bussed in from all over the country. Later the inn became the winter home of Riverside Military Academy and the circle was renamed Military Circle.

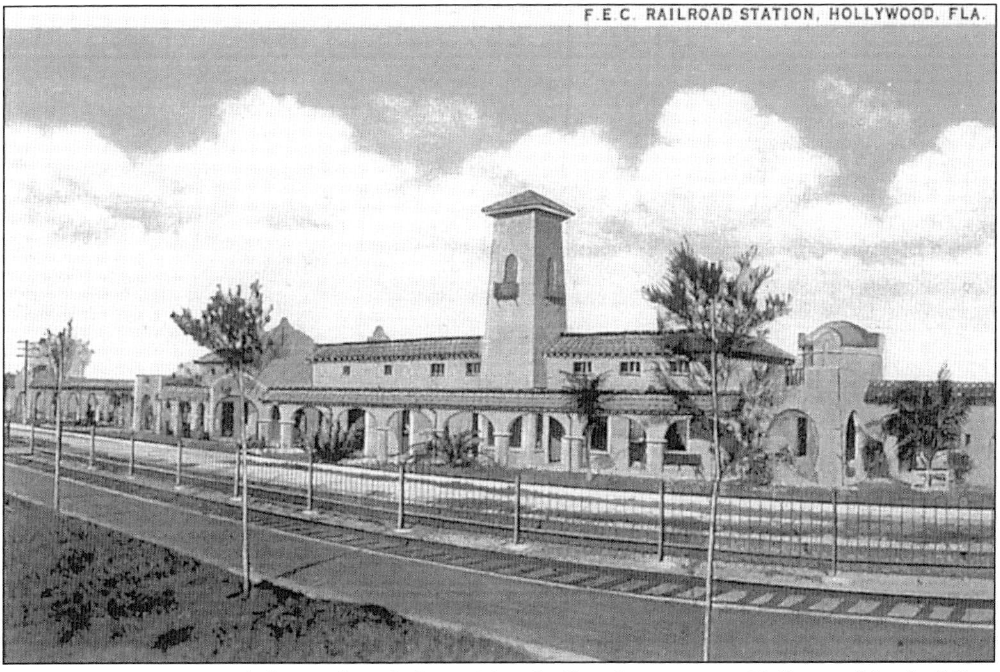

In 1923 Young enticed the Seaboard Coast Line Railroad to stop at Hollywood by building a train station. Its opening was almost stopped because Young's restroom fixtures were way above the quality of the standard bowls and sinks of other stations. The first passenger train *The Floridian* reached Hollywood in 1924.

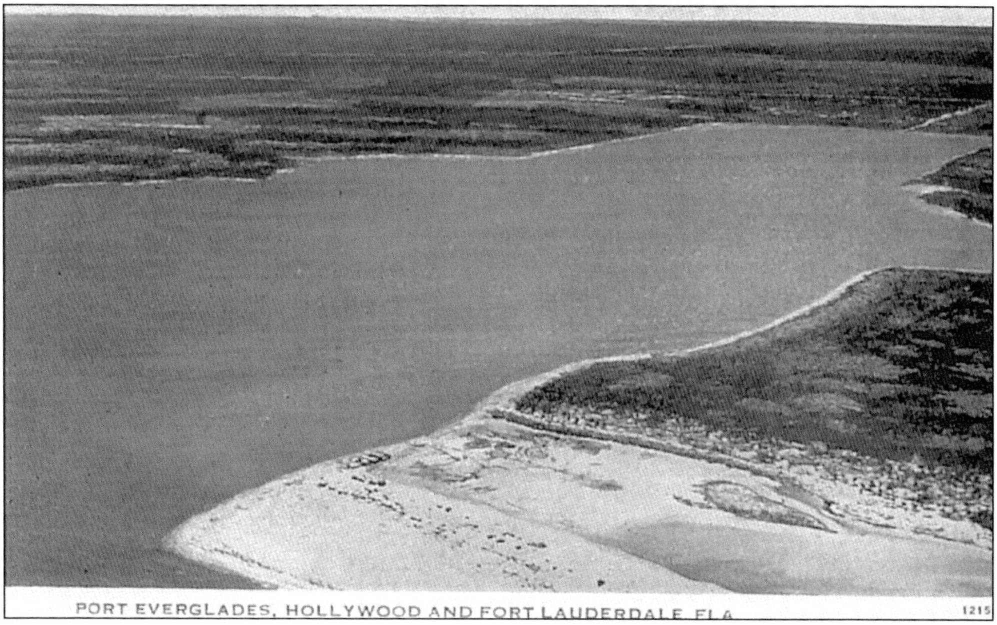

In 1924 the area around Lake Mabel was cleared to build a world-renowned shipping center. Helping with the construction of the future Port Everglades were ten French-Canadian lumberjacks. Their enthusiasm about Hollywood when they returned to Canada began an annual French-Canadian visitation that continues to this day.

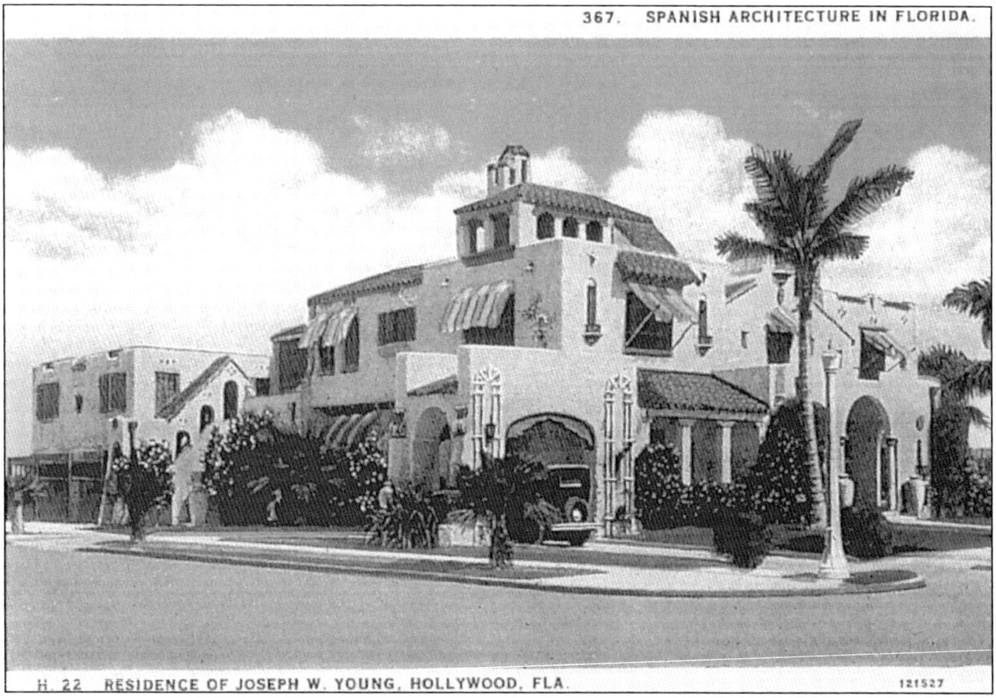

Joseph Young and his family moved into their Spanish-style home at 1053 Hollywood Boulevard in 1925. It was a showplace featuring arched doorways, wrought-iron gates, balconies, and Spanish tile. Young died in this house in 1934 after suffering a massive heart attack.

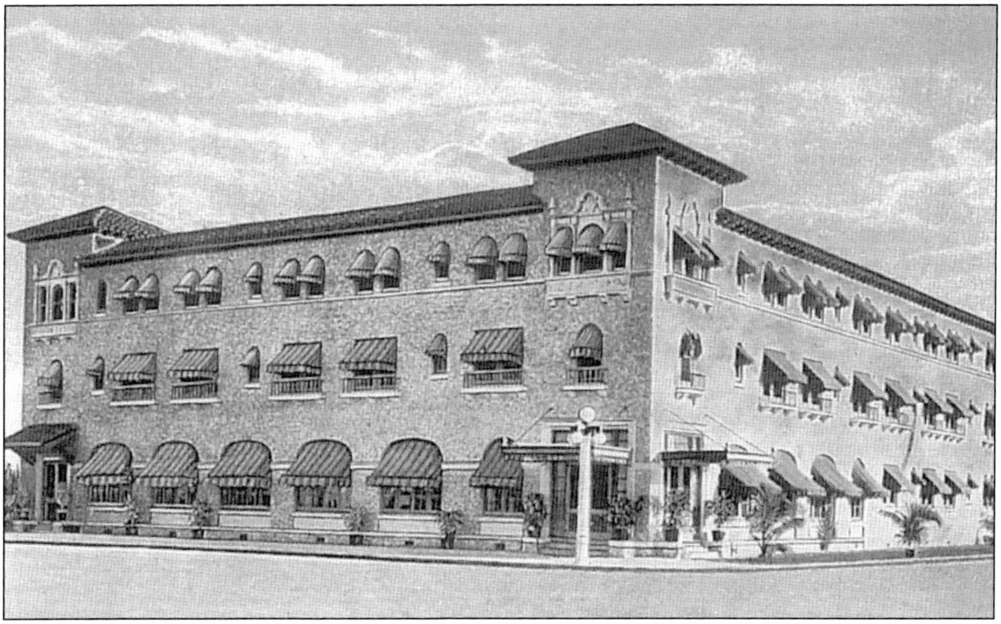

The Great Southern Hotel was built by Young in 1924, at the corner of Hollywood Boulevard and Nineteenth Avenue. The three-story, 100-room hotel cost over $500,000 to construct.

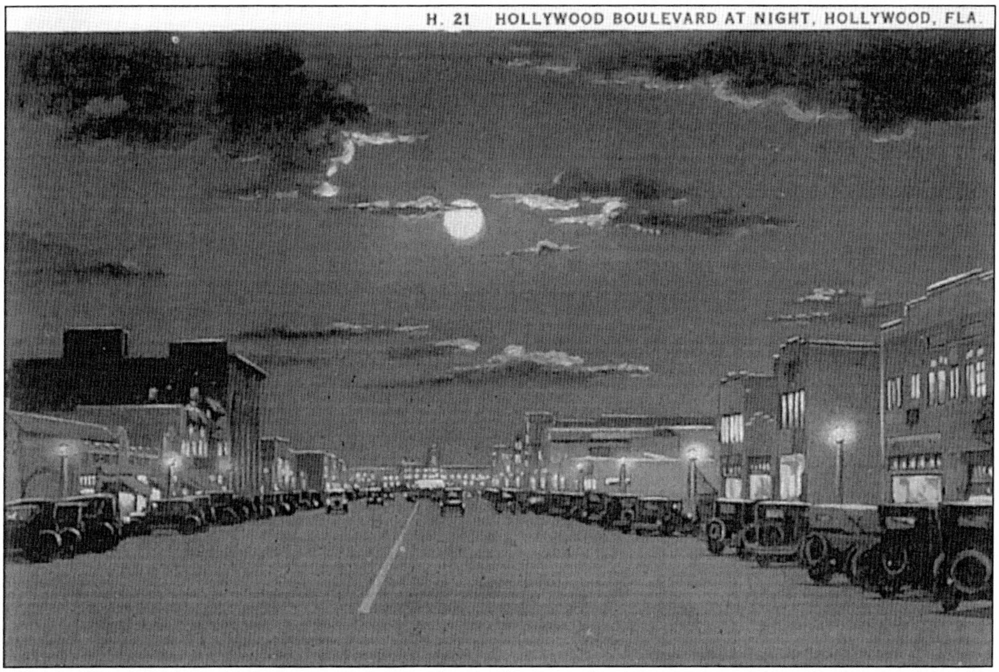

The Hollywood Land Company's land sales technique involved advertising Hollywood in the Northeast and Midwest and bringing people in to see the new city for themselves. By 1925 Hollywood-by-the-Sea had seen so much growth that the nearby towns of Dania and Hallandale both asked to be annexed.

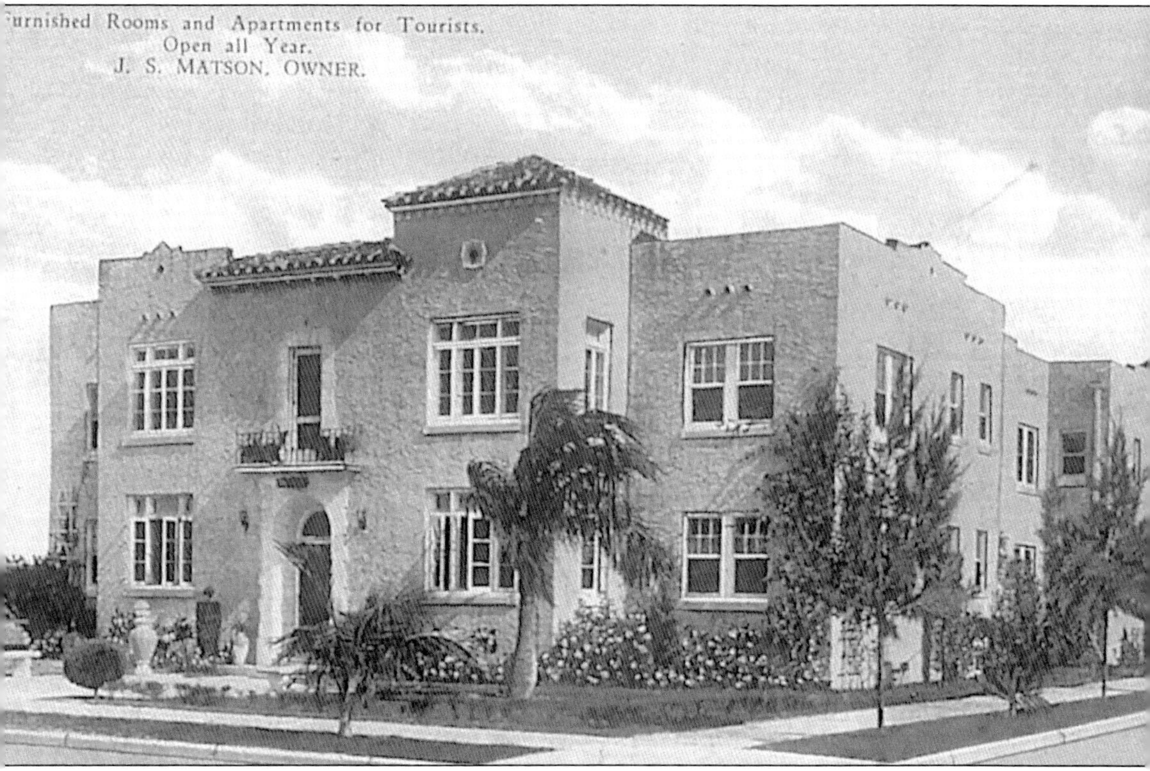

Hollywood's rapid growth created a need for residence hotels. The Flora was built in 1924 at a cost of $60,000. It was considered dignified and upper class, and was privately owned with J.S. Matson as proprietor. Located on the southeast corner of Polk Street and Seventeenth Avenue, it faced the Country Club entrance. The Flora had eight family suites and eight single rooms, each with its own bath. From November to May suites rented for $90-100 per month, while the June to October rates were only $20-25 per month. Single rooms, the temporary home of many a working man, rented for $3 per night for one person, or $4.50 per night for two. The Flora still stands in the same spot today, though it faces the golf course rather than the Country Club entrance. Now beige with tan trim, the building remains in lovely condition.

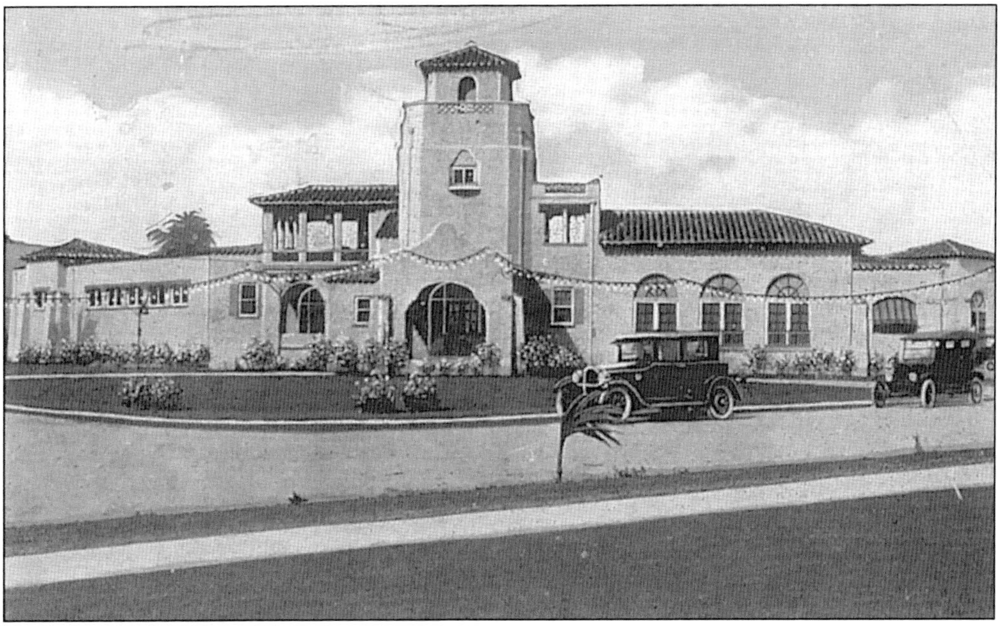

The Hollywood Golf Club, located at Seventeenth and Polk Streets, opened in 1924. President Warren G. Harding enjoyed playing golf at this course, and he visited Hollywood several times. The downtown circle was named Harding Circle in his honor and it kept that name for many years.

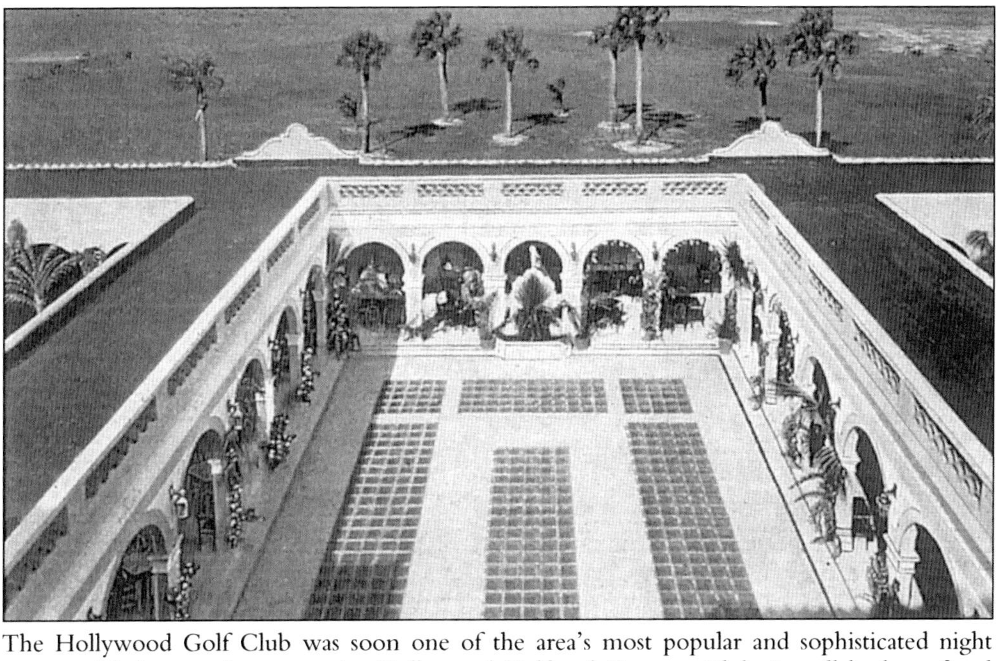

The Hollywood Golf Club was soon one of the area's most popular and sophisticated night spots, and it became known as the Hollywood Golf and Country Club. Its roll-back roof and illuminated dance floor were legendary. On New Year's Eve over 300 couples celebrated under the stars on this patio, while multi-colored lights glowed through the glass-blocked floor.

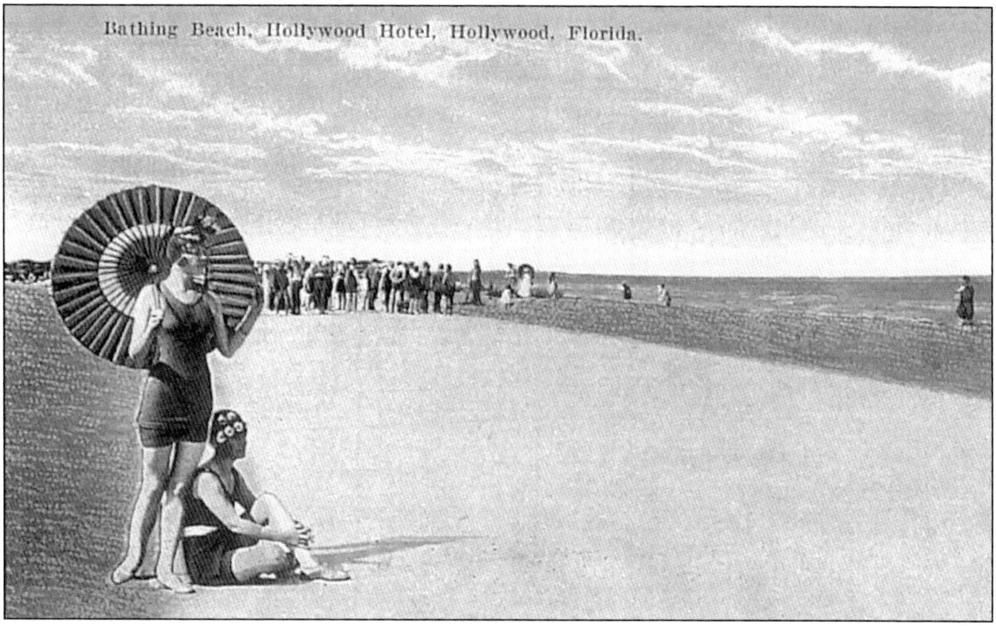

One of Hollywood's greatest assets has always been its beautiful Atlantic Ocean coastline. Early visitors enjoyed the sandy beach and the ocean water. The health benefits of living near the sea were emphasized by lecturers during the Chautauqua-like speeches given to prospective land buyers.

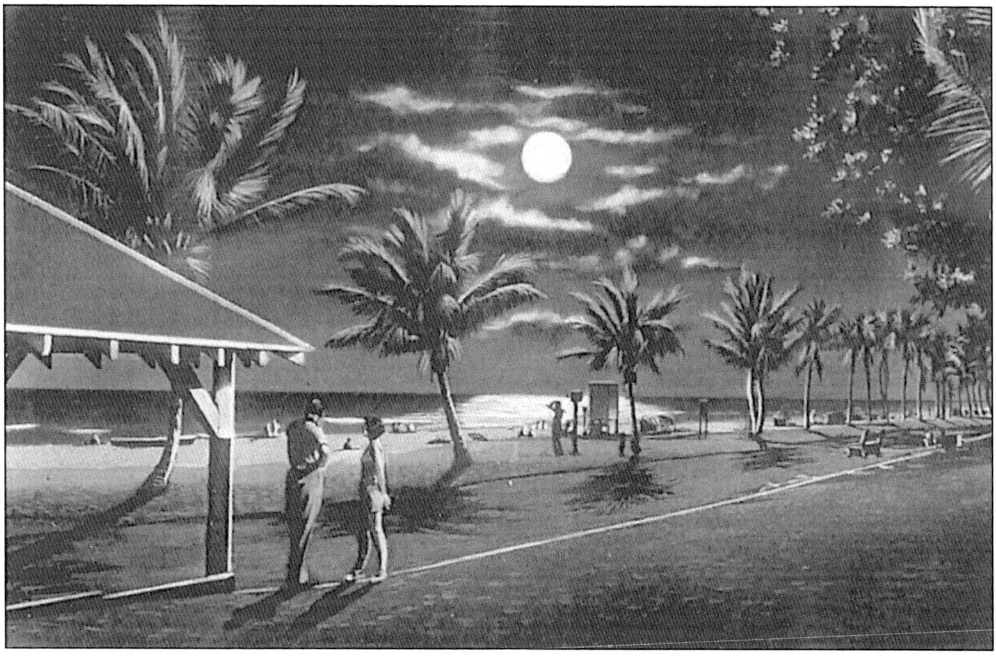

There is nothing quite as relaxing as a moonlight stroll along the beach. The sounds of the waves and the palm fronds, the salty evening breeze, and the cawing of seagulls made visitors want to stay forever. The wide, paved Broadwalk divided the beach from the exclusive hotels and shops that sprang up along the oceanfront.

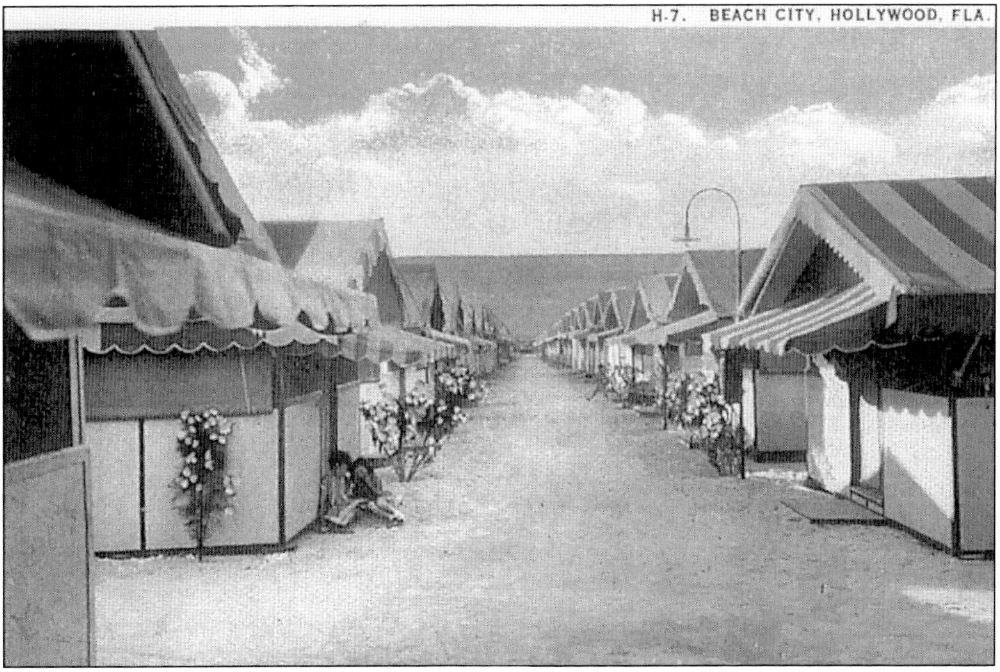

The beach was so attractive to some that they wanted to stay right on the sand, so a tent city was built in the mid-1920s, bordered by Washington Street and the Broadwalk. Each unit had a furnished living room, bedroom, and bath, and many had kitchenettes as well. Maid service was provided.

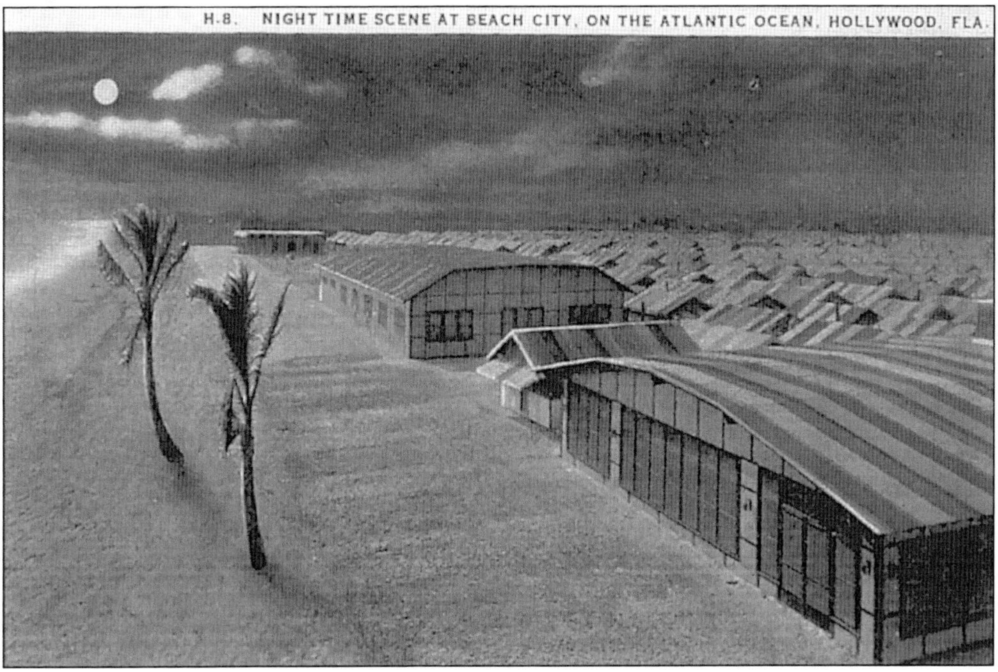

The cottage-type structures had wood frames and wood floors with colorful, striped canvas roofs and awnings. Their upper walls were screened. Several hundred "tents" were aligned in orderly rows with streetlights every 50 feet. They were filled to capacity during the 1925–26 season.

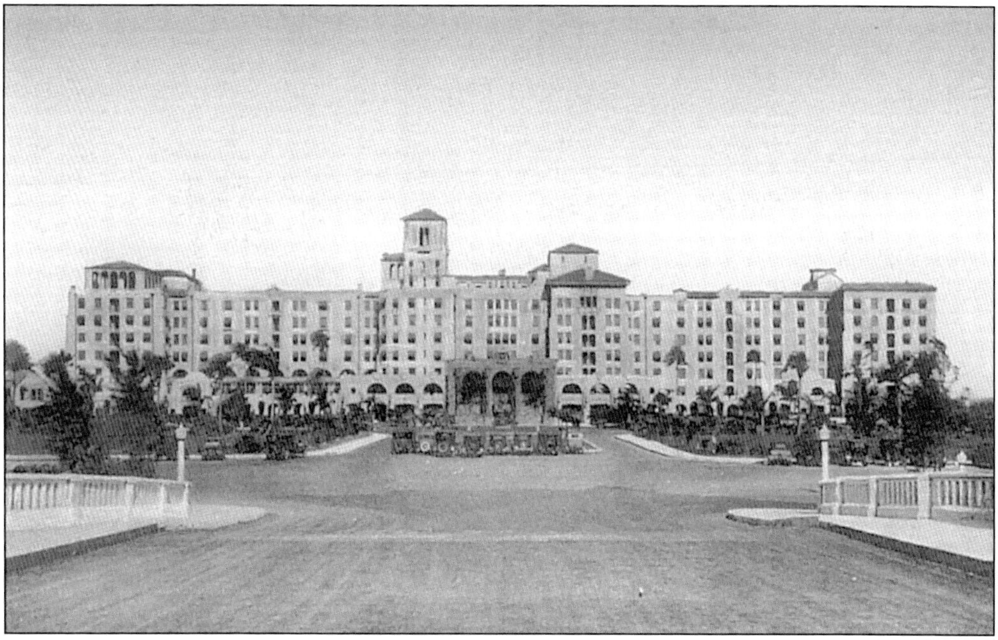

One of Young's major goals was to build an elegant hotel directly on the oceanfront, at the eastern edge of Hollywood Boulevard. Since it was called the Hollywood Hotel on the architect's drawings, the Hollywood Hotel on the downtown circle changed its name to the Park View and the new one became the Hollywood Beach Hotel.

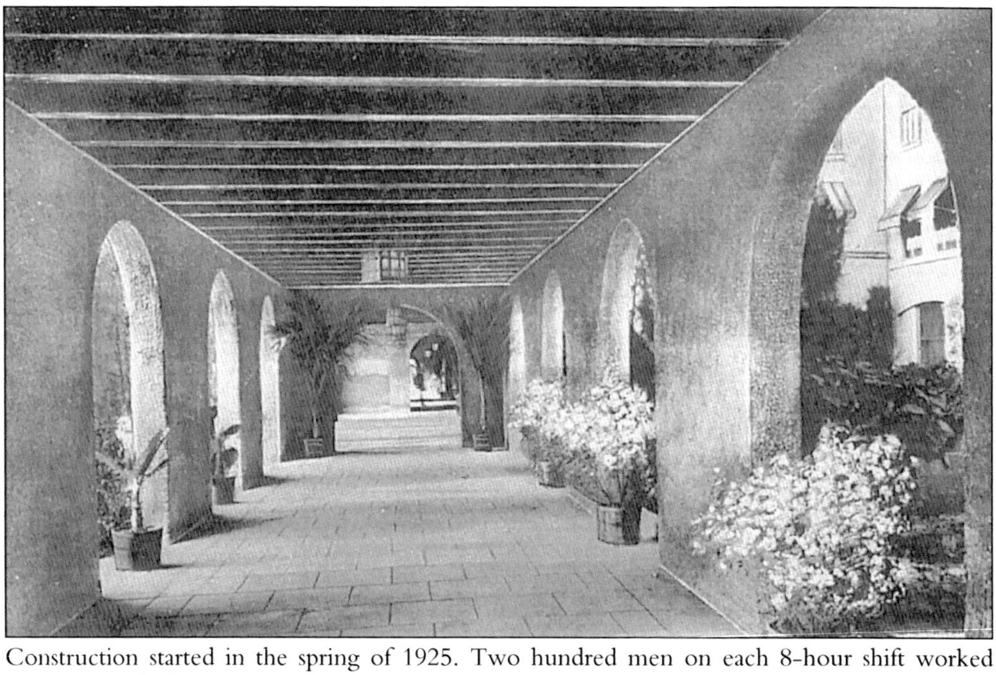

Construction started in the spring of 1925. Two hundred men on each 8-hour shift worked around the clock to ensure that the "90-Day Wonder," as local residents called it, was ready to open for the 1925–26 winter season. This view of the west porch shows the attention to atmosphere that was a hallmark of the new hotel.

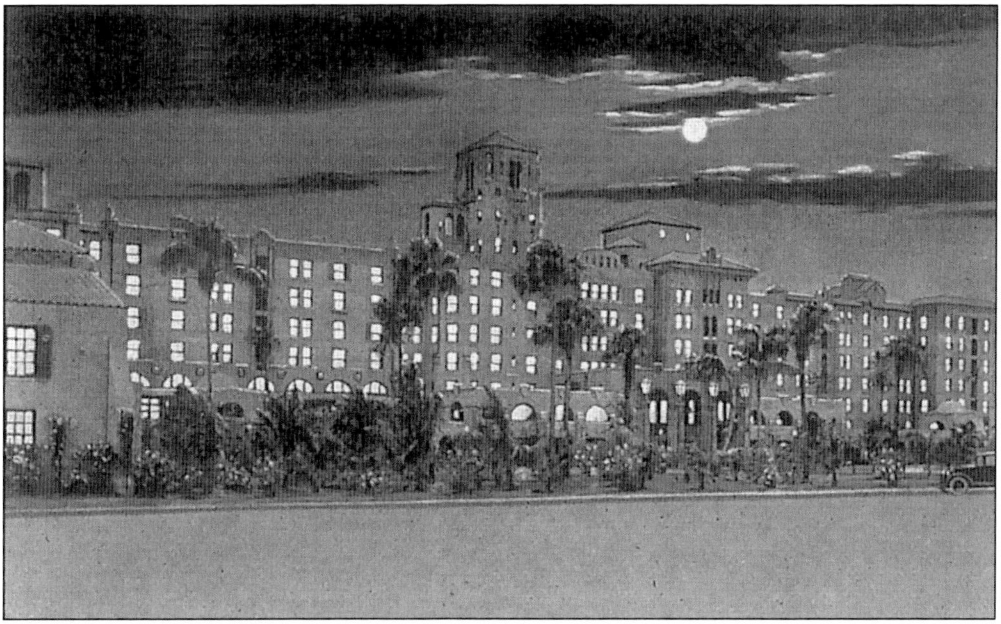

Since workmen labored at all hours, lights were kept lit all night. They were so bright that the hotel could be seen from a half-mile away. The Hollywood Beach Hotel did open in time for the season, although it wasn't until February of 1926 that many of the details were completed.

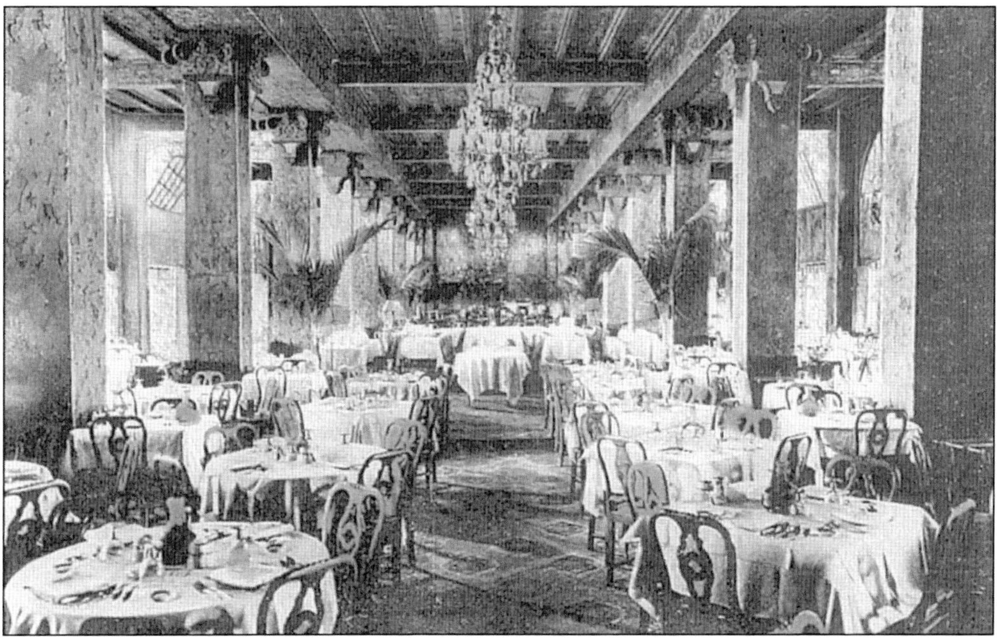

It's easy to imagine the overwhelmingly positive feelings of visitors from the Northeast and Midwest. Young brought everyday people to Hollywood by the thousands, paying for everything but their hotel rooms, to admire its beauty. The main dining room at the Hollywood Beach Hotel was the site of many a sales discussion.

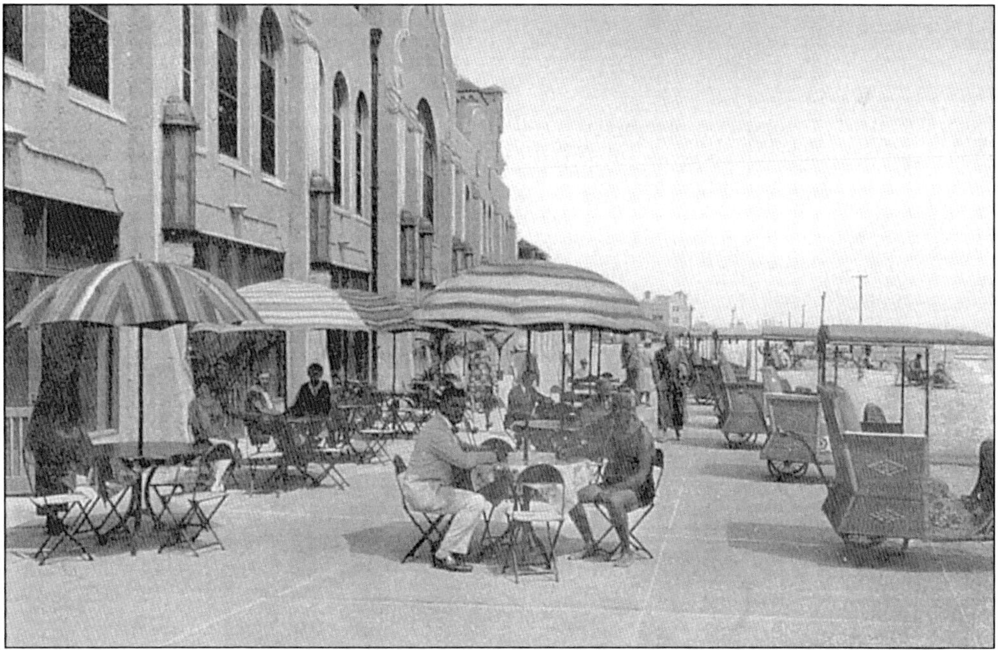

Between 1921 and 1926 the Hollywood Land Company bought 27 White Buses at $8,000 each to bring prospective buyers to Hollywood. The bus caravans generated lots of excitement. Sales pitches were made along the Broadwalk as would-be Floridians sat under beach umbrellas gazing at the ocean's waves.

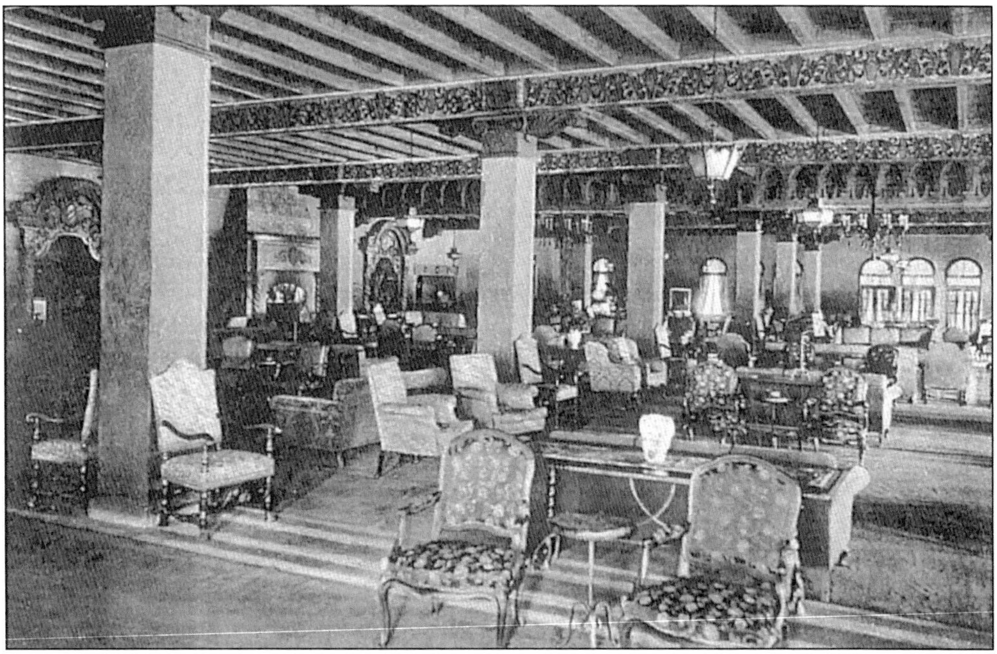

Chautauqua-type lectures were given at sales pavilions and luncheons. Upper-crust guests were often entertained in the Hollywood Beach Hotel's lounge. Everyone wanted to sell real estate, and the boom created so many jobs that employers had trouble finding workers.

All guests' lunches were provided by the Hollywood Land Company. The meals consisted of a ham sandwich, a chocolate cupcake, an orange, and a cup of cafe au lait. After lunch, dazzled visitors might have relaxed on the Hollywood Beach Hotel's upper promenade as they considered making Hollywood their new home.

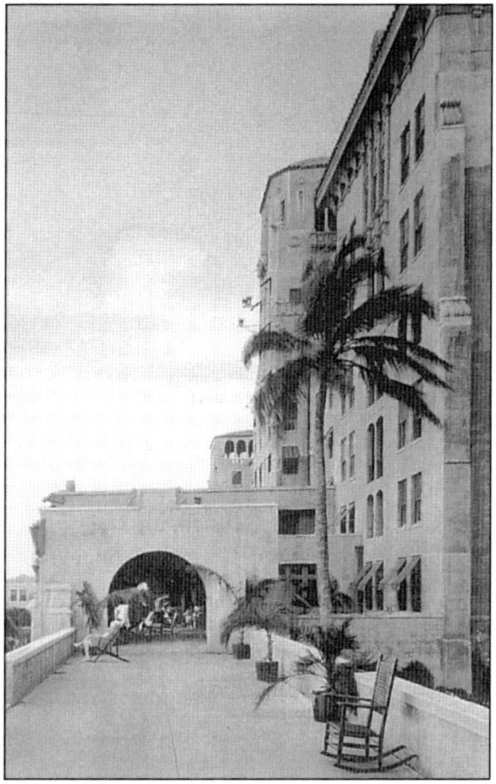

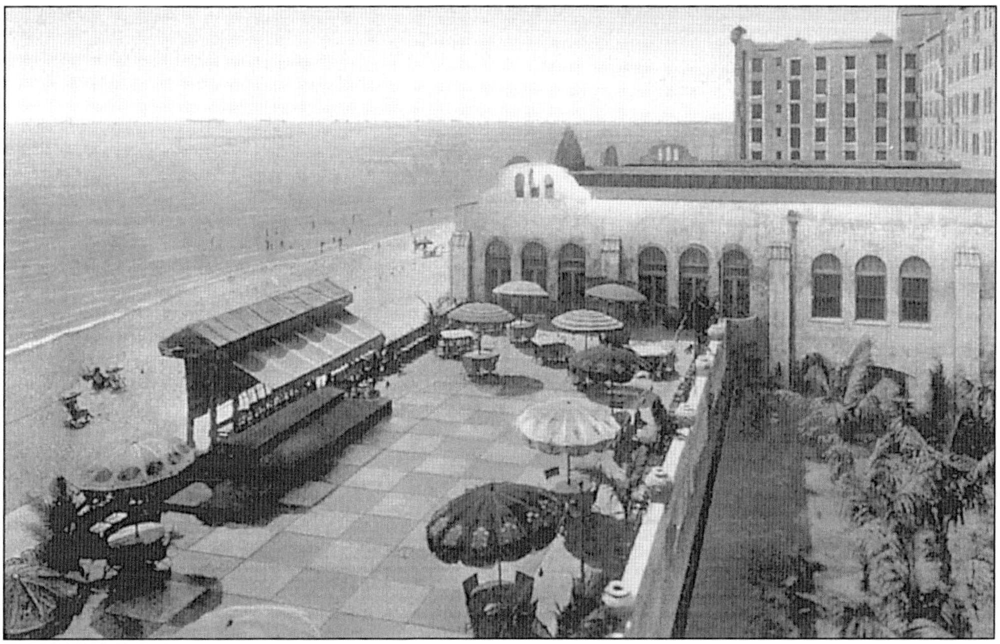

Marimba band dances held in the evenings continued to sweep the out-of-towners off their feet. The north deck of the Hollywood Beach Hotel was a favorite spot for chatting and relaxing after long days of touring the area. Prospective home-buyers were assured that the area was safe from hurricanes, being protected by the Gulf Stream.

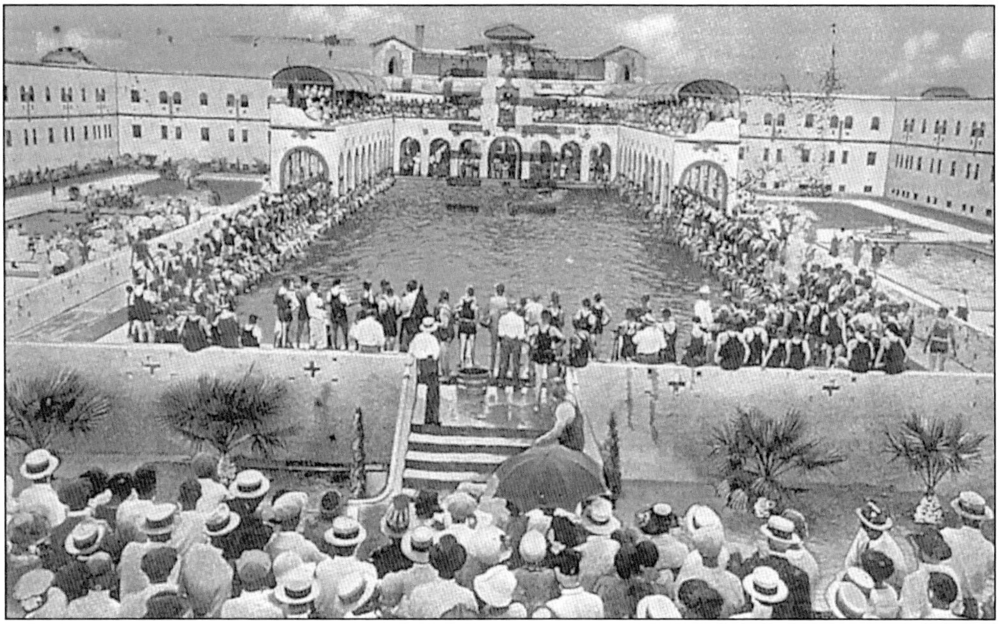

The Hollywood Beach Casino, on the Broadwalk near Johnson Street, had 824 dressing rooms, 80 showers, and a shopping arcade. The 3-story building had an Olympic-sized pool and gardens. The Broadwalk arched just in front of the building to form a tunnel for showers and provide a bather's route to the ocean and casino.

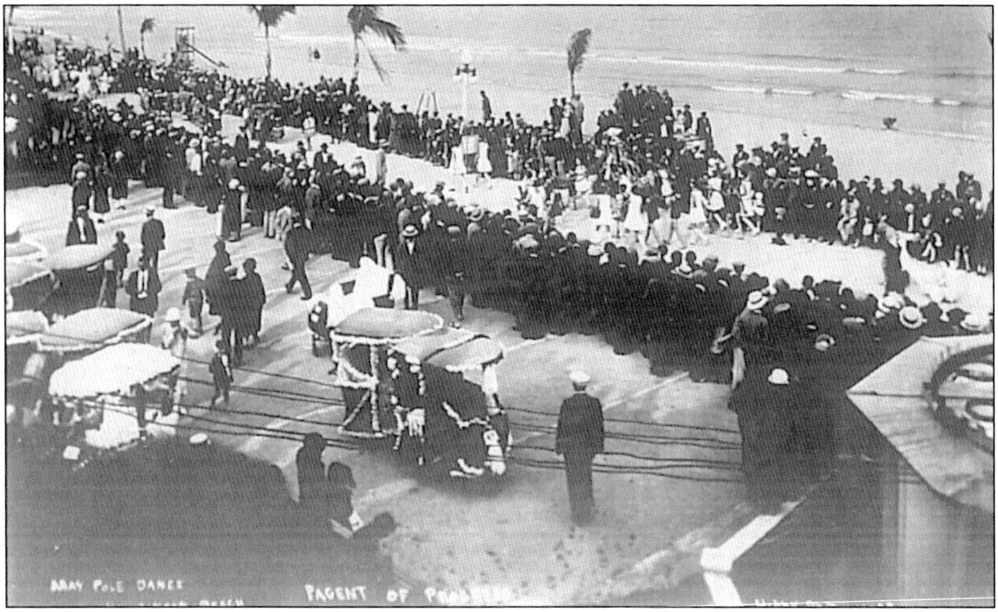

In February of 1926 Hollywood held a Pageant of Progress, which became the annual Fiesta Tropicale in later years. Hollywood, which hadn't even existed six years before, had by some accounts become the county's largest city with 20,000 people. Neighboring Fort Lauderdale had a population of 16,000 at that time.

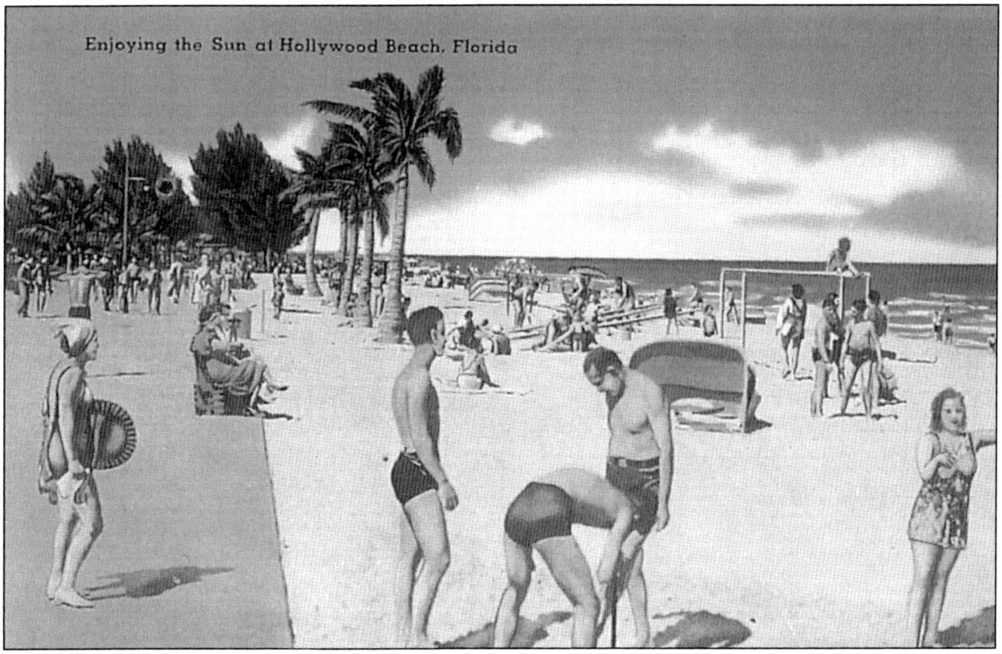

September 17, 1926, began just like every other day. Beachgoers, both locals and tourists, enjoyed the sand and surf.

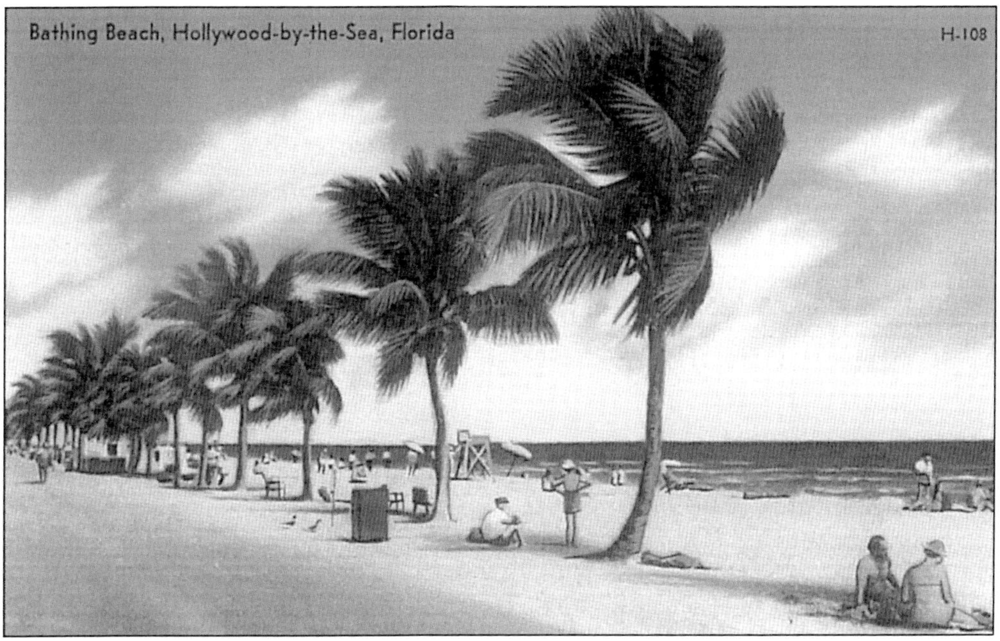

Later in the day, however, the wind picked up. The area's most damaging hurricane had begun. Winds over 140 miles per hour toppled buildings. The tent city was blown away. Over 18 inches of salt water covered Federal Highway and sand buried the ground floor of the Hollywood Beach Hotel.

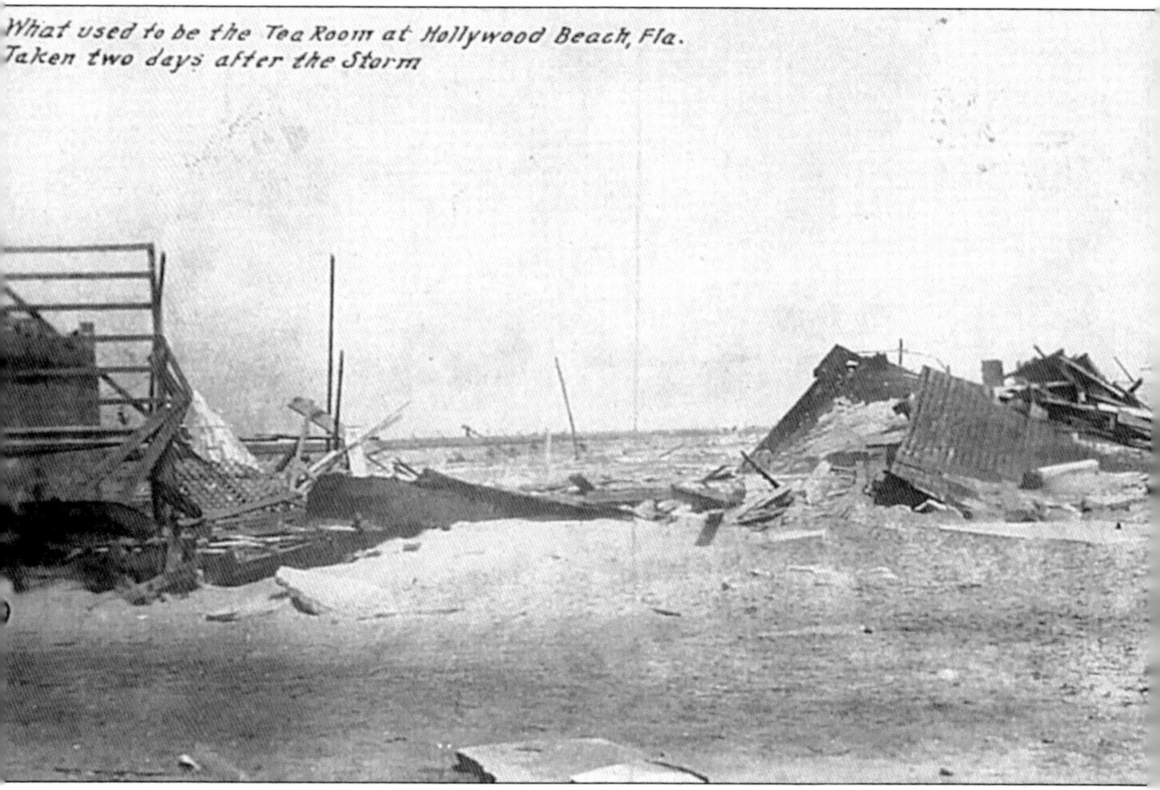

This postcard shows the remains of the Tangerine Tea Room on the beach, two days after the storm. The hurricane had killed 400 people, destroyed millions of dollars worth of property, and frightened away potential residents, effectively ending the land boom. Young's concrete Broadwalk was disintegrated and some of its pieces still lie at the bottom of the Intracoastal Waterway. Joseph Young's glamour days were over. The hurricane's destruction left him unable to make loan payments to Highway Construction, which had installed streets and sidewalks in Hollywood Hills. That firm, headed by Samuel Horvitz, was the forerunner of Hollywood, Inc. Horvitz bought 24,000 of Young's homesite lots for $35,000 at a sheriff's sale. Hollywood was bankrupt. Dania and Hallandale were de-annexed to escape liability from debt. While many residents fled back to their northern homes, a large number stayed and began to rebuild their city.

Two

Changing Landmarks

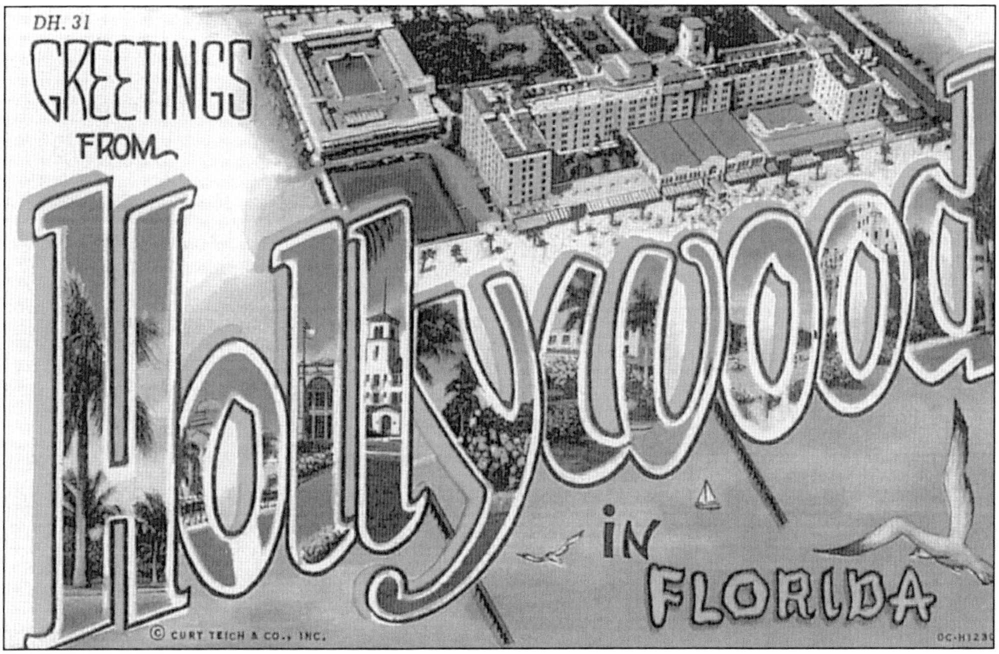

All cities and towns change over time. Well-known buildings are renovated or torn down and replaced by new ones. Familiar businesses disappear and scenery gives way to inevitable growth and development. Hollywood is certainly no exception to this rule. From its beginning it has known great change. Originally called Hollywood-by-the-Sea, the area became known as the city of Hollywood when it incorporated in 1925. But the "Hollywood-by-the-Sea" moniker can still be seen on even the most modern of postcards. This "Greetings from Hollywood in Florida" postcard is from the linen era (1940s). Hollywood, California, had gained such fame that its Florida sister had to ensure that postcard recipients knew where the senders were staying. This chapter pairs postcards of the same scene—but from different eras. My goodness, Hollywood, how you have grown!

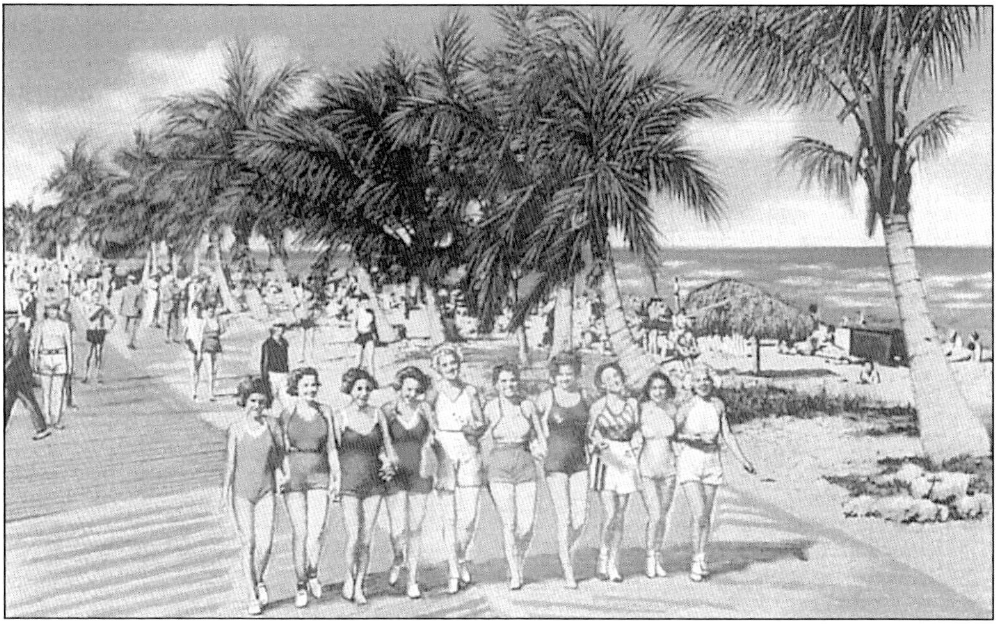

Ladies along the Broadwalk at the beach loved to show off their modern bathing costumes. Mailed in 1936, the postcard's message to Roy reads, "My boy, you ought to be here. You could get a "bird" here any time. We live in a little bungalow—electricity, water for $3 a night."

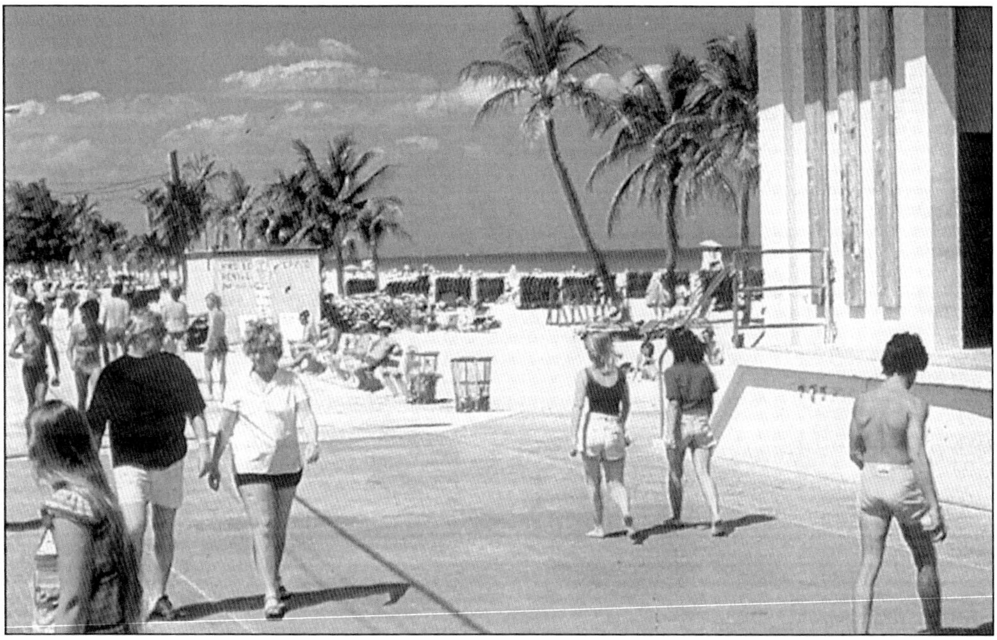

The Broadwalk at Johnson Street looked a bit different some 30 years later. Bathing suits were skimpier and people dressed much more casually. The thatched-roof tiki huts were replaced by wood-and-canvas cabana chairs.

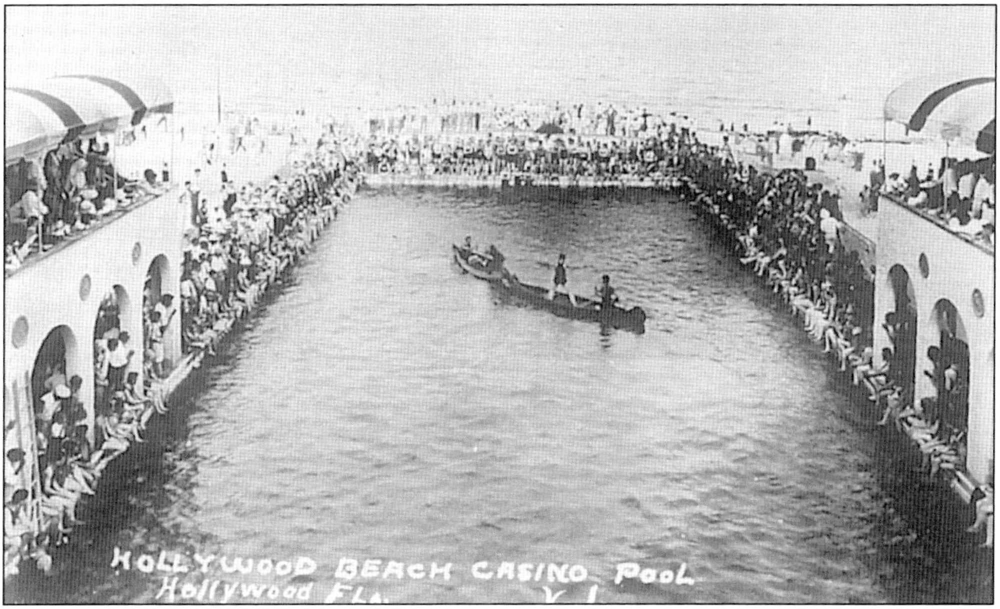

As soon as the Hollywood Beach Casino Pool opened on the Broadwalk at Johnson Street in the 1920s, it became one of the most popular recreation centers in southeast Florida. Scores of people gathered to watch a variety of water shows, including canoe-tilting and log-rolling competitions.

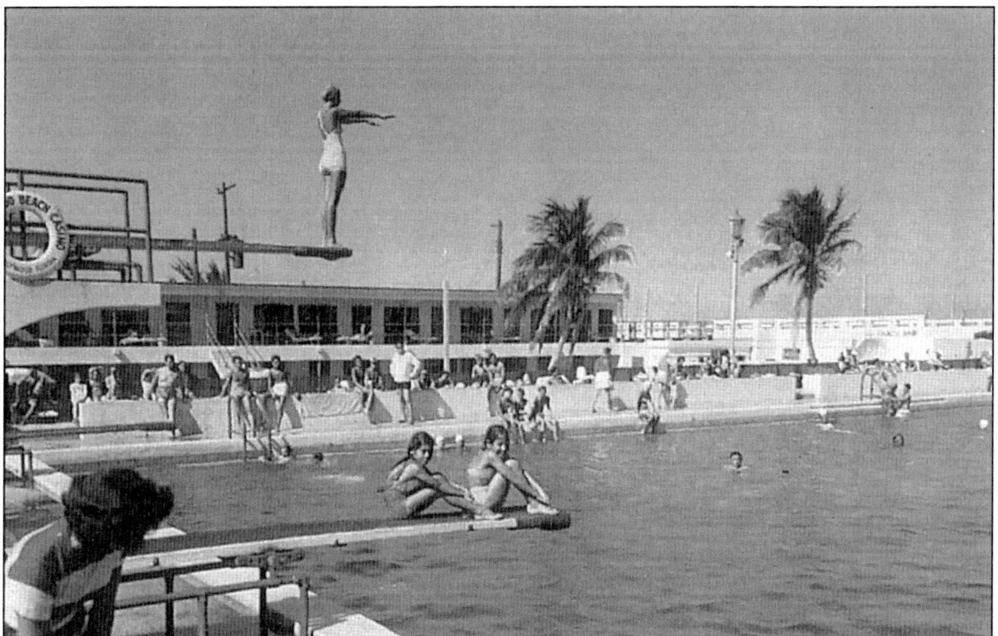

In 1946 the city awarded a 25-year lease to John Porto, who built a new fire station to serve the beach area. The casino was no longer open for gambling, but its pool remained at the heart of the city's recreational activities. A wading pool and playground for children were added. This view is from the 1950s.

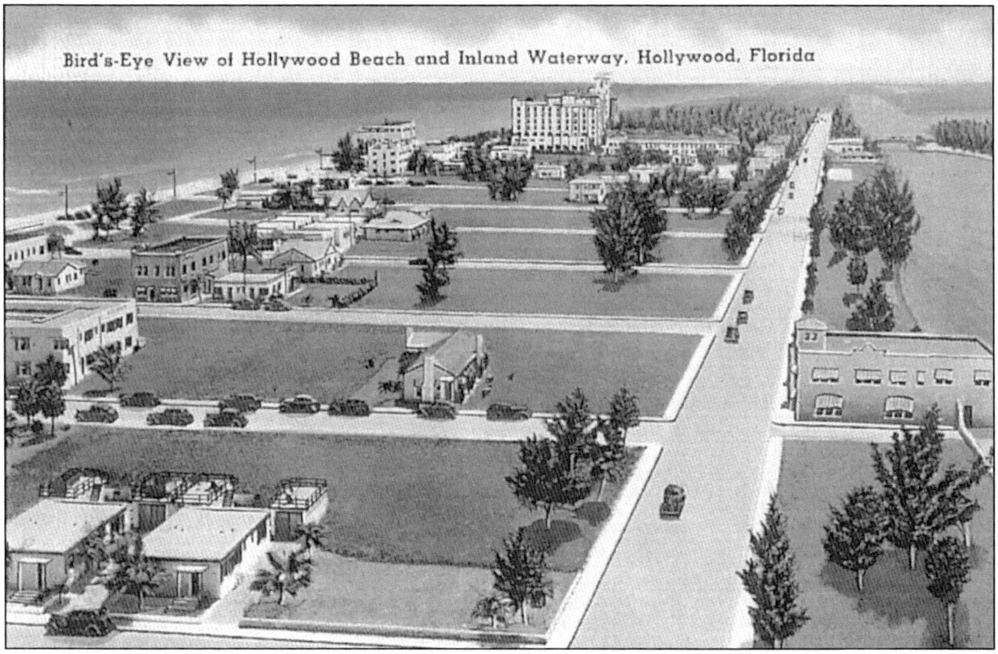

Hollywood's beach and the inland waterway, now known as the Intracoastal Waterway, had lots of green space in the 1930s. On this postcard in 1938, Laura wrote, "Doesn't this look like a fine place in which to spend one's old age, or rather one's play-time?"

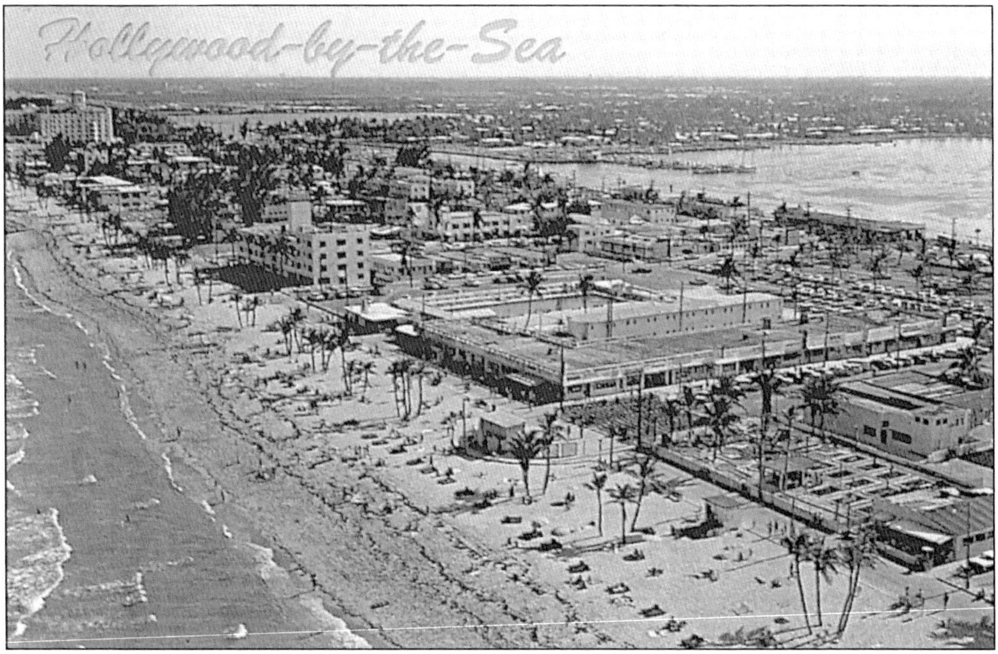

By 1970, when this postcard was mailed, the beach around Johnson Street had been completely built up. In both views, the Hollywood Beach Hotel is at the far end of the scene. Phil and Agnes wrote, "It was good to get away from all the snow." Perhaps some things never change!

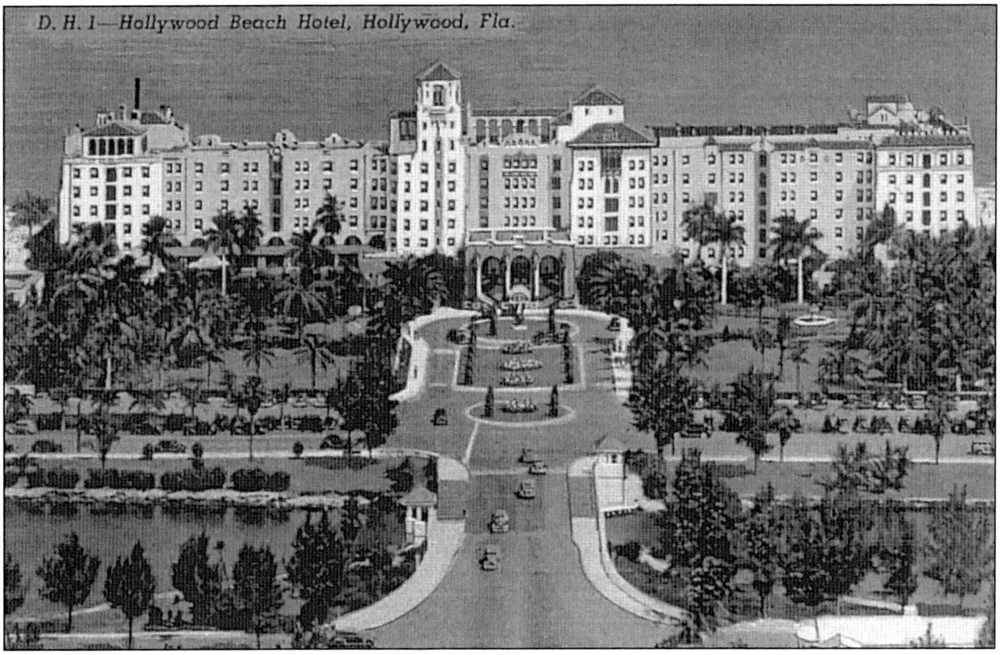

This view shows the Hollywood Beach Hotel in the 1940s. A small, wide bridge brought visitors across the Intracoastal Waterway from the downtown area to the beach along Hollywood Boulevard. The majestic hotel with its luxuriant gardens was a breathtaking sight.

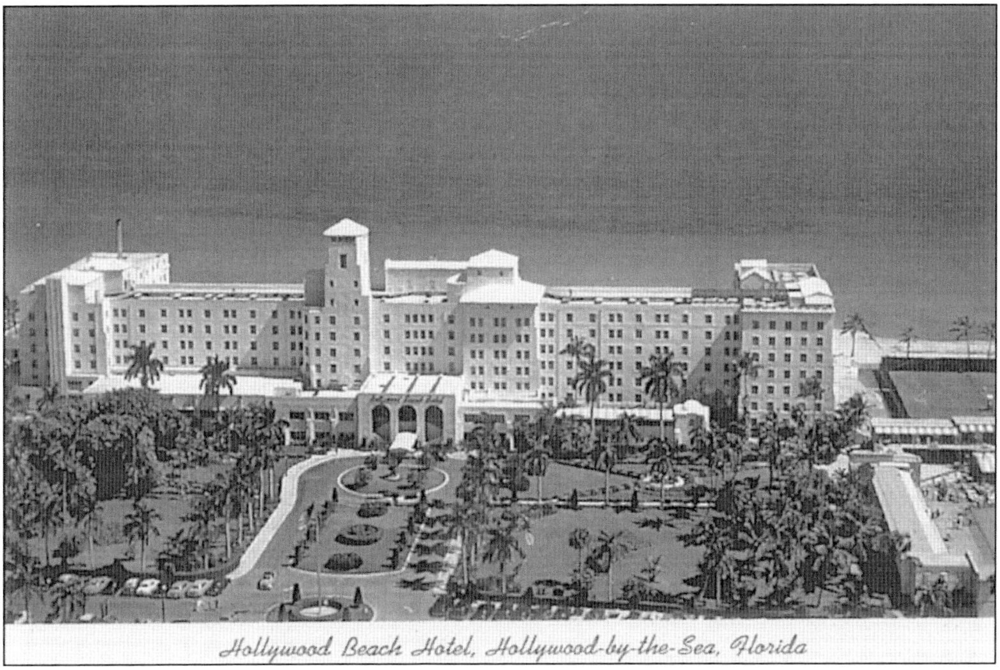

The hotel kept much of its glamour into the 1960s. This postcard uses the Hollywood-by-the-Sea name to emphasize the beach area. Today the bridge has been redesigned, and a highway crosses directly in front of the hotel. The awesome view of the hotel where the road meets the ocean is no longer.

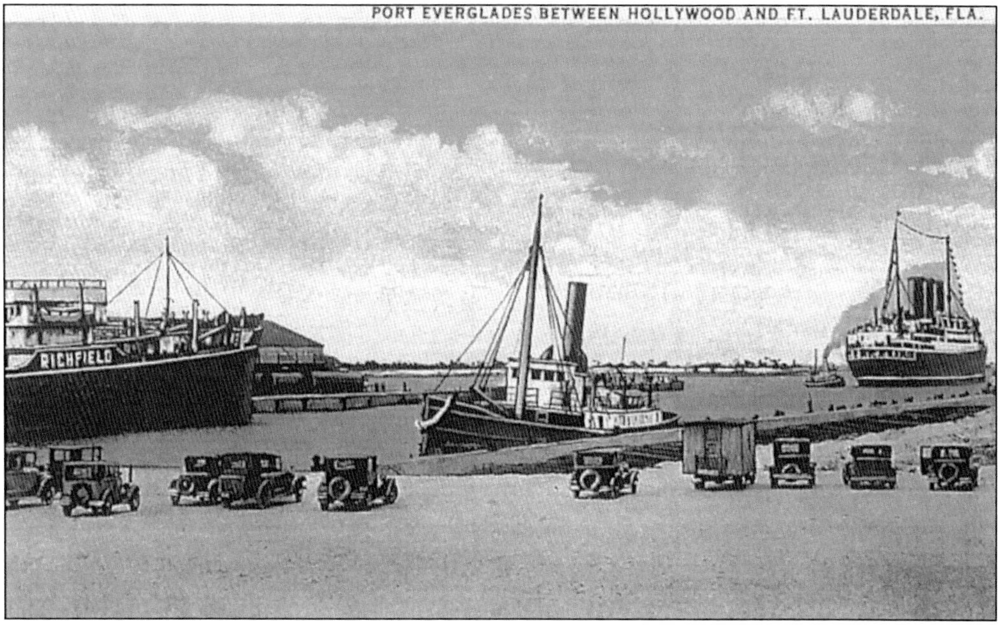

Port Everglades was originally called Lake Mabel, then Bay Mabel, Hollywood Harbor, Port Florida, and finally, Port Everglades. The port opened in 1928, financed primarily through bond issues. In 1936 President Franklin Roosevelt arrived here on a U.S. Navy ship while taking a vacation cruise and was warmly greeted by hundreds of residents.

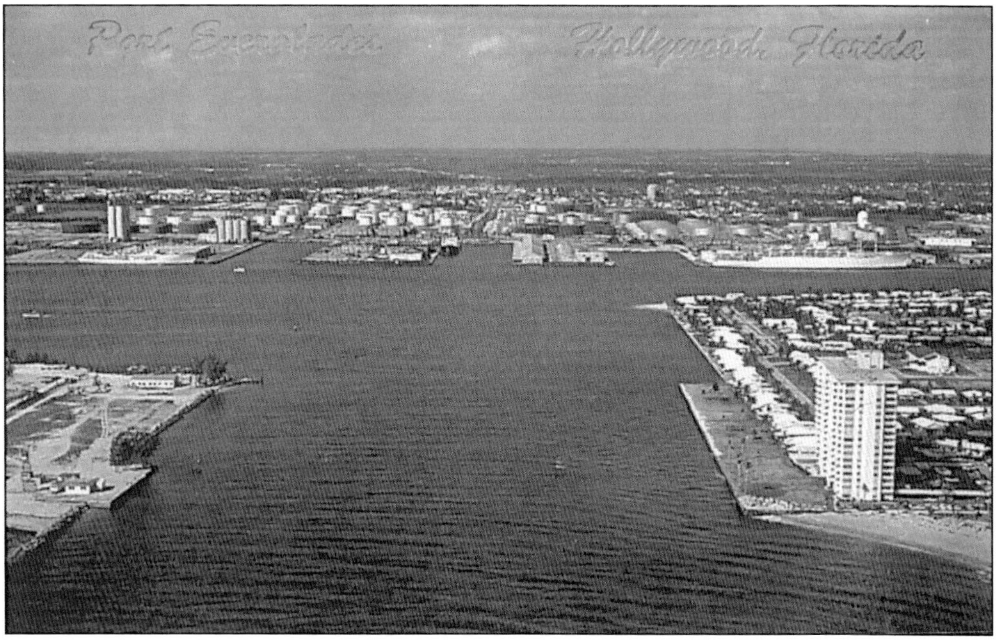

Shared by Hollywood and Fort Lauderdale, 85% of the harbor is within the Hollywood city limits, though the main land-side gate of the port is in Fort Lauderdale. By the 1960s the 755-acre Port Everglades was the South's leading international cruise port. It is also Florida's deepest harbor.

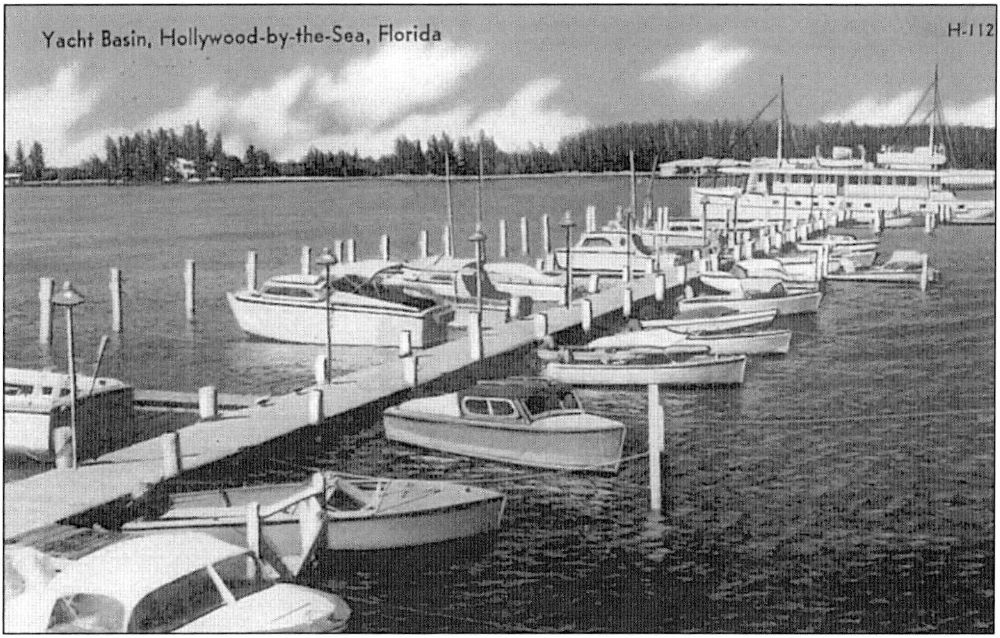

The Hollywood Yacht Basin is on the west side of the Intracoastal Waterway north of the Hollywood Beach Hotel. It was originally intended as a place for tourists and residents to tie their boats, but when a new law made on-board toilets a requirement to use the facilities, most of the boat owners took their crafts elsewhere.

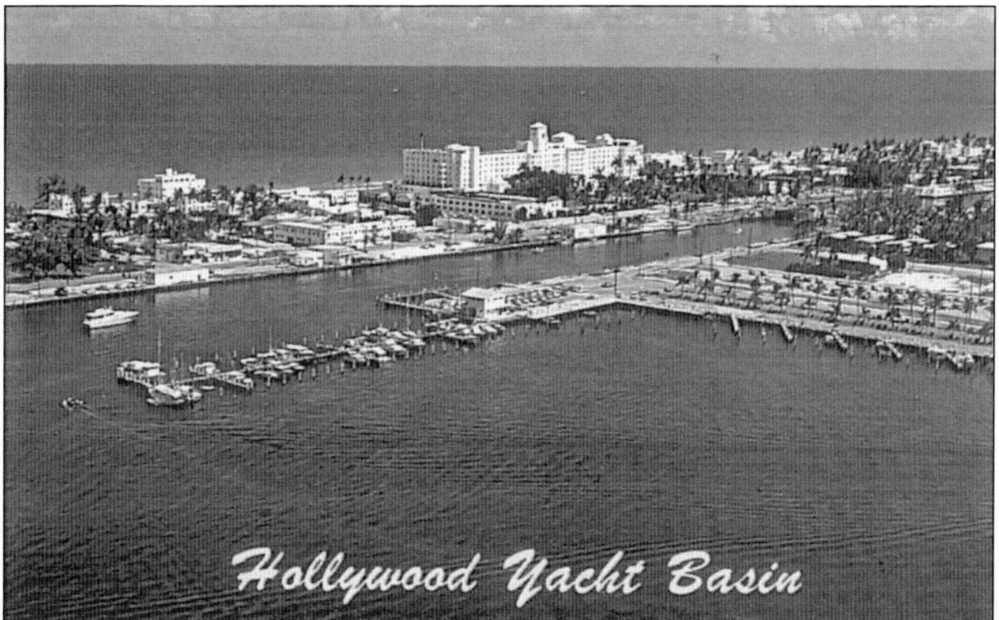

In later years the Coast Guard Auxiliary met in a small room at the yacht basin. There was never a problem getting volunteers for coast guard patrol; perhaps the nude beach not far from the marina helped the volunteer effort. This 1960s view, with the Hollywood Beach Hotel as a landmark, helps provide perspective.

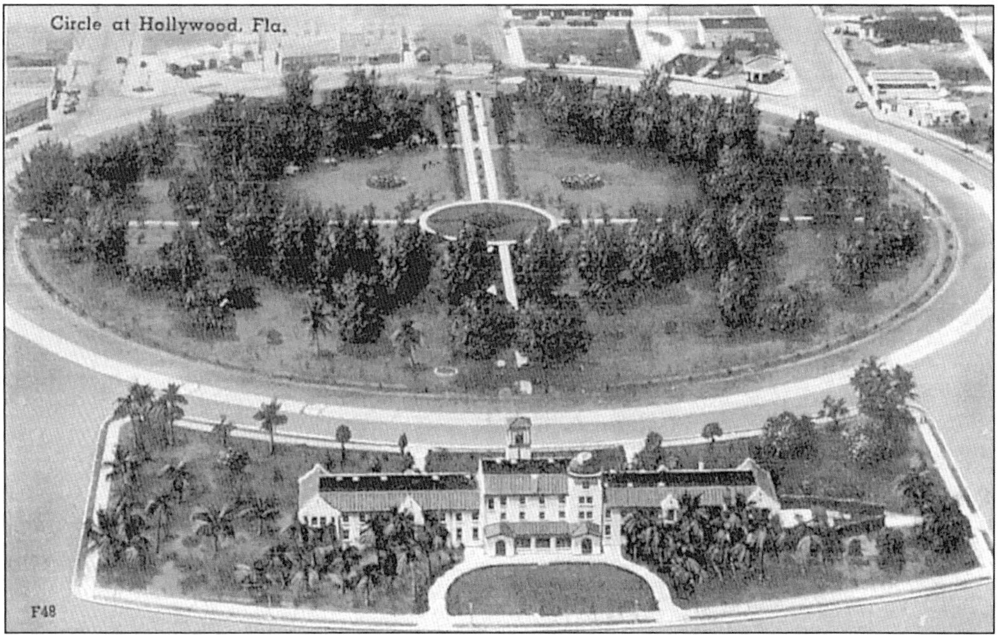

This late 1930s view of the downtown circle is captioned, "18 miles north of Miami, Florida on U.S. Highway #1, the Hollywood Circle studded with Australian Pines and Florida Palms presents a picturesque sight to the traveler." The Hollywood Hotel stands proudly at the foot of this image.

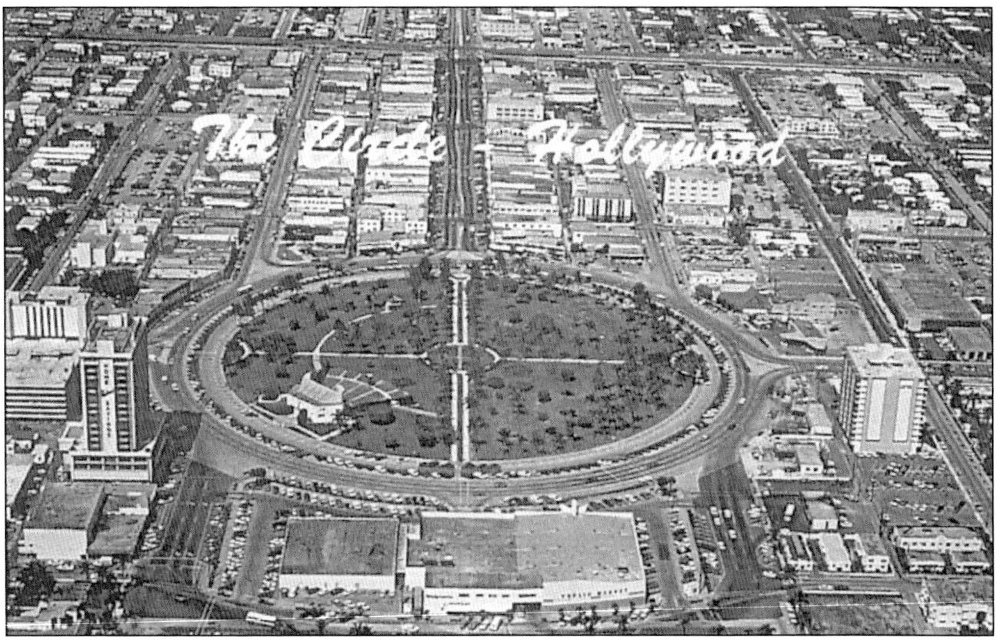

What a difference 30 years makes! Publix Market can be seen on the spot where the Hollywood Hotel (later the Park View and then the Town House) once stood. The band shell has been added and tall buildings such as Home Federal Savings dot the downtown landscape.

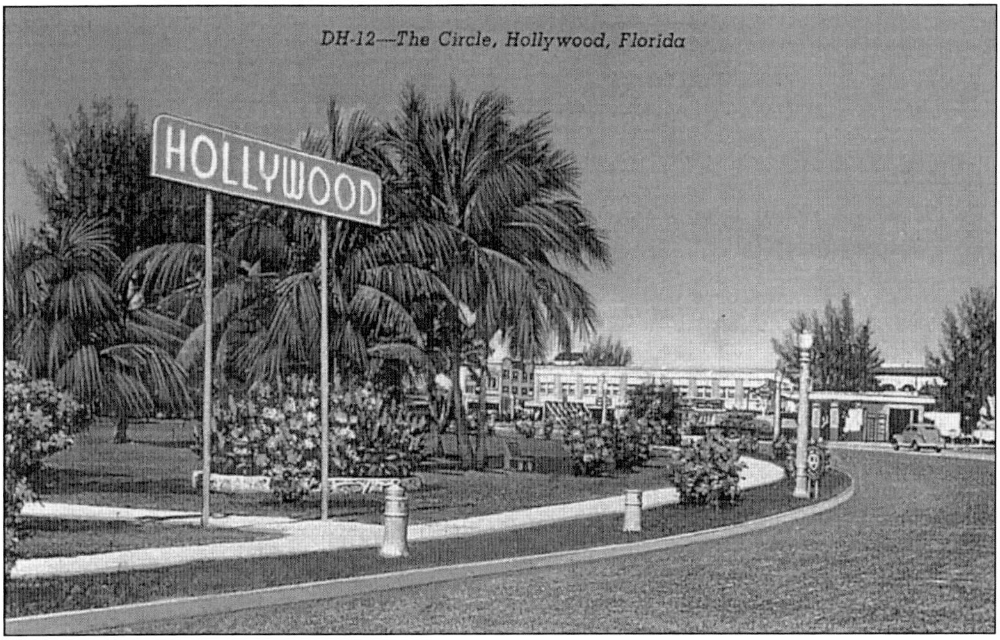

Originally intended as a restful place of beauty, the downtown circle, then called Harding Circle, became a park in 1923. Tropical flowers create a garden atmosphere in the middle of the bustling shopping and business center. The town's Memorial to War Dead is located here.

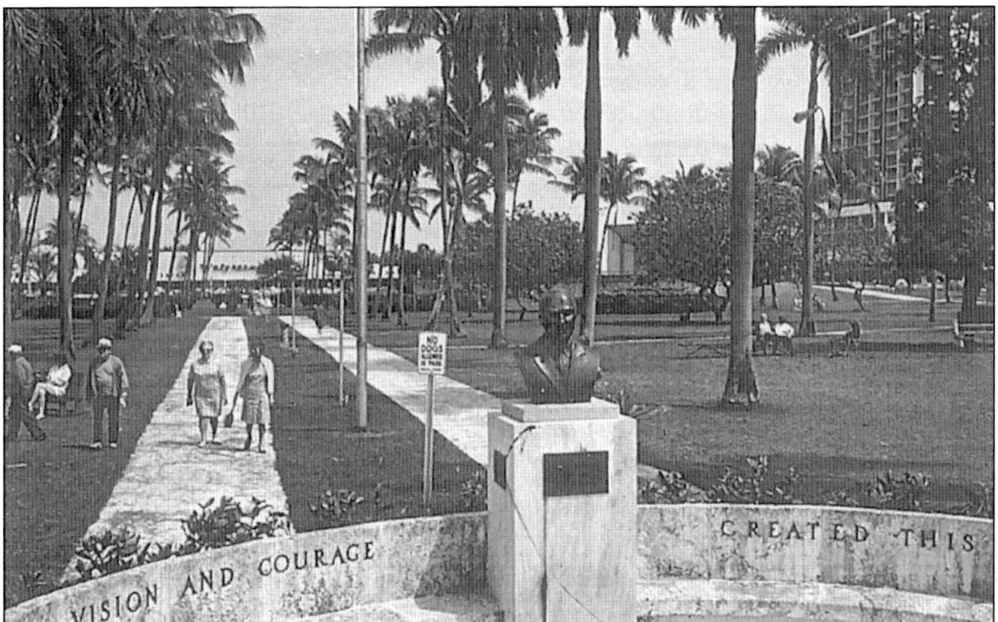

In 1935 the city renamed the circle the Joseph W. Young Circle and designated August 4th (Young's birthday) as Founder's Day. A bust of Joseph Young, atop a marble pedestal and bench area, reminds Hollywoodians of their city's history. "His vision and courage created this city" is the inscription.

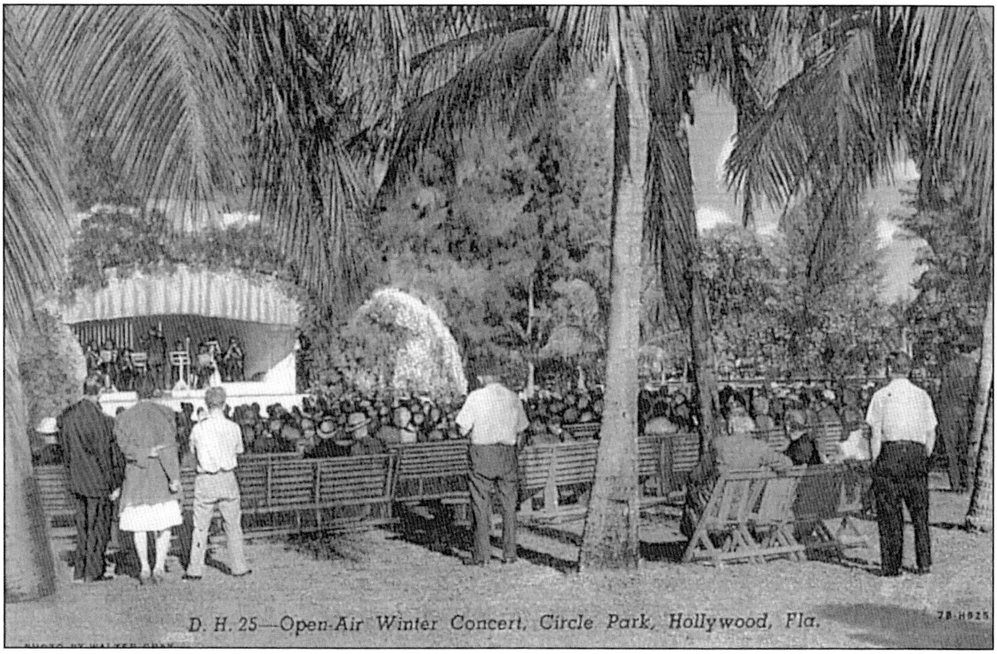

The bandstand was built in the downtown circle by the City in 1934. In a sense, it was a celebration of the success of the townspeople who had worked together to rebuild Hollywood after the Hurricane of 1926. During those years simple entertainments replaced the lavish amusements of the boom days.

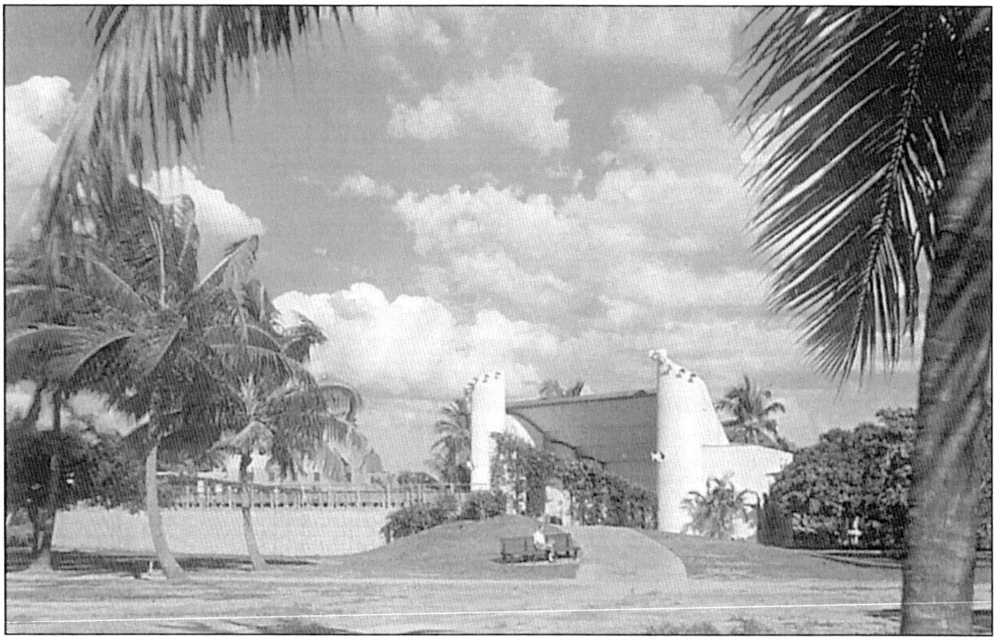

The municipal band shell in Young Circle Park has been improved over the years, and still continues to offer free evening entertainment all year long. Pageants and contests are held here as well.

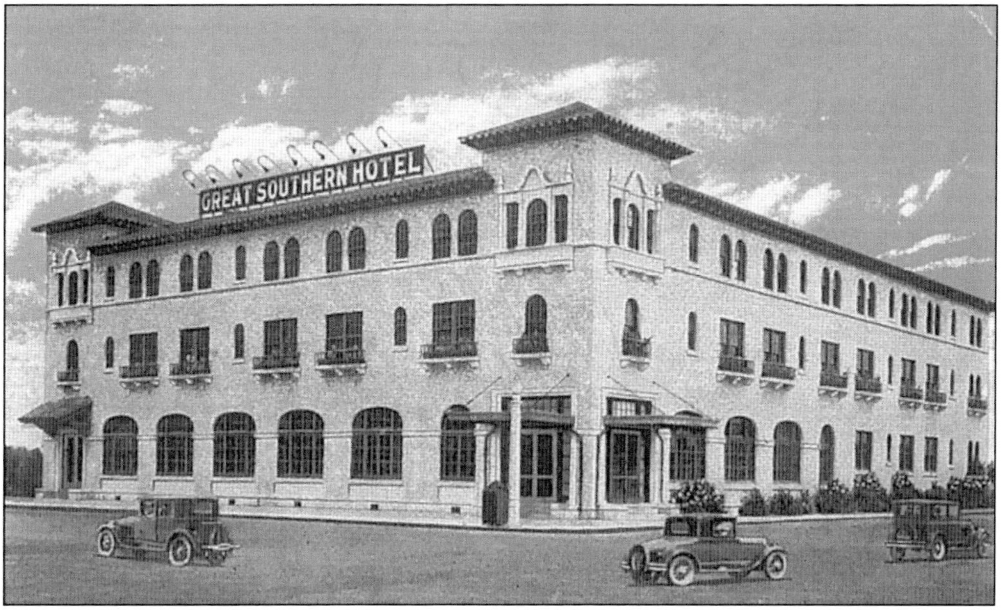

The Great Southern Hotel, built in 1924, was listed on the architect's drawings as Young Hotel. Standing at the corner of Hollywood Boulevard and Nineteenth Avenue, the three-story, 100-room hotel had a construction cost of over $500,000. It was used as an emergency hospital after the Hurricane of 1926.

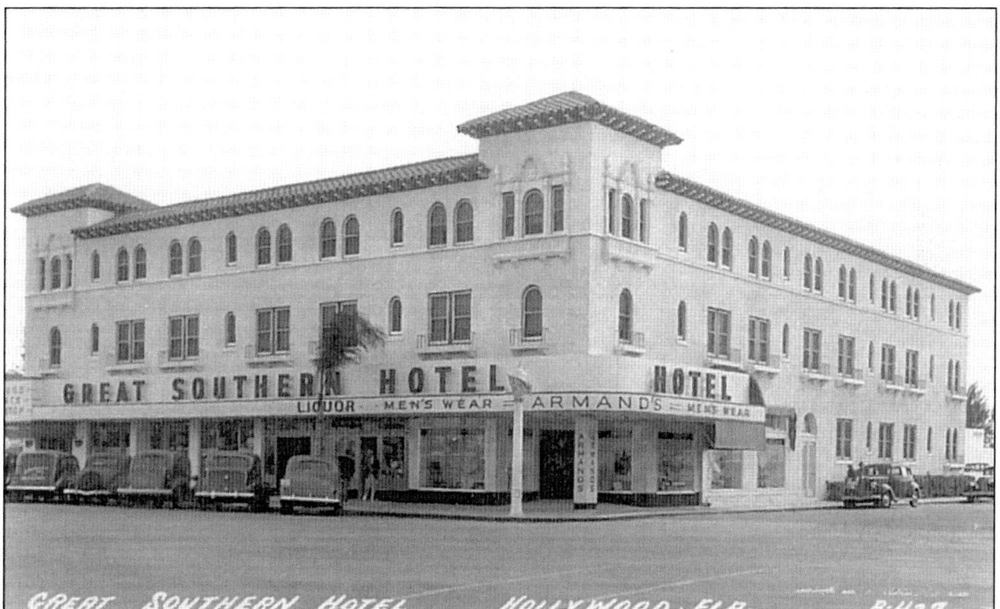

During the 1930s the hotel was remodeled and the Hollywood Boulevard side of its ground floor was converted into a row of stores. In this view a liquor store and Armand's Men's Wear occupy the retail spaces.

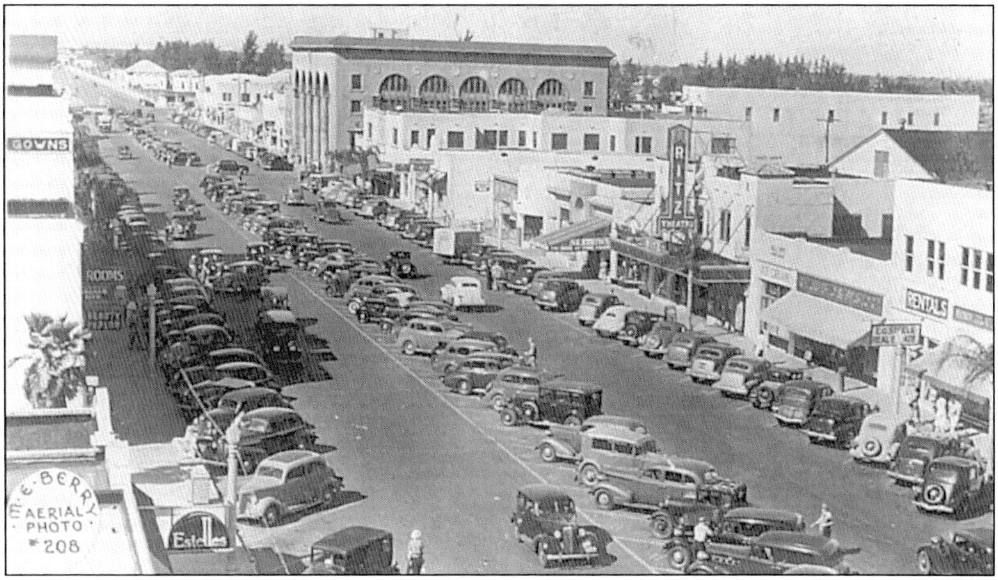

This fabulous 1930s westward view along Hollywood Boulevard shows many shops. The meat department of the Atlantic and Pacific (A&P) store, E.O. Steele Real Estate, the ice cream shop next to the Ritz Theatre, Sexmith's Fine Foods, Hollywood Cafe, and Estelle's are just a few that can be seen.

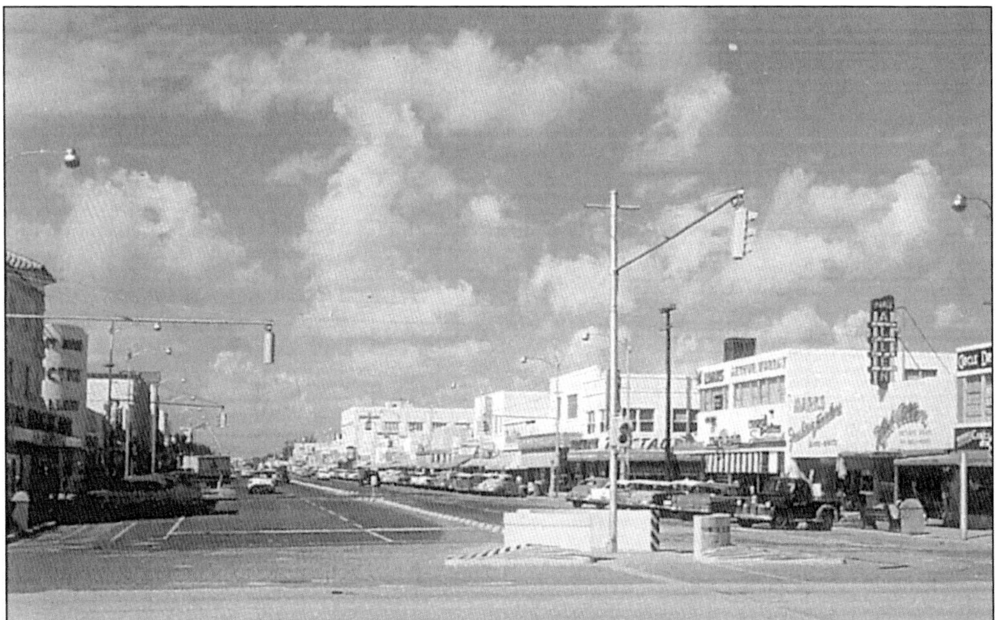

By the time this view was created, 35 years after the image at the top of the page, many traffic lights had been added. Middle-of-the-street parking, since re-established, had been eliminated. Looking west from Young Circle, we can see the Circle Dress Shop, Allen's, the Royal Palm, and other business establishments.

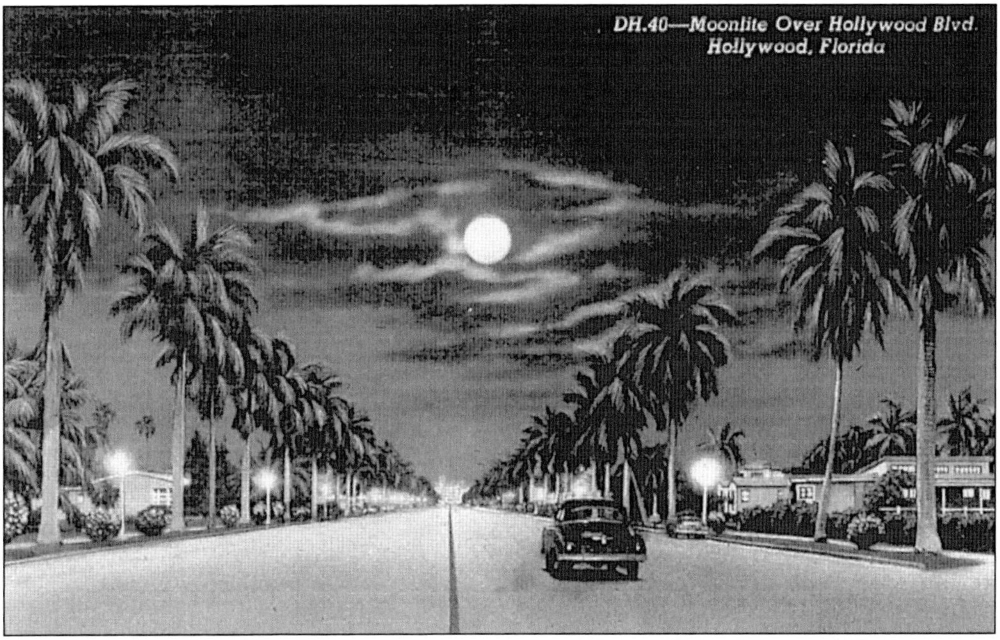

Moving west along Hollywood Boulevard brings us to the residential area and the beginning of Hollywood Hills. Ruth, on this postcard from the 1940s, wrote, "What a nice way to live—warm and clean. So glad I let my wonderful Vince talk me into coming."

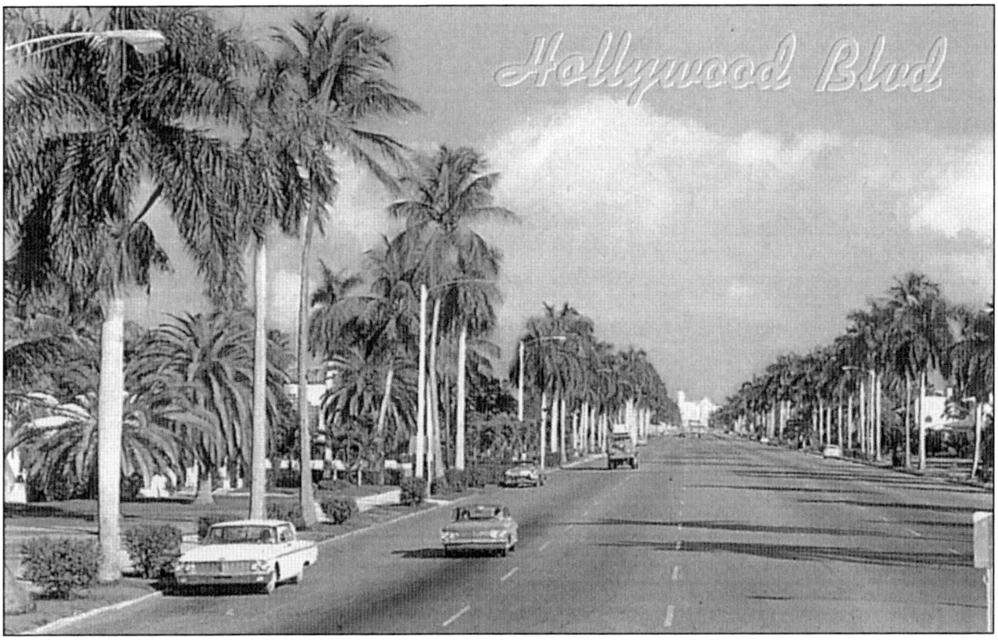

Little had changed along Hollywood Boulevard by the late 1960s. The broad roadway and stately palm trees continued to add to the glamour of its homes. Modern streetlights had replaced the older ones.

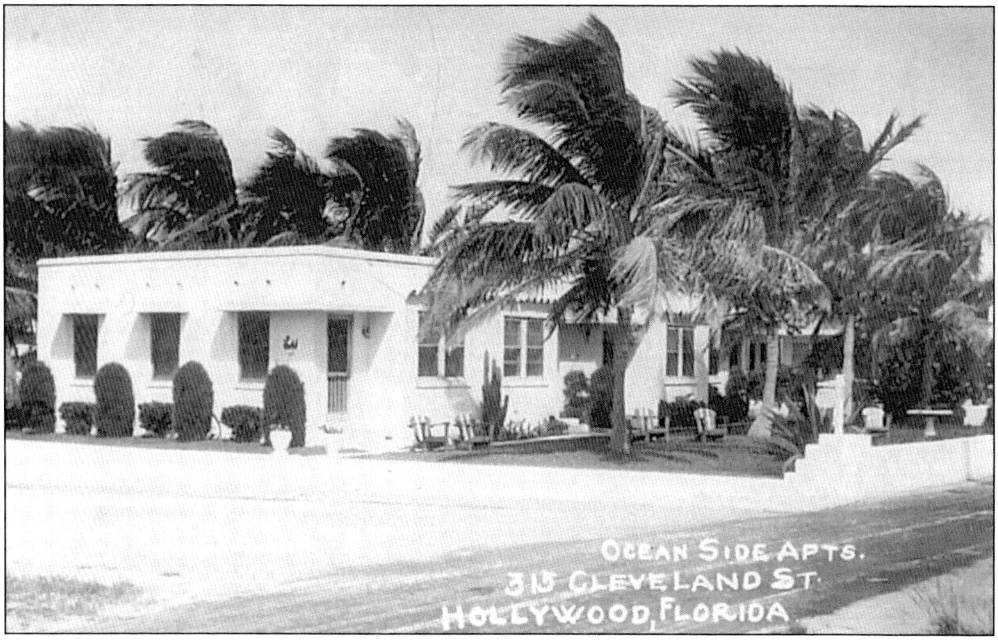

Ocean Side Apartments, located at 315 Cleveland Street, began as a ranch-style building with one-room efficiencies facing the ocean. The "apartment-motel" concept was very popular, since it allowed the accommodation of visitors whether they planned to stay for just a few days or for the entire winter season.

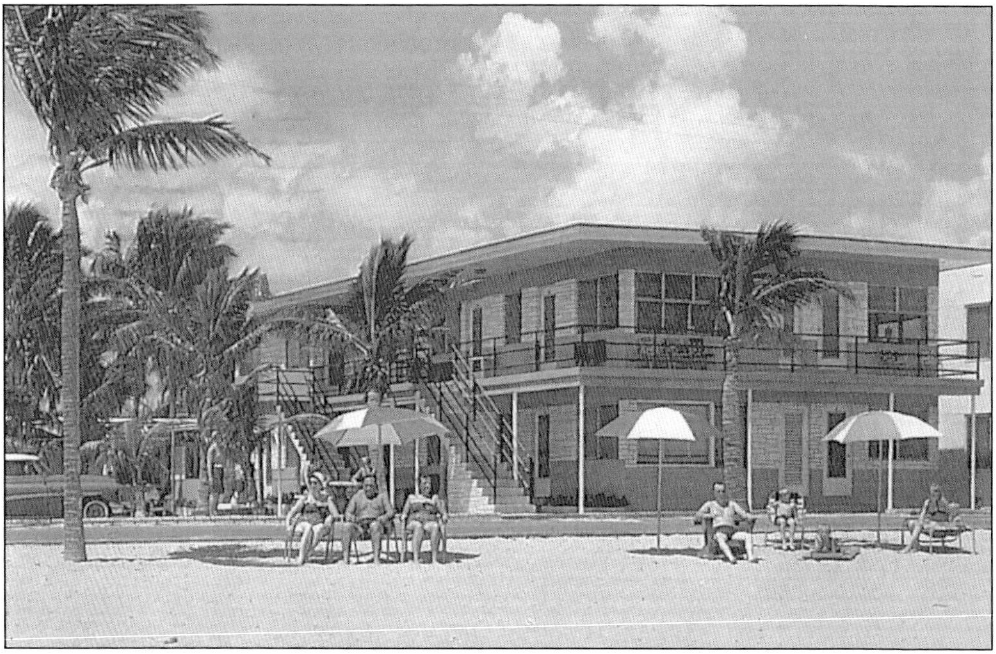

By the 1960s Oceanside Apartments had streamlined its name and added a second story. It had 21 motel rooms and furnished apartments with televisions and air-conditioning. Bright blue trim, colorful beach umbrellas, and shuffleboard courts added to its charm.

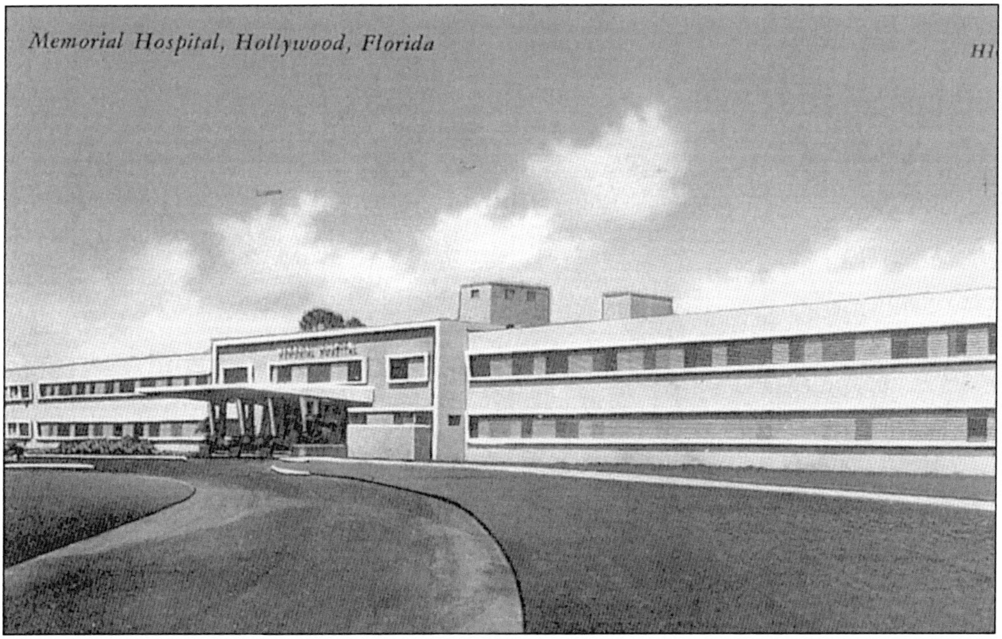

Memorial Hospital opened its doors in 1953 with 32 doctors and 28 nurses on staff, and 100 beds available. Located on Johnson Street at Thirty-fifth Avenue, the two-story building treated 12 patients on its first day. By the late 1950s the annex, obstetrical care, and autopsy buildings had been added and a $4 million expansion was planned.

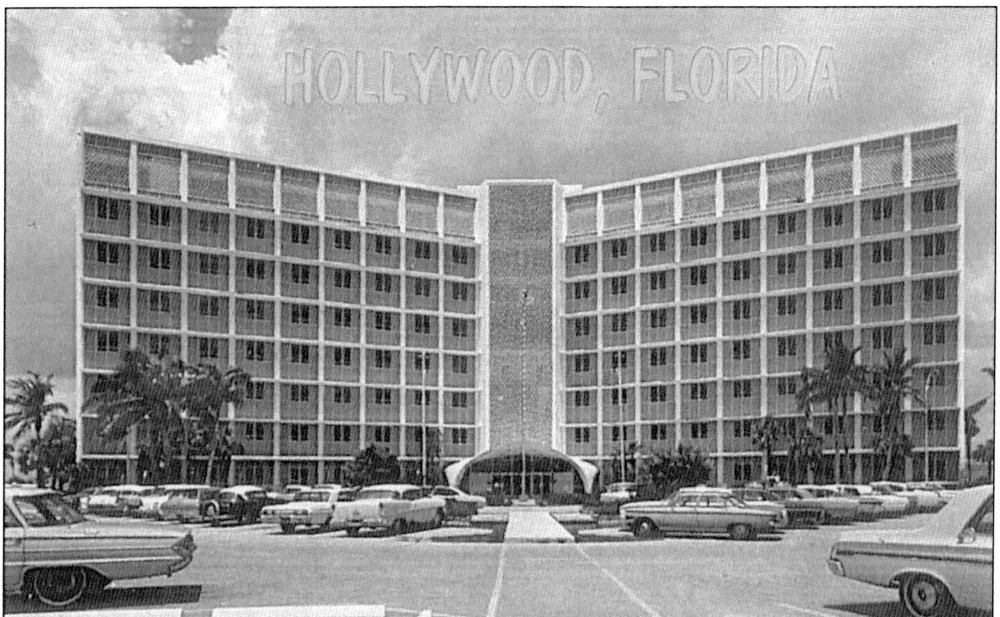

By 1963 the hospital had grown to eight stories. More additions came in 1967 and 1974. By 1982 Memorial was one of Florida's five-largest hospitals, with more than 380 doctors and 800 nurses. That year there were 25,000 admissions and 54,000 emergency cases. Still located on the same spot, the hospital has continued to expand.

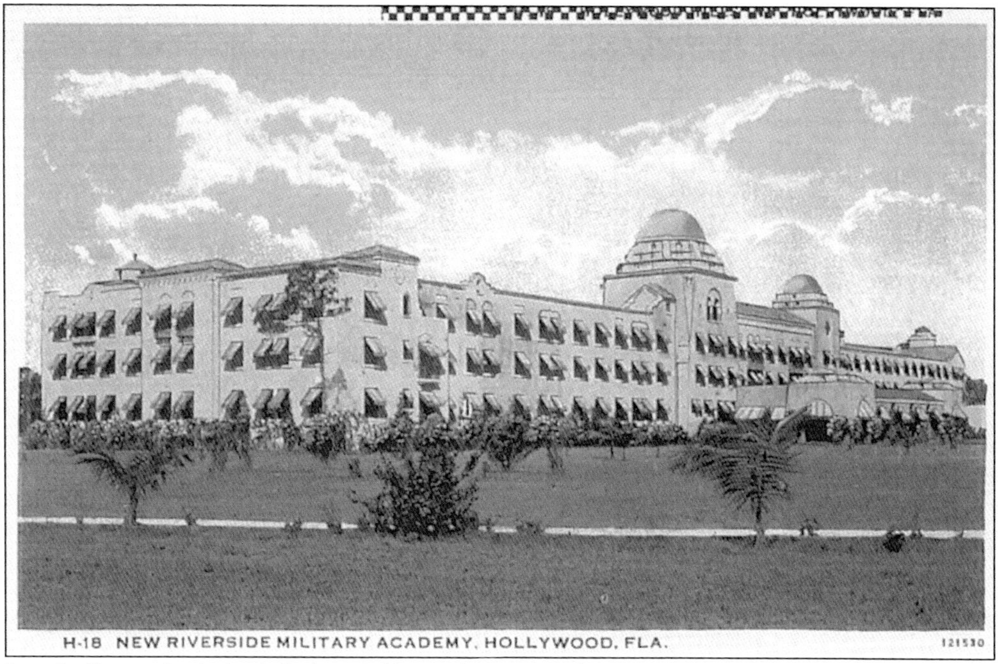

Joseph Young had deeded the Hollywood Inn on the westernmost circle to the City of Hollywood after the disastrous 1926 Hurricane. Late in 1931 the Riverside Military Academy of Gainesville, Georgia, bought the inn for $1, and in 1932 it became the academy's winter home. This postcard was re-captioned after the purchase.

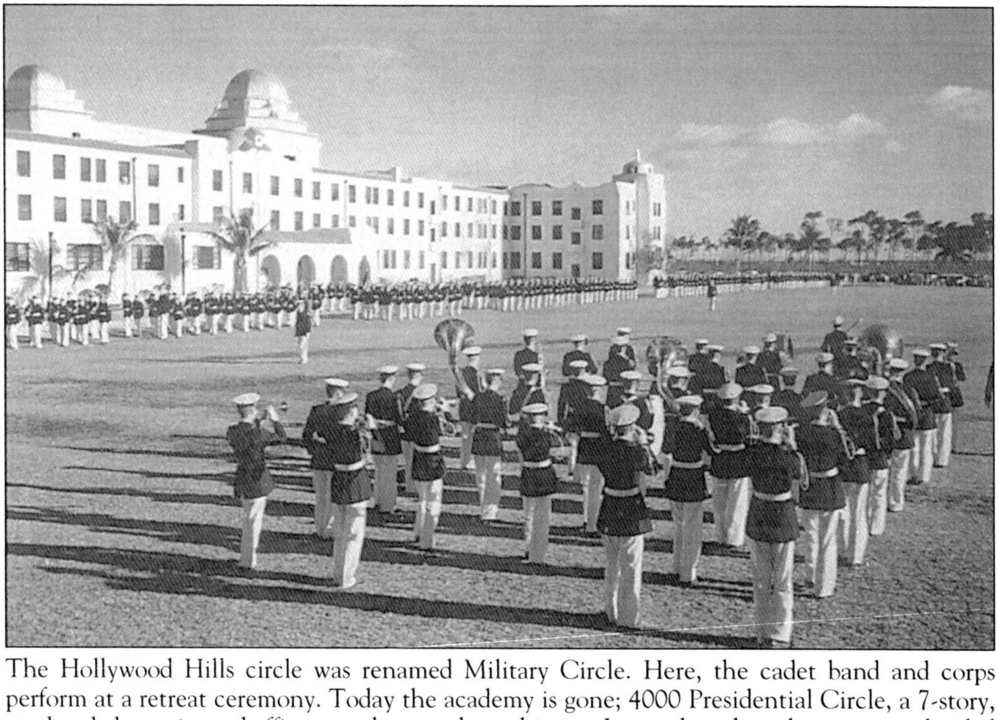

The Hollywood Hills circle was renamed Military Circle. Here, the cadet band and corps perform at a retreat ceremony. Today the academy is gone; 4000 Presidential Circle, a 7-story, steel and glass-mirrored office complex stands on this site. Its north and south towers are divided by a domed atrium.

Three

HOMES AND HOTELS

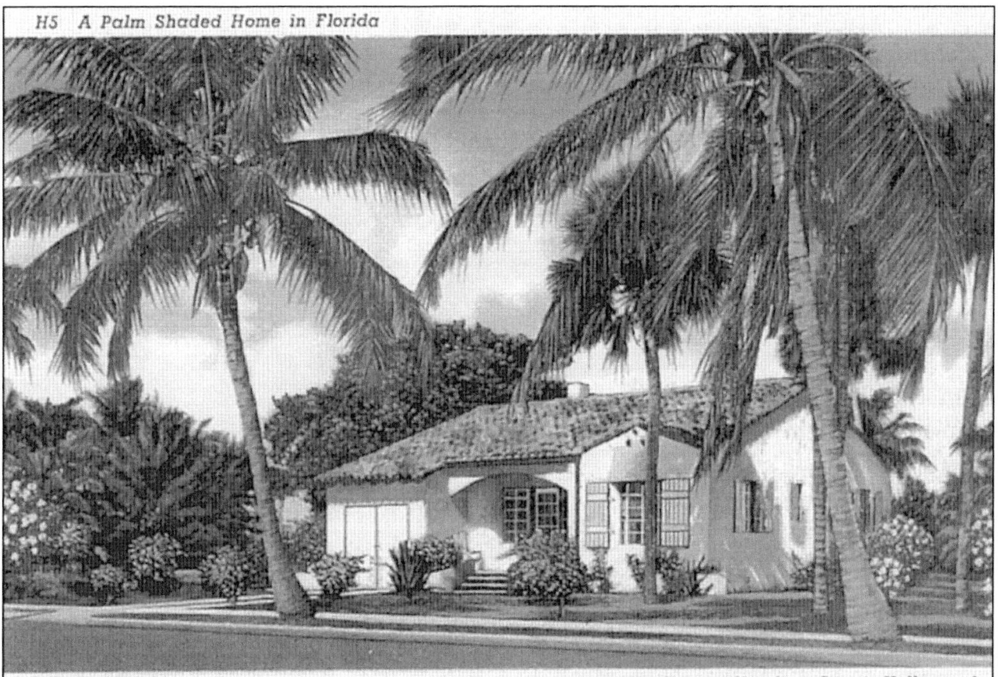

During the winter of 1925–26, at the peak of the land boom, Hollywood Land Company brochures announced that Hollywood had 30,000 residents. The devastating Hurricane of 1926, however, along with the stock market crash of 1929 and hundreds of bankruptcies and foreclosures in the early 1930s, brought the population down to 2,869. Until his financial woes in the 1930s, Young's Hollywood Land Company had built all of Hollywood's streets and sidewalks one section at a time as each area of the planned city was opened for sale. World War II resurrected the city; the influx of U.S. Navy training and operating facilities brought many jobs and offset the loss of tourist dollars due to gasoline and tire rationing. Thousands of servicemen and their families came to Broward and settled here after the war. This postcard shows a lovely bungalow, shaded by palm trees, on Harrison Street in the 1940s.

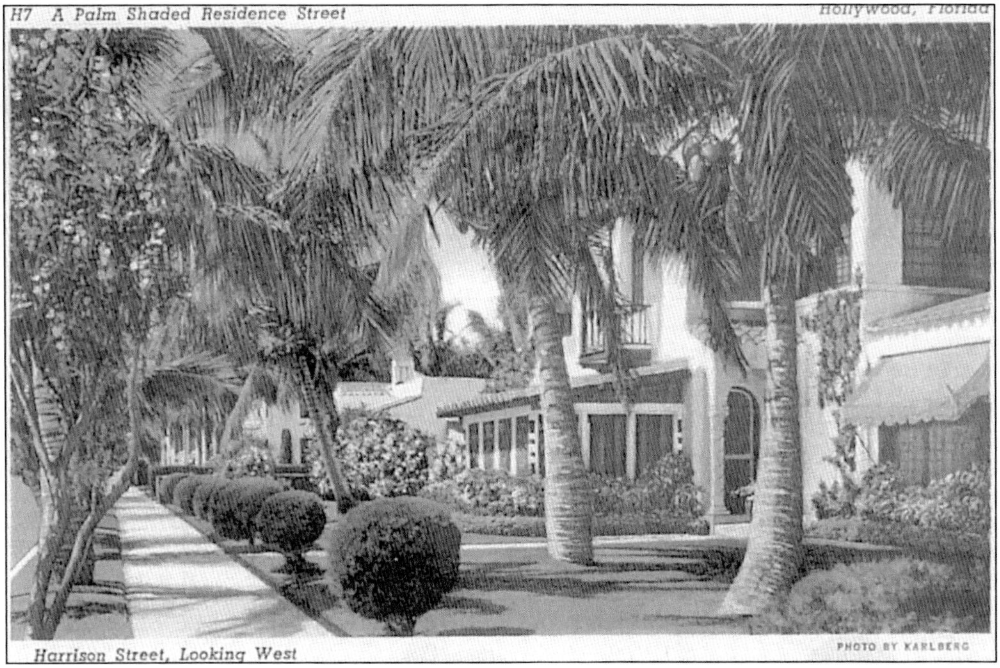

Though residential streets such as the one pictured above can look peaceful, excitement may be just around the corner. In 1924 the Beery family spotted a 6-foot alligator in the middle of the street. Riding in the back seat of the family car, "Ol' Al" was taken home to 1818 Monroe. Mr. Beery built a wire-fenced pool and his new pet ate table scraps and got to know each member of the family. The Beerys scrubbed his hide until it gleamed.

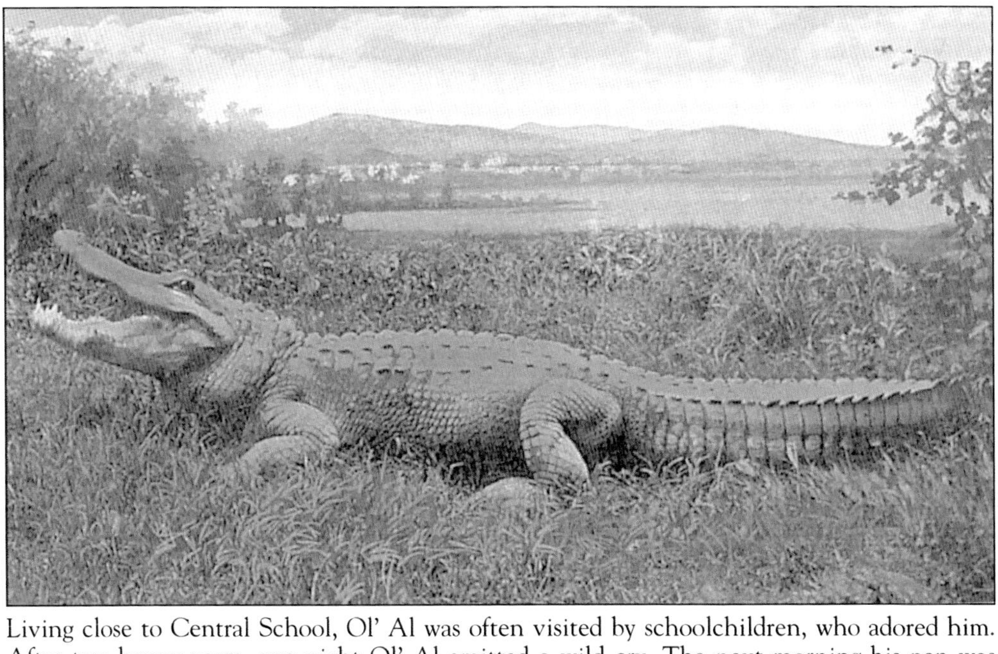

Living close to Central School, Ol' Al was often visited by schoolchildren, who adored him. After two happy years, one night Ol' Al emitted a wild cry. The next morning his pen was empty. A bridge tender at the Dania crossing of the Intracoastal Waterway reported a gator with a polished hide swimming to freedom, shortly after dawn.

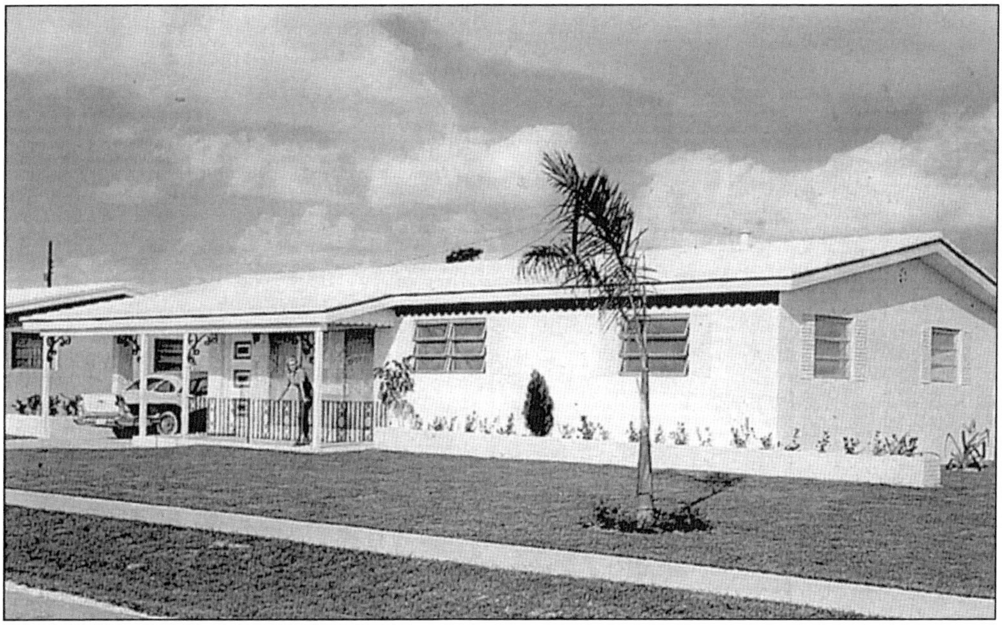

Real estate development was brisk in the 1950s. Hollywood Inc. escalated Hollywood's development in 1953 when William Horvitz (Sam's 27-year-old son) became its president. By 1970 Hollywood boasted 106,873 residents. This postcard shows a Dean Homes model in Boulevard Heights, "as modern as tomorrow."

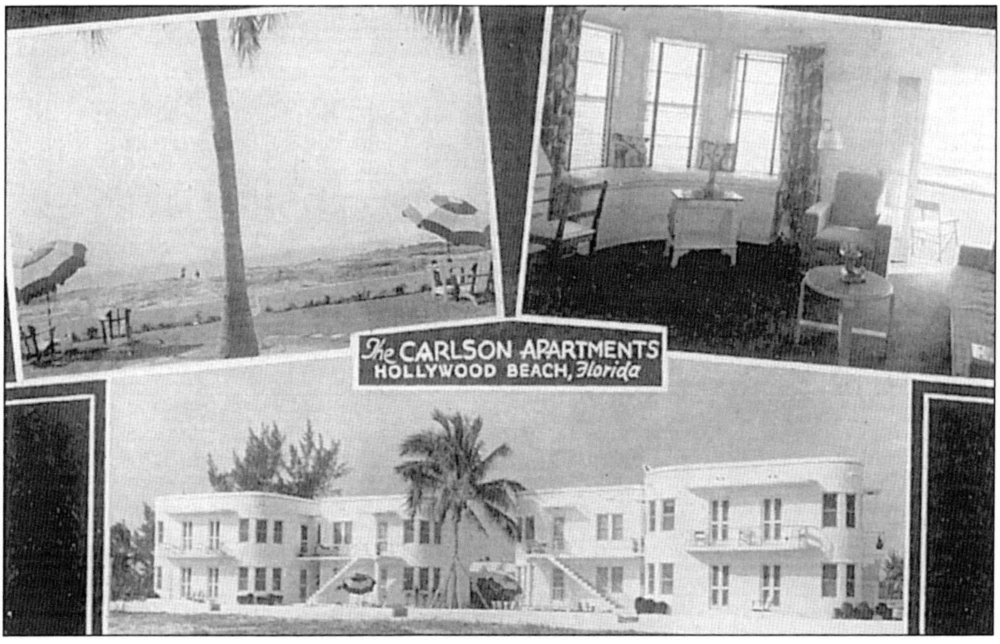

In addition to single-family homes, apartment buildings sprang up rapidly. Servicemen stayed in Hollywood after their discharge and needed accommodations while they saved money to bring their families to Florida. A large number of Northerners and French Canadians began to stay in Hollywood as "snowbirds" during the winter season.

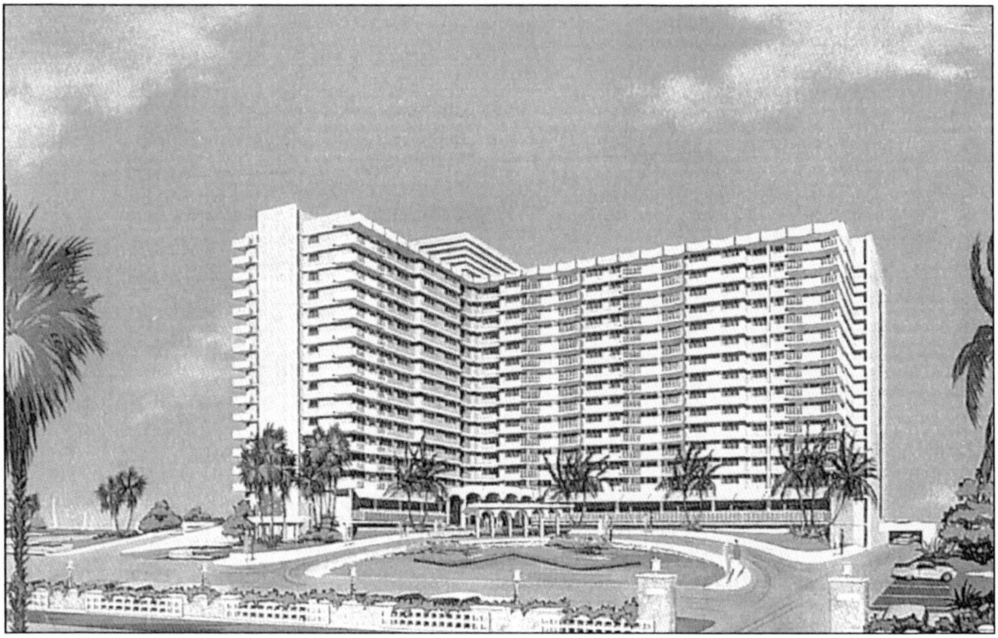

During the 1970s huge highrises, most sold as condominiums, were built along Hollywood's beaches. Presidential Towers at 2501 South Ocean Drive, one block north of the Diplomat Hotel, boasts 17 stories, a private beach, an olympic pool, a shopping concourse, and a restaurant on site.

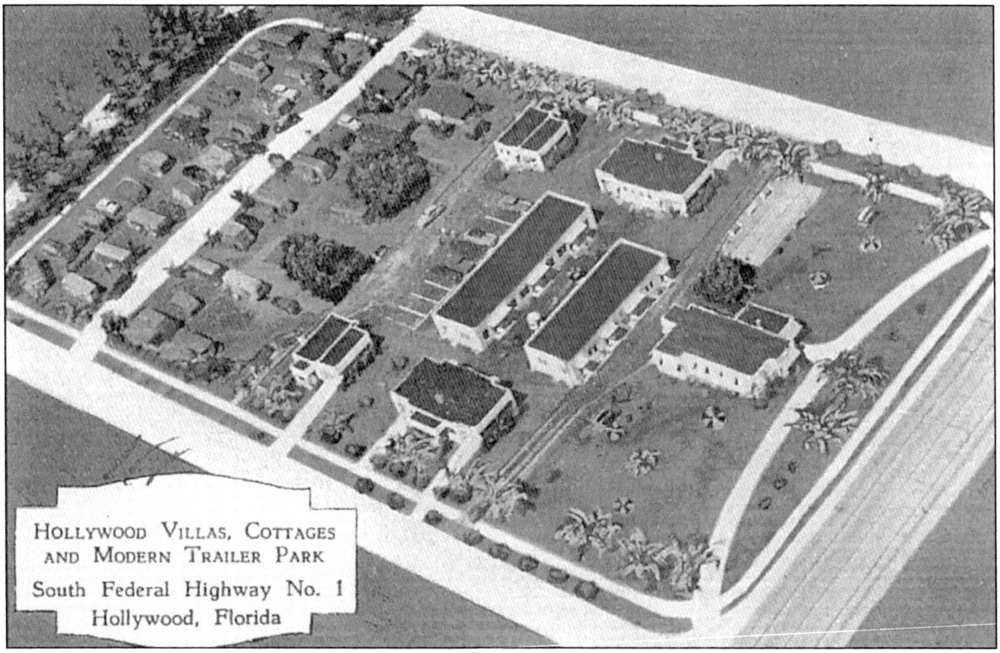

For those needing something less extravagant, Hollywood Villas, Cottages, and Modern Trailer Park was located on South Federal Highway, one mile south of the downtown circle. Daily or weekly rates were available for one-, two-, and three-room apartments with electric kitchens, private baths, and steam heat.

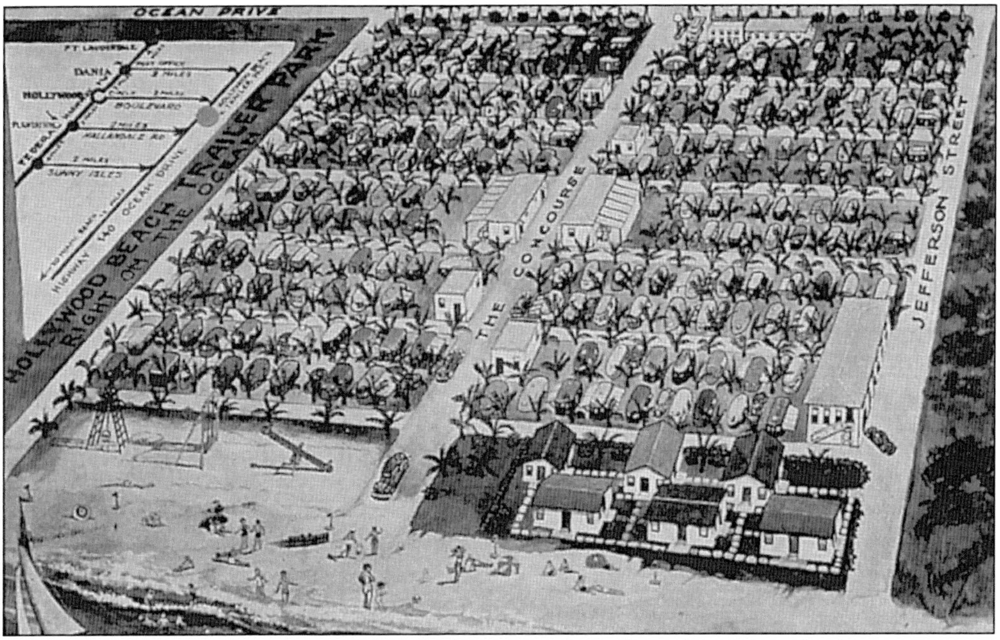

The Hollywood Beach Trailer Park was, and remains, the only trailer park with a large amount of ocean frontage. This 1950s view combines a drawing of the park with a map of the major streets in the area. The park was "up to the minute in equipment" and had "soft certified water."

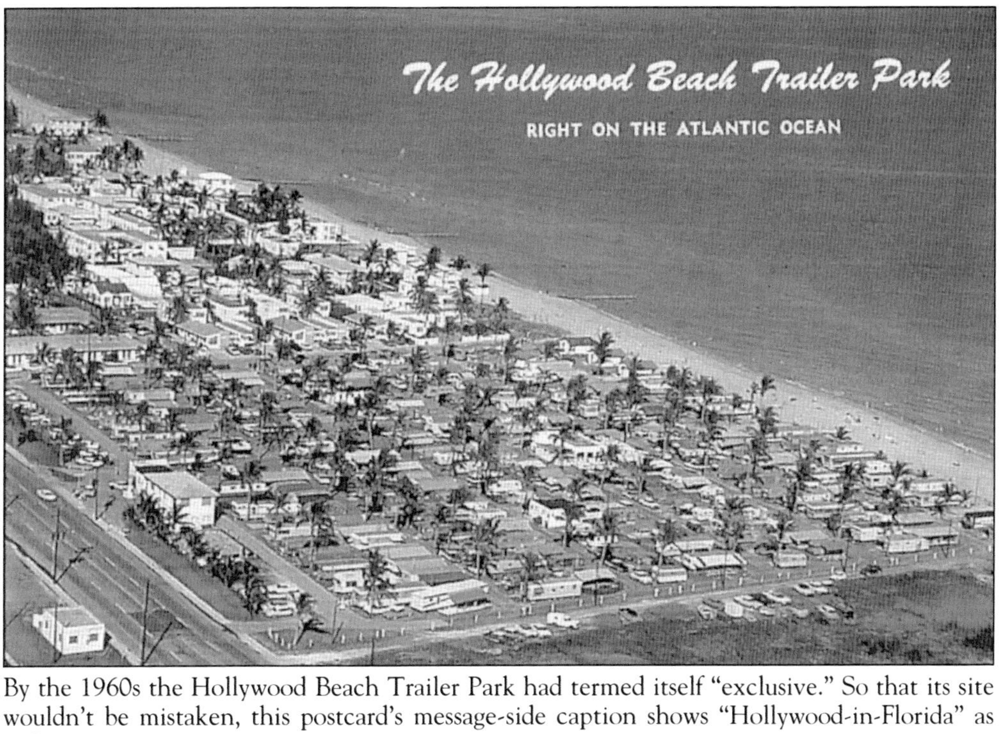

By the 1960s the Hollywood Beach Trailer Park had termed itself "exclusive." So that its site wouldn't be mistaken, this postcard's message-side caption shows "Hollywood-in-Florida" as its location.

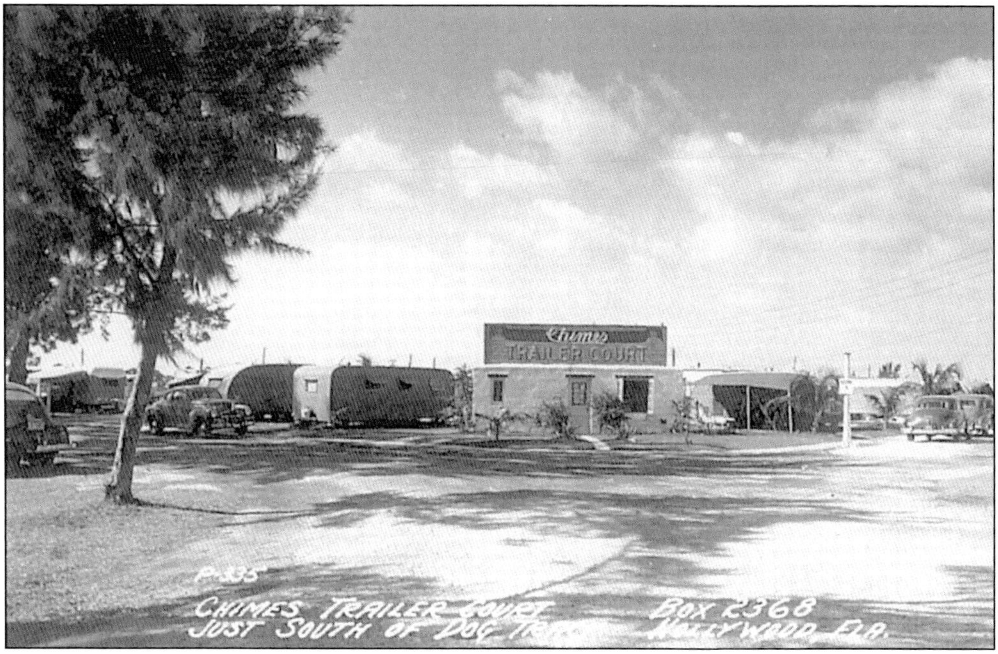

Trailers and mobile homes have always been very popular, in spite of their unfortunate tendency toward destruction in hurricane winds and Florida's frequent lightning storms. The Chimes Trailer Court was located just south of the dog track.

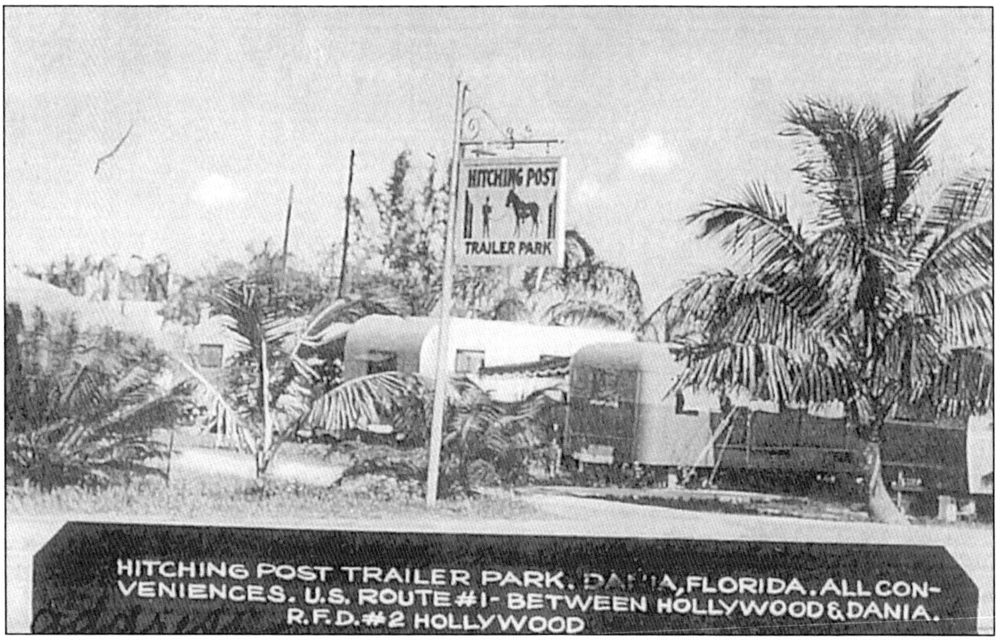

Then, as now, many "snowbirds" traveled to Florida in their trailers or recreational vehicles. Their homes-on-wheels allowed them to remain for as long or as short a time as they wished, without the need to unpack or find a motel they liked. The Hitching Post Trailer Park was located on U.S. Route 1, between Hollywood and Dania.

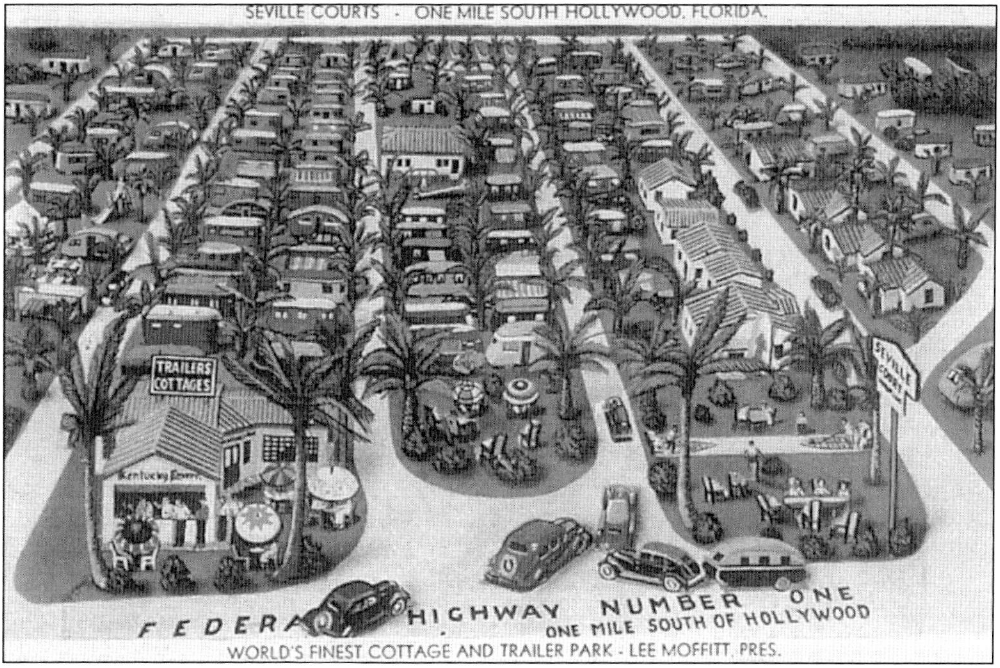

To accommodate both short-term travelers and long-term residents, Seville Courts offered villas and trailer sites. Asserting itself as the "World's Finest Cottage and Trailer Park," it was located on Federal Highway, one mile south of the downtown circle.

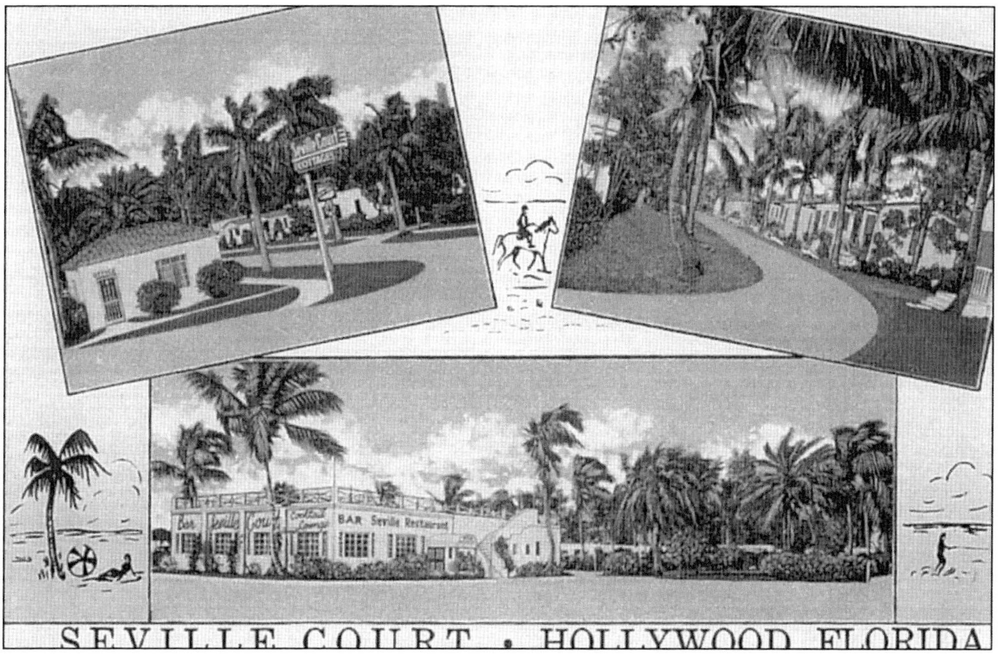

This view from the 1940s features Seville Court's cottages and lovely, palm-lined residential streets. Amenities included the attractive Seville Restaurant and Cocktail Lounge (pictured at the bottom) as well as a swimming pool, fishing, and proximity to the Gulfstream Park Race Track.

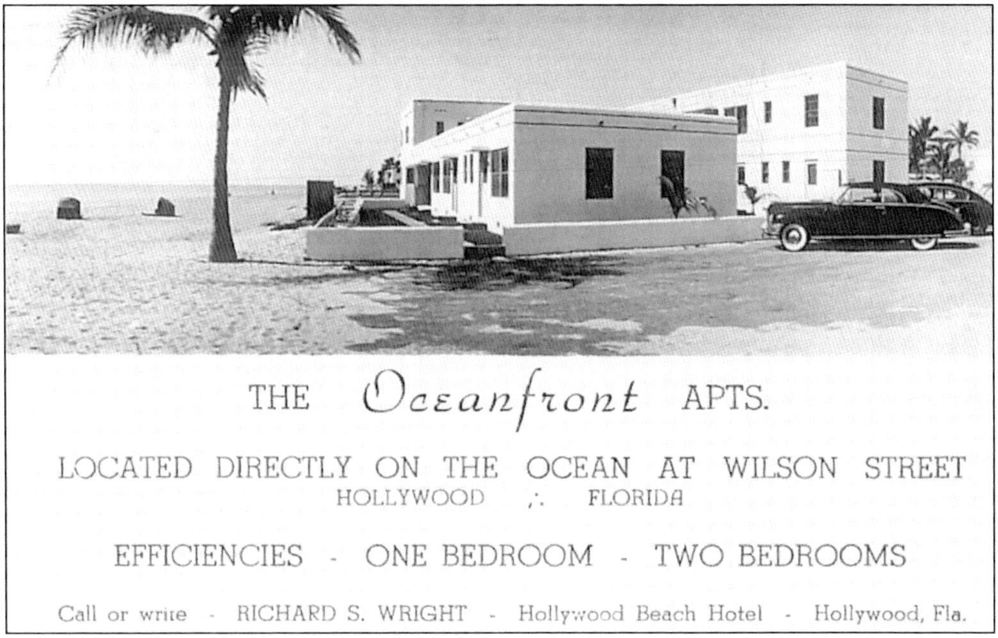

The fine line between apartments and motels has always been blurry in South Florida. Both could typically be rented by the day, week, month, or season. The real distinction came down to having a kitchen. The Oceanfront Apartments at Wilson Street appears to have been managed by the Hollywood Beach Hotel in the 1940s.

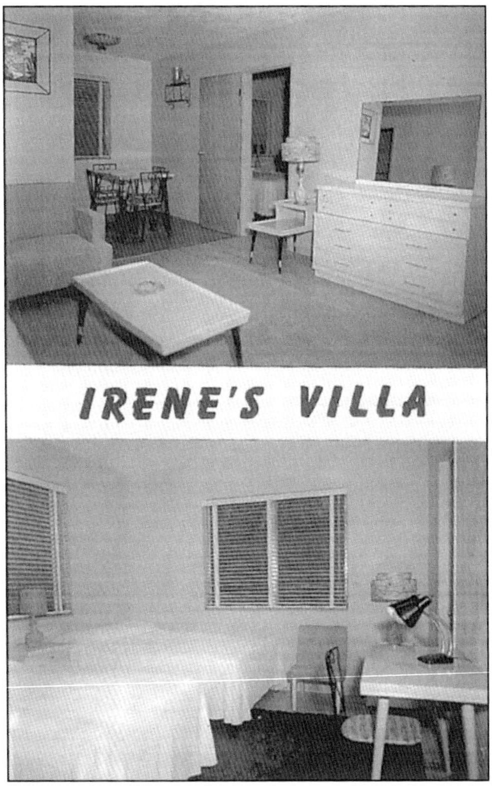

Irene's Villa, located at 328 Roosevelt Street, offered fully furnished efficiencies as well as one- and two-bedroom apartments. Sam and Irene Young promised reasonable rates. The attractive furnishings were typical of the 1950s.

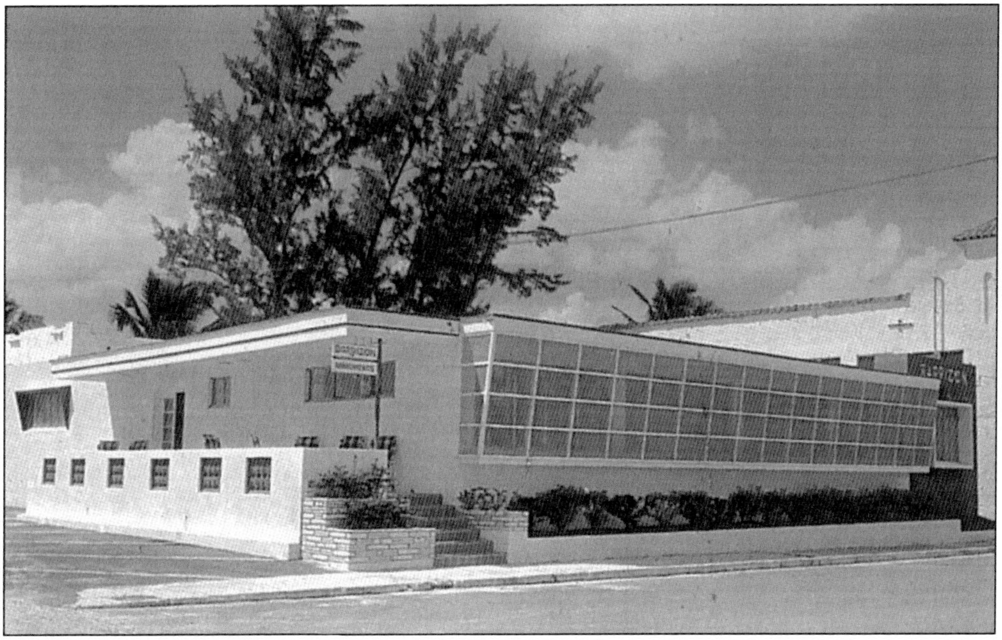

While buildings had a wide range of shapes and styles, most emphasized their windows, especially if they offered a view of the Atlantic Ocean. Barbizon Apartments at 308 Monroe (at the corner of Surf Road) advertised its "fully and tastefully furnished spacious studio apartments," ocean-view porch, and phone service.

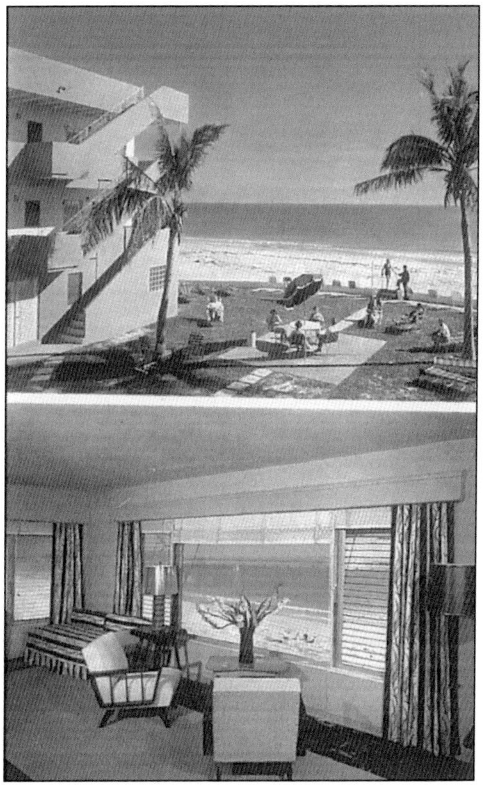

The Sands Motel and Apartments at 2404 N. Surf Road offered tile baths throughout, air-conditioning and heating, television in the lobby, two large patios, and deck shuffleboard. Its main feature was the beautiful 150-foot beachfront. "For your place in the Sun," reads the postcard, "Tel. 2-9308."

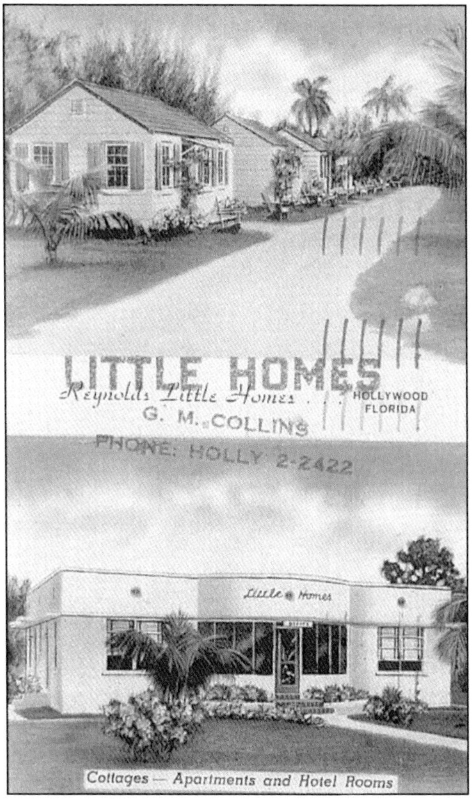

Reynolds Little Homes, located at 1845 N. Eighteenth Avenue, offered suites with private baths and heating. Its phone number was 180W. Before automatic dialing became available after WW II, four-digit phone numbers ended either in the letter J (one long ring) or W (two short rings). G.M. Collins purchased the homes in the 1950s and its new name and phone number are overprinted. A strip shopping center is presently on the site.

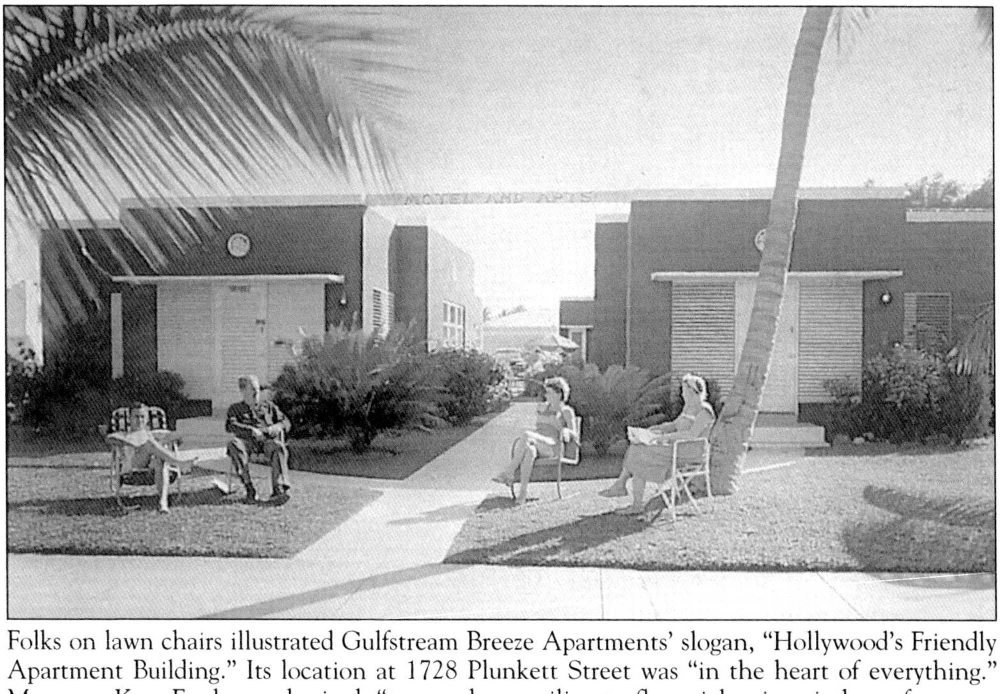

Folks on lawn chairs illustrated Gulfstream Breeze Apartments' slogan, "Hollywood's Friendly Apartment Building." Its location at 1728 Plunkett Street was "in the heart of everything." Manager Ken Frash emphasized "tremendous ceiling-to-floor jalousie windows for cross ventilation." Efficiency kitchenette units were $65 per week.

The Bali Hai, at 310 McKinley Street, modestly described itself as the "vacationer's year-around paradise." Their suites featured air-conditioning, radio, and 21-inch televisions. Free off-street parking, as well as plane and train pick-up service, were important amenities during the crowded winter tourist season.

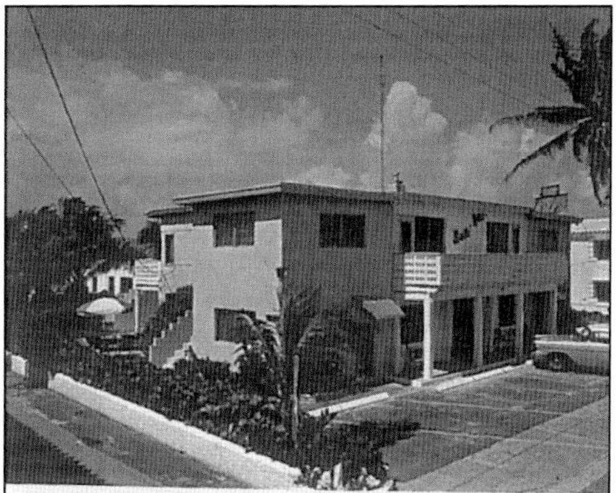

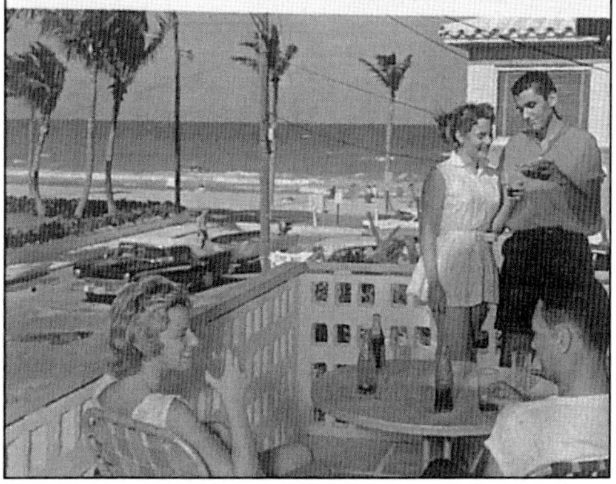

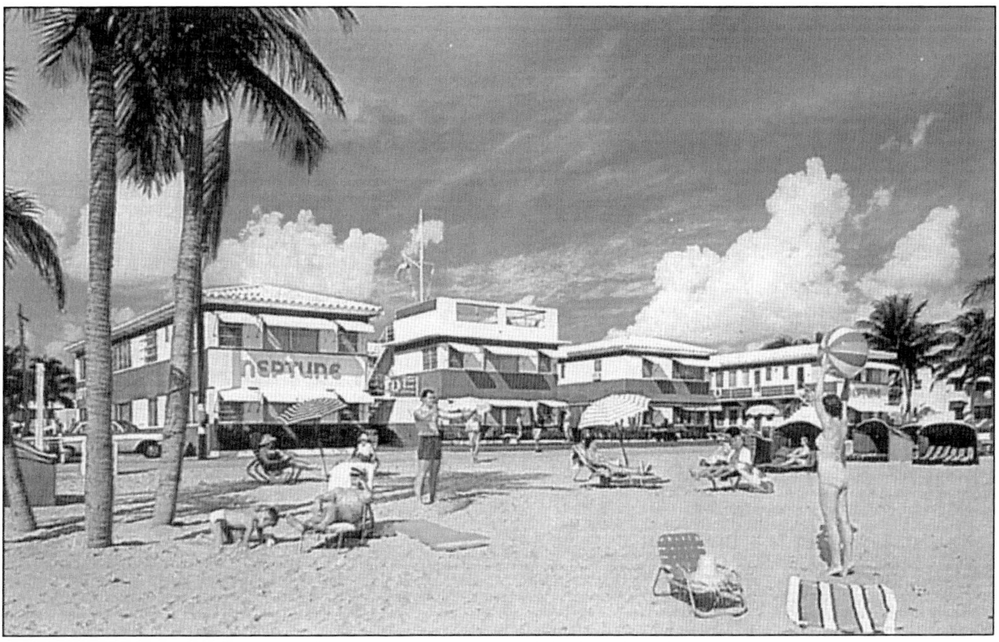

In the early 1960s Neptune Apartments at 2012 N. Surf Road advertised privacy and quiet. Free cabanas, a sun deck, shuffleboard, boating, snorkeling, skin diving, and fishing were also offered. Still on the same site today, the Neptune Hollywood Beach Club offers residence hotel and time-share units.

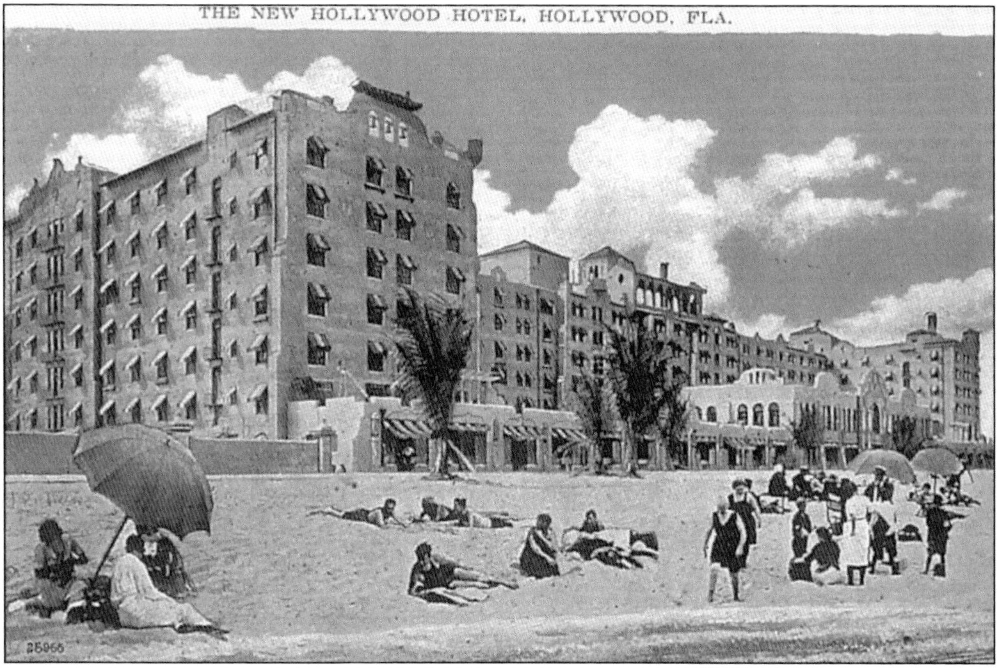

Early views of the Hollywood Beach Hotel appeared in the first chapter of this book, but the hotel's history certainly didn't end with its severe damage during the 1926 hurricane. In the days, weeks, and months after the disaster, the hotel became a shelter for the homeless and a temporary home for emergency workers.

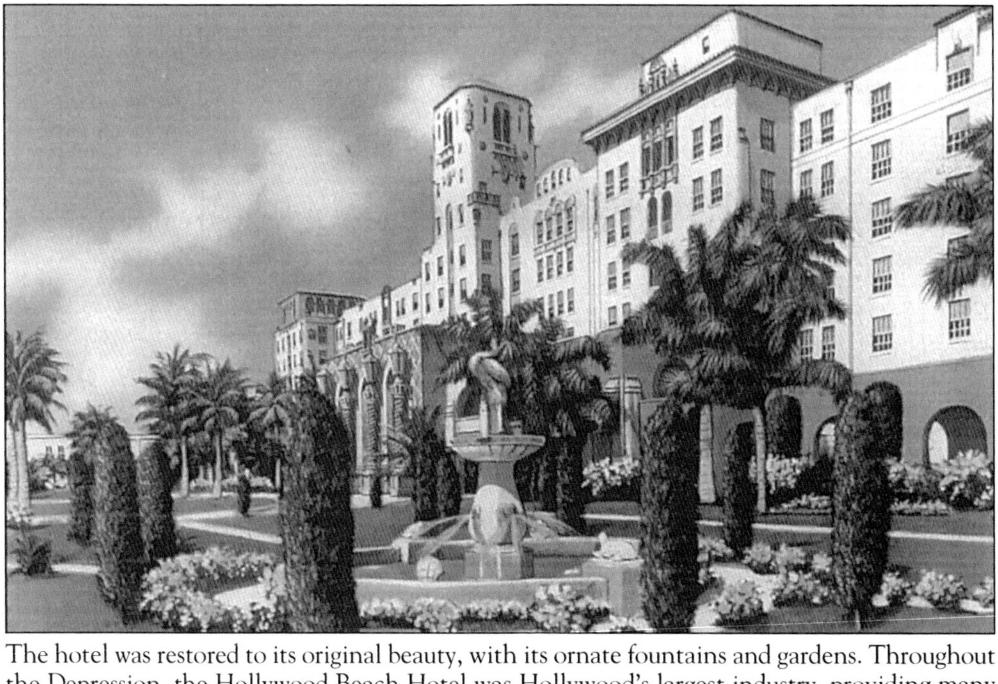

The hotel was restored to its original beauty, with its ornate fountains and gardens. Throughout the Depression, the Hollywood Beach Hotel was Hollywood's largest industry, providing many jobs. But in the 1930s, like many of the Hollywood Land Company's assets, the property went into receivership.

The Hollywood Beach Hotel, along with the Country Club and the Park View Hotel, were bought by brothers Albert and Edwin Rosenthal and E.I. Kaufmann in the 1930s. After WW II, Ben Tobin, the nationally known real estate investor who became president of the Bank of Hollywood, bought the legendary hotel.

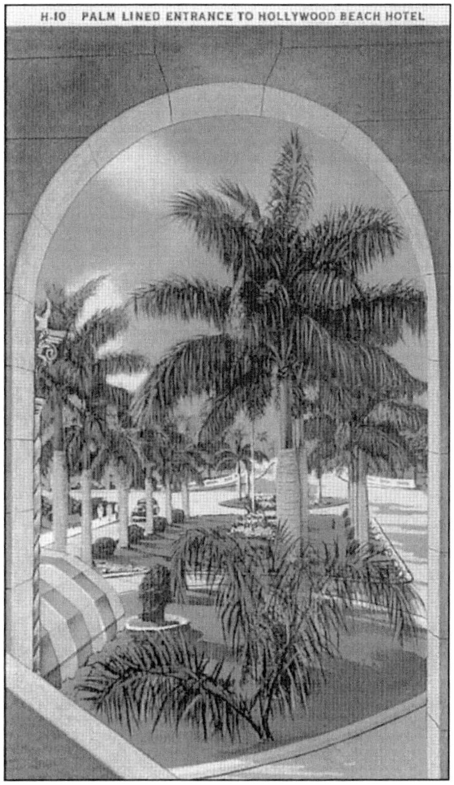

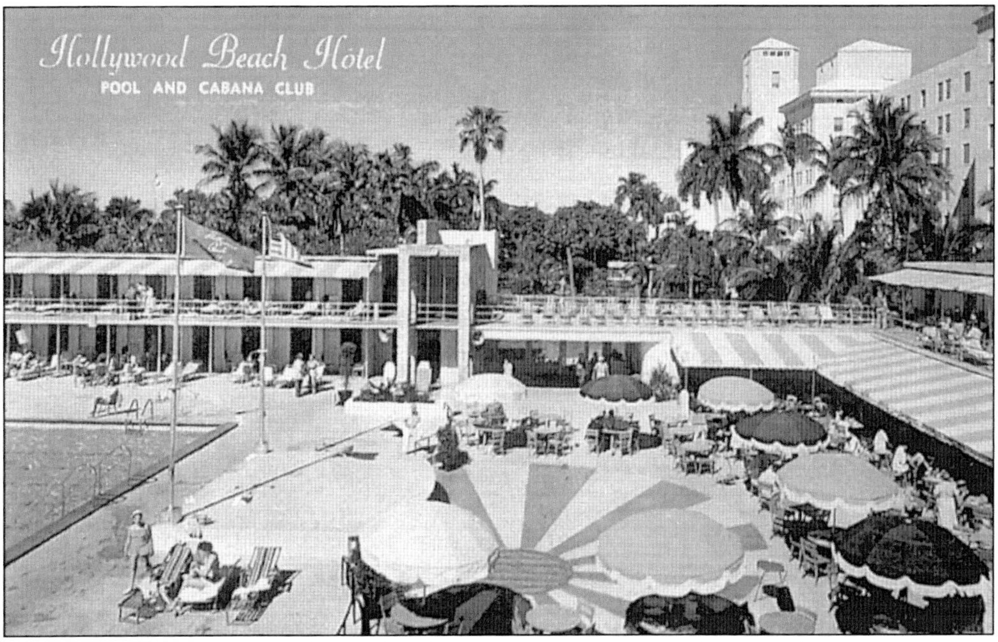

During the 1970s country club and cabana privileges were sold. Many families have fond memories of frequent free barbecues with hot dogs and hamburgers for members. For a time the building housed the Florida Bible College; then its units were sold as condominiums. Today its units are part of a time-share network.

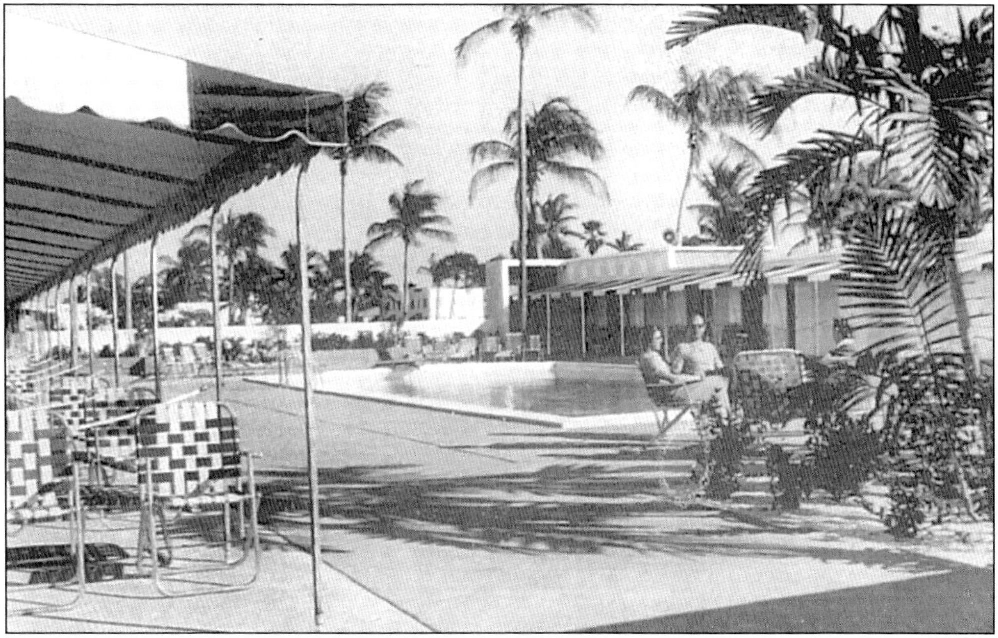

After Ben Tobin purchased the Hollywood Beach Hotel he bought the Park View Hotel at the edge of the downtown circle. The building was remodeled and renamed the Town House in 1947. Under Hollywood Beach Hotel management, it offered pool and cabana club privileges for several years before it was torn down.

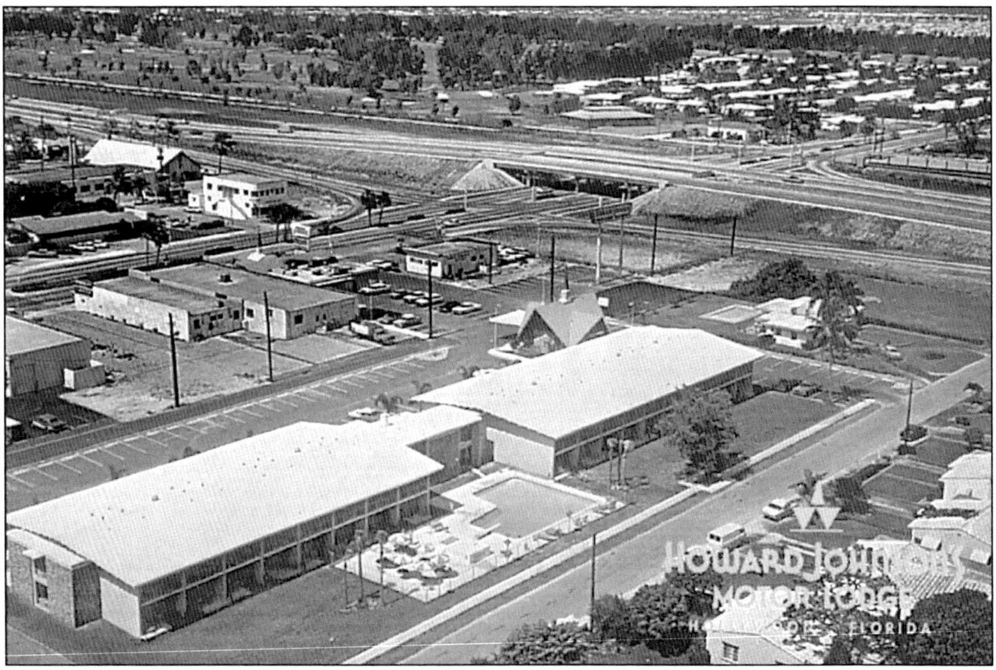

In-town motels like this Howard Johnson's Motor Lodge at the intersection of Hollywood Boulevard and Interstate 95 had no beach amenities to offer. Its advertising emphasized convenience to attractions, and restaurants such as the distinctive HoJo's orange-roofed eatery.

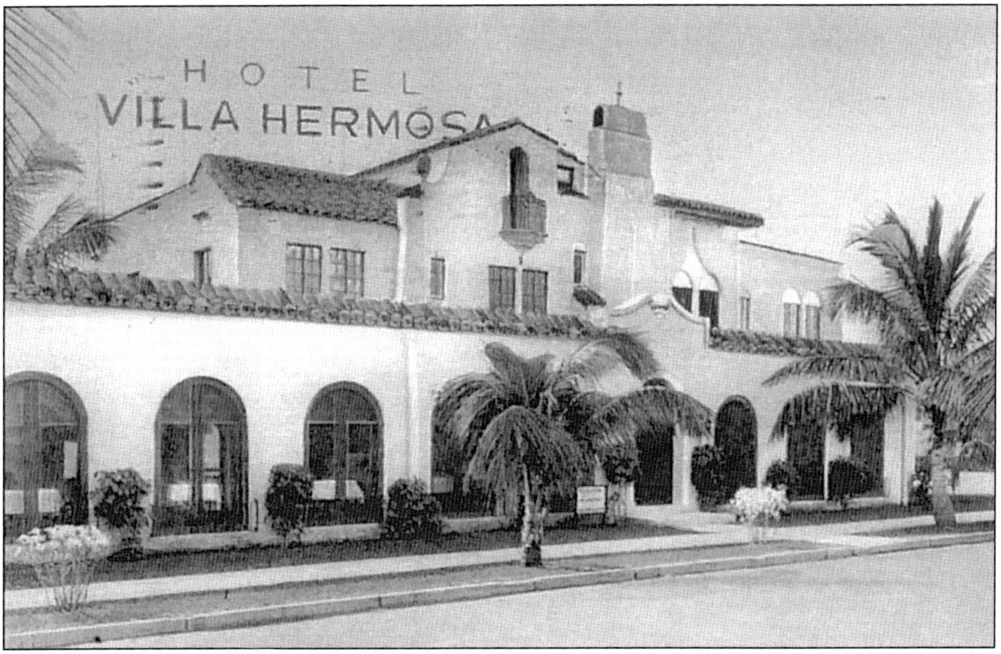

The Hotel Villa Hermosa at 1908 Jackson Street was built in 1925. This glamorous, 40-room hotel was extremely elegant in both its decor and its building design. "The House Beautiful" was its slogan, since it was located in a residential area. A tropical patio and solarium were favorites with its guests.

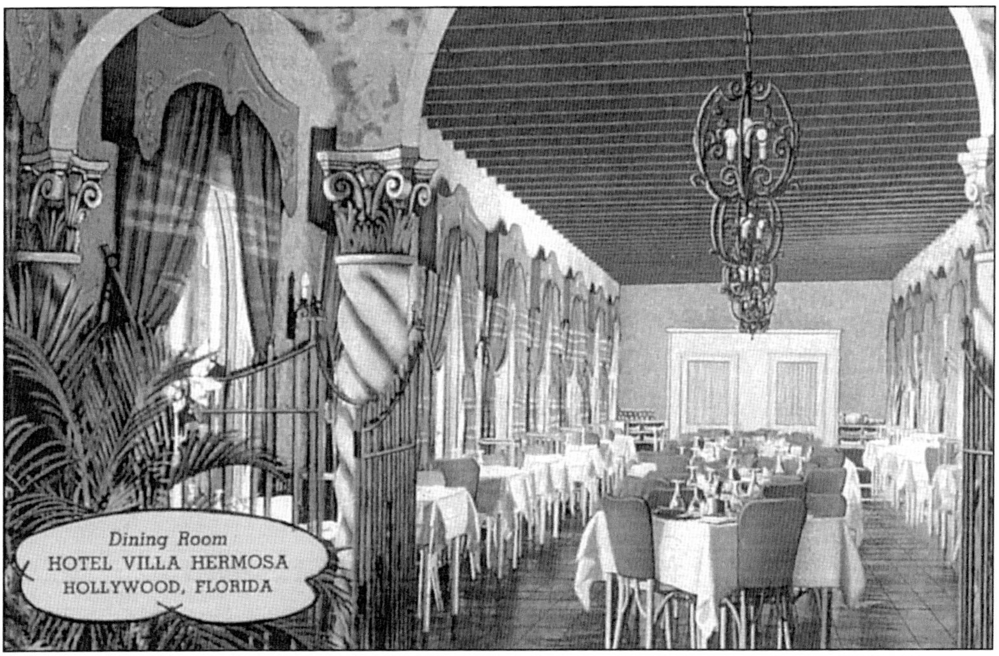

After the 1926 hurricane, owner E.H. Whitson set up a commissary inside the Villa Hermosa for residents of Hollywood and Dania who had been left homeless. Mr. Whitson housed 200 refugees and fed an additional 300 every day, including national guardsmen and Red Cross personnel, in this dining room.

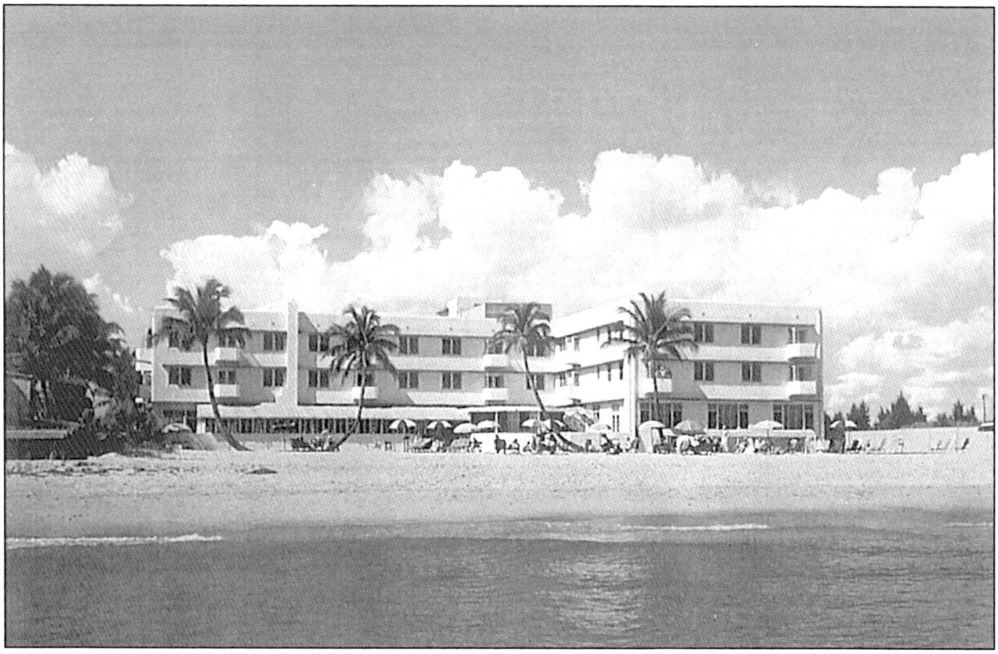

Sea Crest Manor was a luxury hotel as early as the 1940s. Boasting "a delightful atmosphere for refined people," it was located along a stretch of private beach.

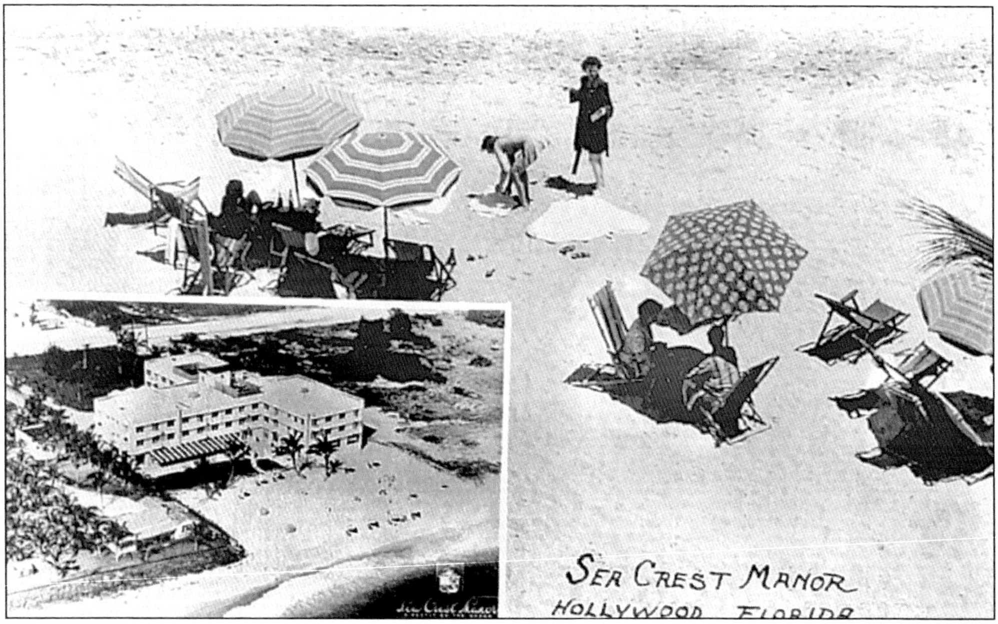

The hotel offered many amenities to its guests and was a perfect getaway in which to relax. Marion wrote, in 1944, "Ned is up on the roof for a massage and is already a new man."

The oceanfront Howard Johnson's Motor Lodge sits on Route A1A, between Taft and Carolina Streets. It is the only beachfront Howard Johnson's in the Miami-Hollywood area.

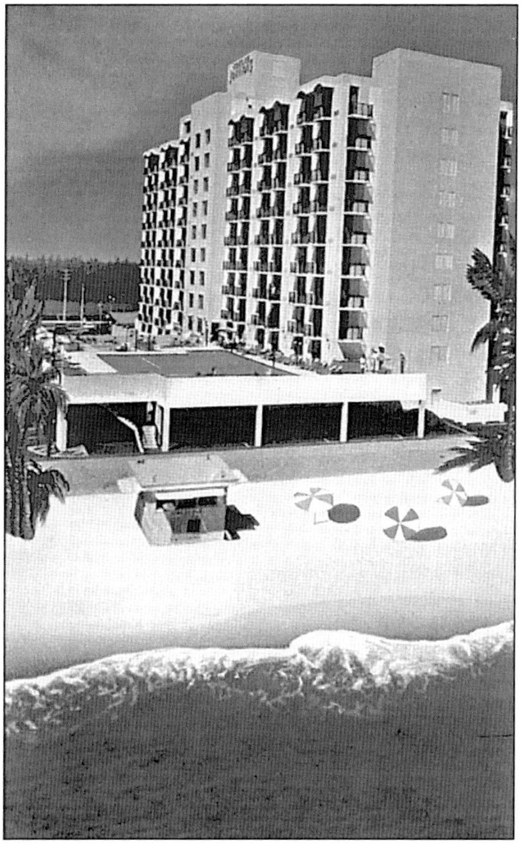

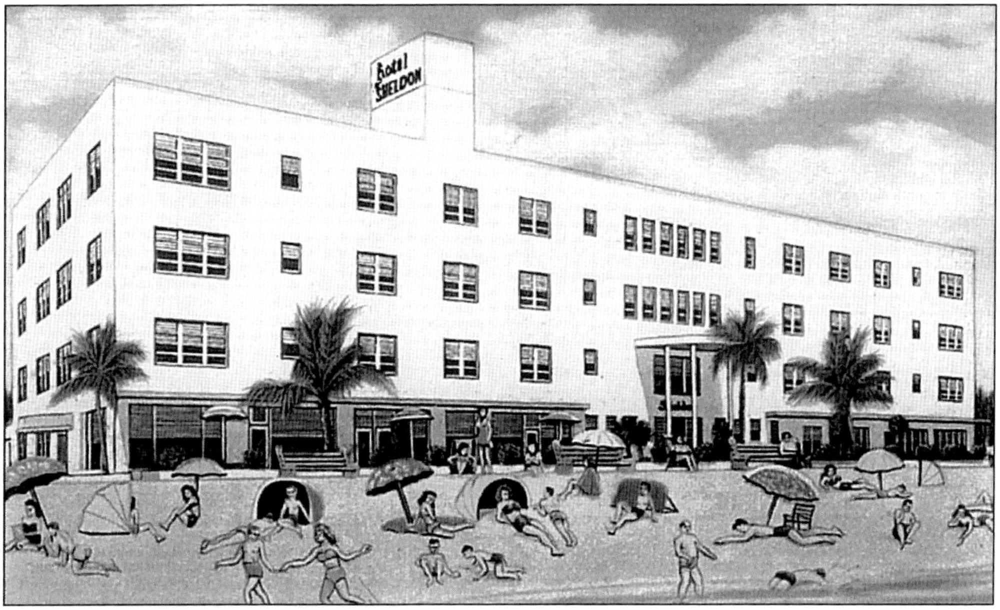

This 1940s postcard shows the modern, fireproof Hotel Sheldon. Its features included all-outside rooms with an ocean view, telephone and elevator service, a solarium, a private beach, and a cocktail lounge.

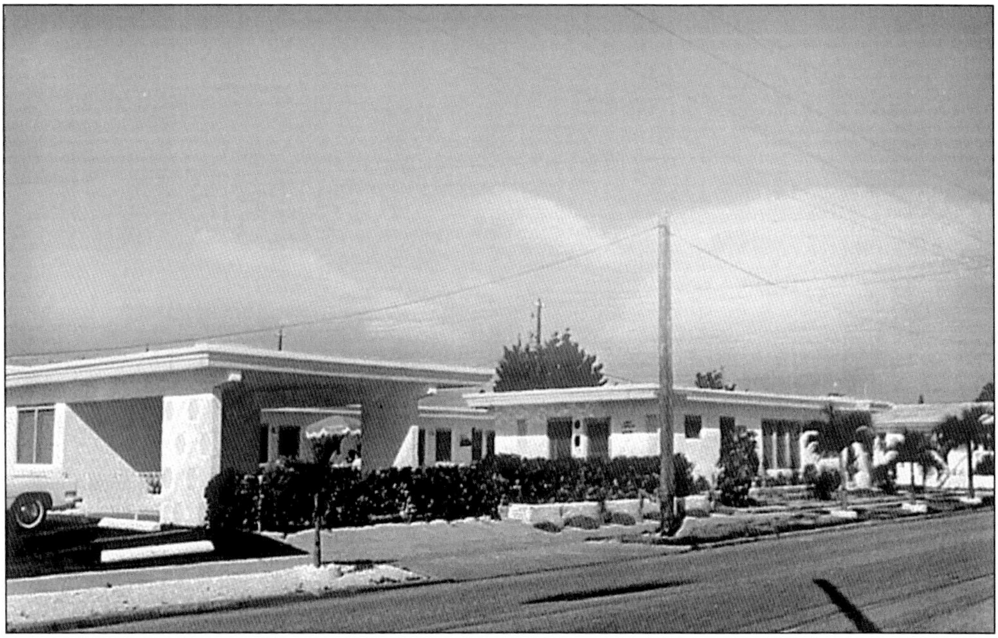
The Tower Motel, located at 1905 Lincoln Street, was one of the many that catered to French-Canadian visitors. It was owned and managed by Georges and Claudette LaPorte, who were proud to say "Nous parlons Francais." Along with air-conditioned apartments and motel rooms, they offered television, electric heat, and a pool.

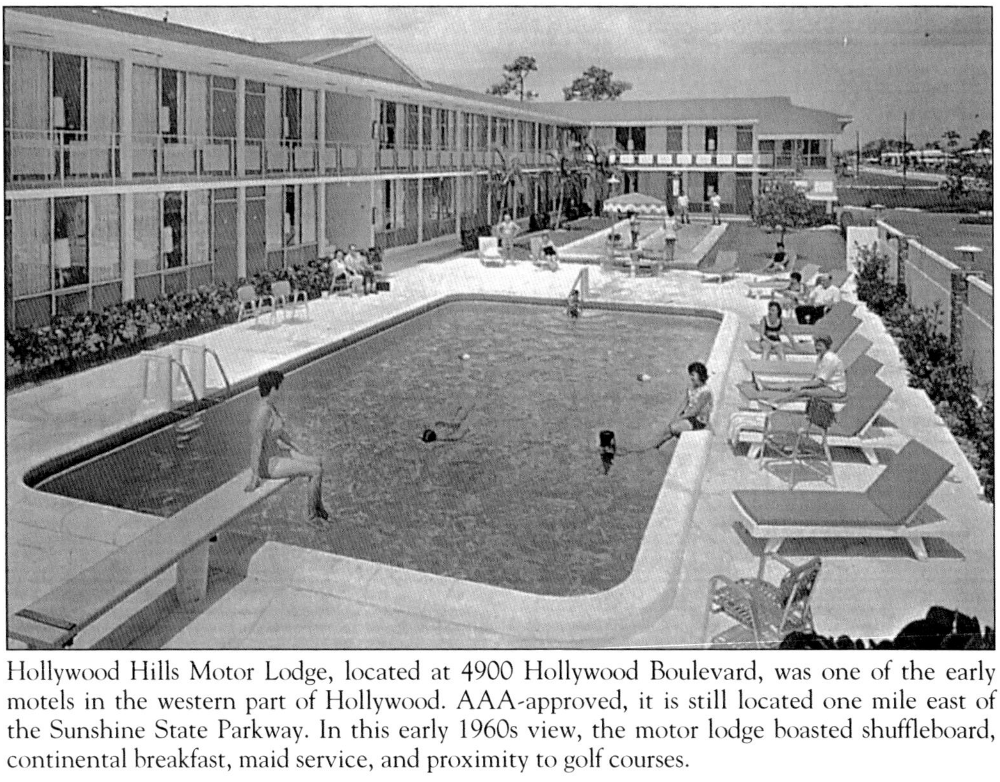
Hollywood Hills Motor Lodge, located at 4900 Hollywood Boulevard, was one of the early motels in the western part of Hollywood. AAA-approved, it is still located one mile east of the Sunshine State Parkway. In this early 1960s view, the motor lodge boasted shuffleboard, continental breakfast, maid service, and proximity to golf courses.

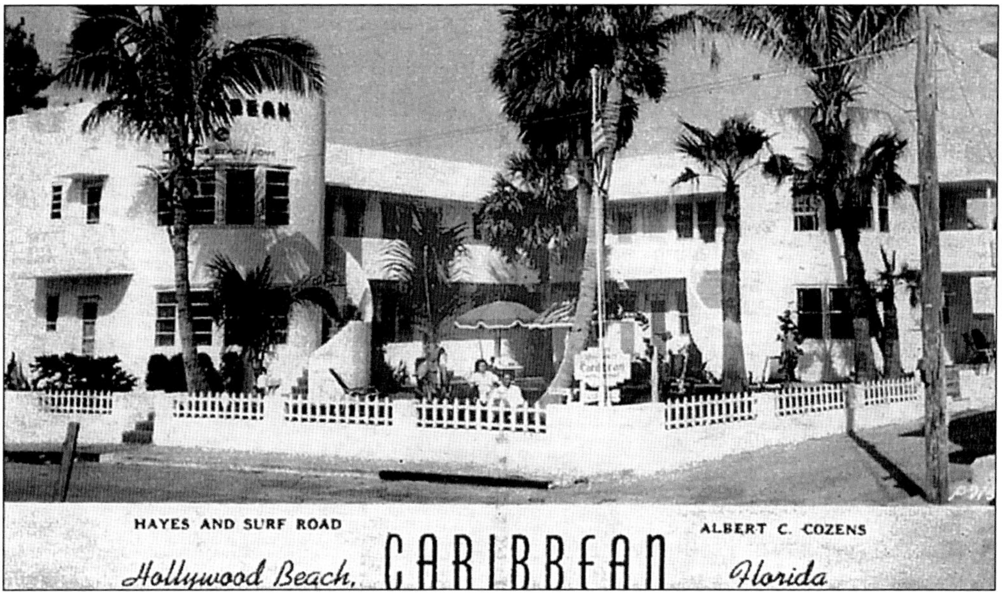

The Caribbean, located at Hayes Street and Surf Road, was managed by Albert C. Cozens during the 1950s, when this postcard was produced. It is still there today and looks very much the same.

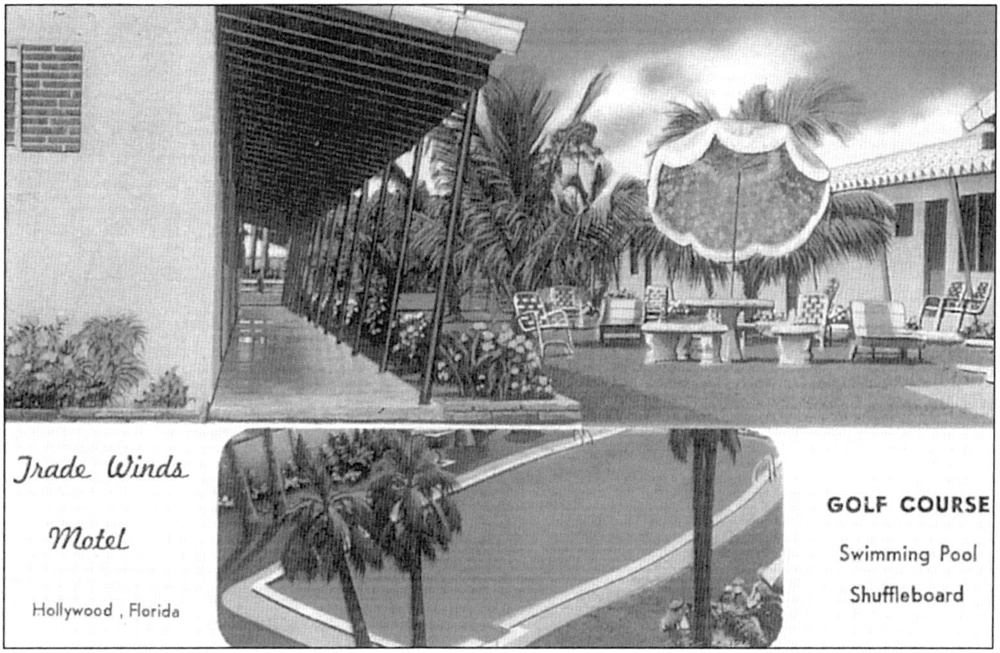

This is a 1940s view of the Trade Winds Motel, located at 2734 Johnson Street. Owners Dufek, Pagano, and Parker would arrange for guests to be met at their train, plane, or bus and transported to the motel, which offered panel-ray heat, a TV lounge, tile baths, a swimming pool, and cross ventilation with optional air-conditioning.

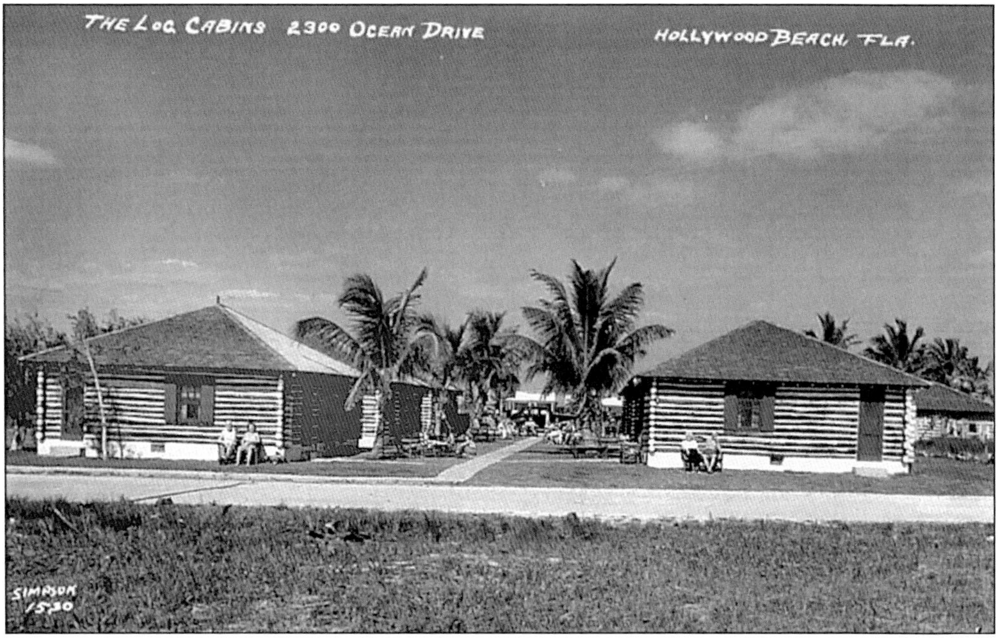

The Log Cabins were located at 2300 Ocean Drive. This real photo postcard from the 1950s shows smiling men, women, and children seated in wicker chairs next to each building. Today Ruffy's Restaurant stands on the site.

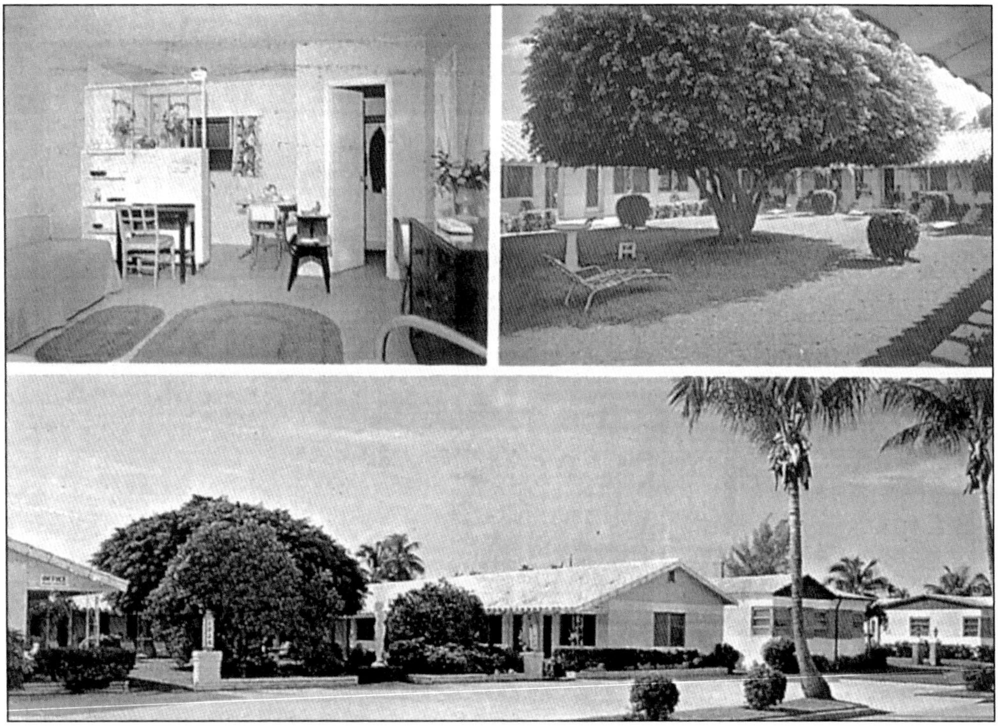

The Rio Motel, located at 1824 Washington Street, offered 36 motel rooms and efficiencies in a residential setting. Owner-managed, it featured a coffee shop and shuffleboard court. Nicely furnished units and large shade trees attracted many visitors.

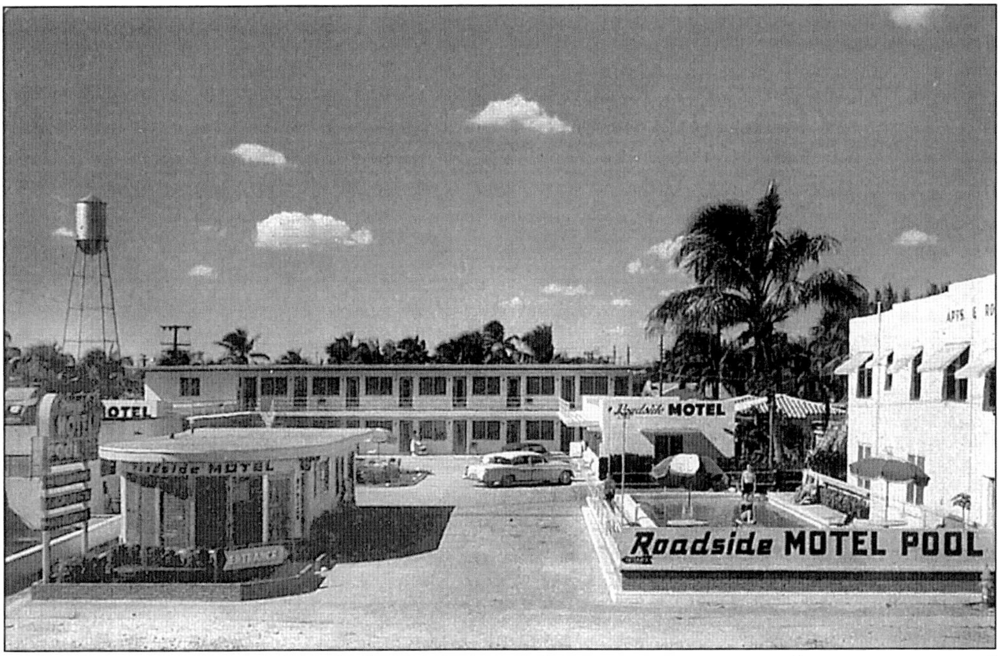

The Roadside Motel was perfectly designed to appeal to passing motorists and was a stereotypical Florida motel. Located at 906 North Federal Highway, it offered parking right at your door, a swimming pool, an adjacent restaurant, and proximity to the horse and dog tracks as well as the "Hi-Li" Fronton.

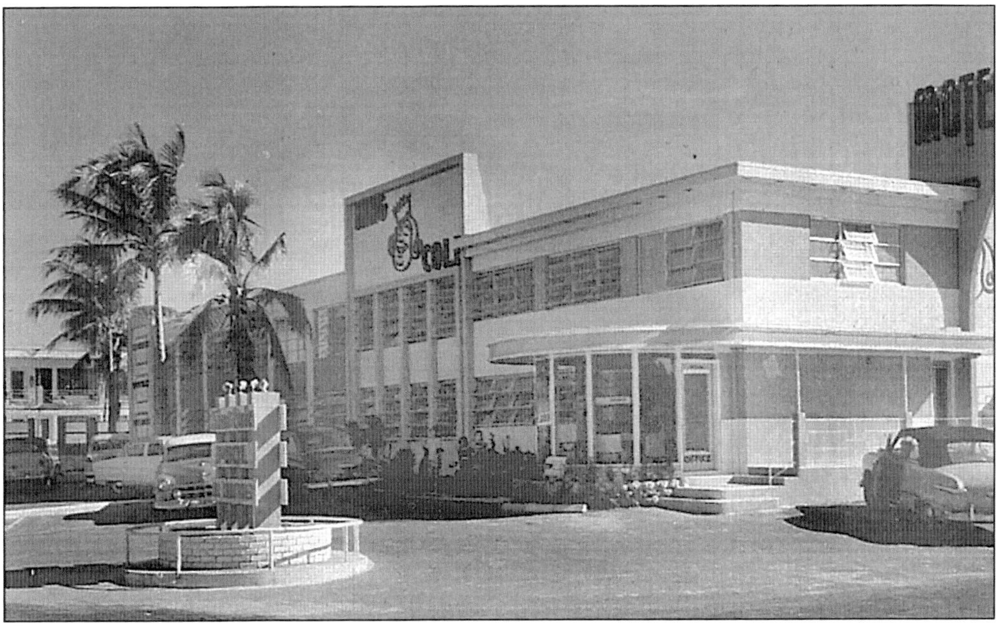
The King Cole Motel still stands at the corner of Thomas Street and A1A. In this 1950s view the building is white with orange and turquoise trim. Today the King Cole is tan with green trim and a green awning shades its entryway. Its "Nous Parlons Francais" sign extends a warm greeting to French-speaking guests.

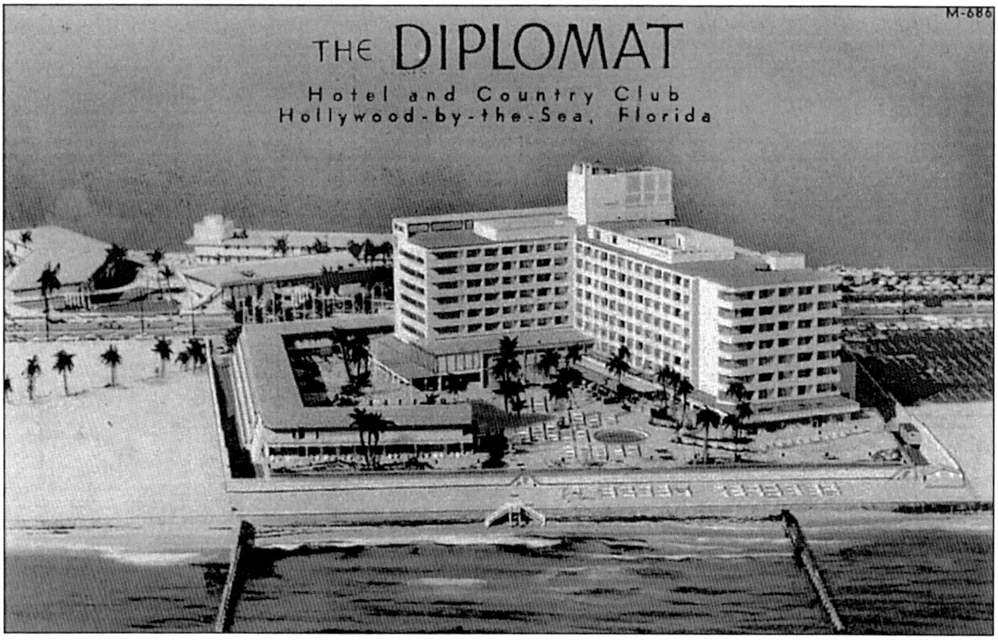

The Diplomat Resort and Country Club was a Hollywood landmark for many years. In 1957 Philadelphian Samuel Friedland, founder of the Food Fair supermarket chain, opened the resort, which included a 150-room hotel, golf course, and clubhouse along the beach at 3515 South Ocean Drive.

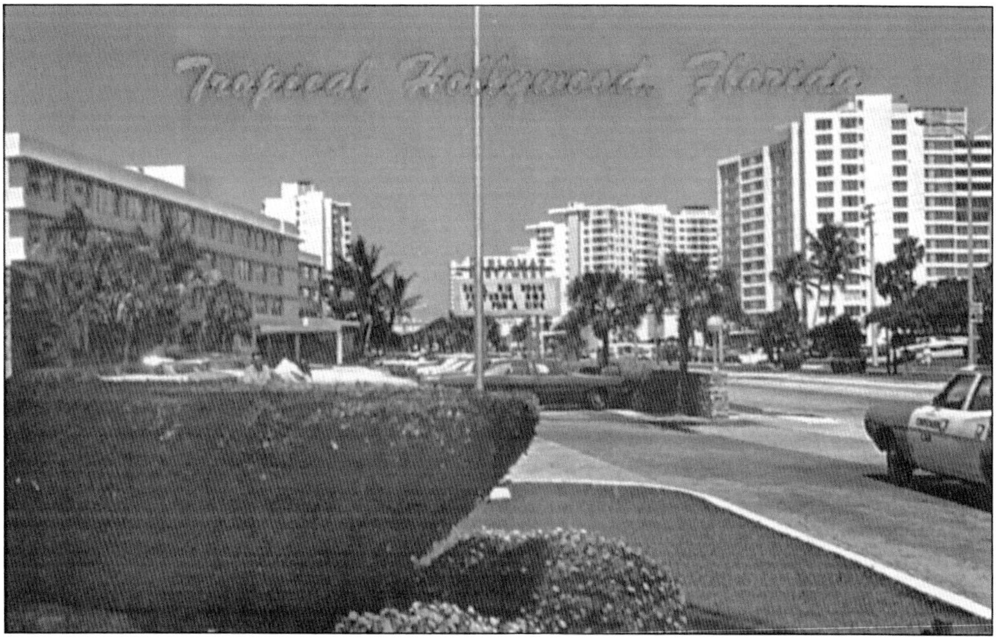

Other than the Hollywood Beach Hotel, a sprinkling of small apartment motels, and lots of sand and water, there was virtually nothing between Miami and Fort Lauderdale. It was a risky project, but it succeeded. Soon other luxury hotels and apartments joined the Diplomat along A1A.

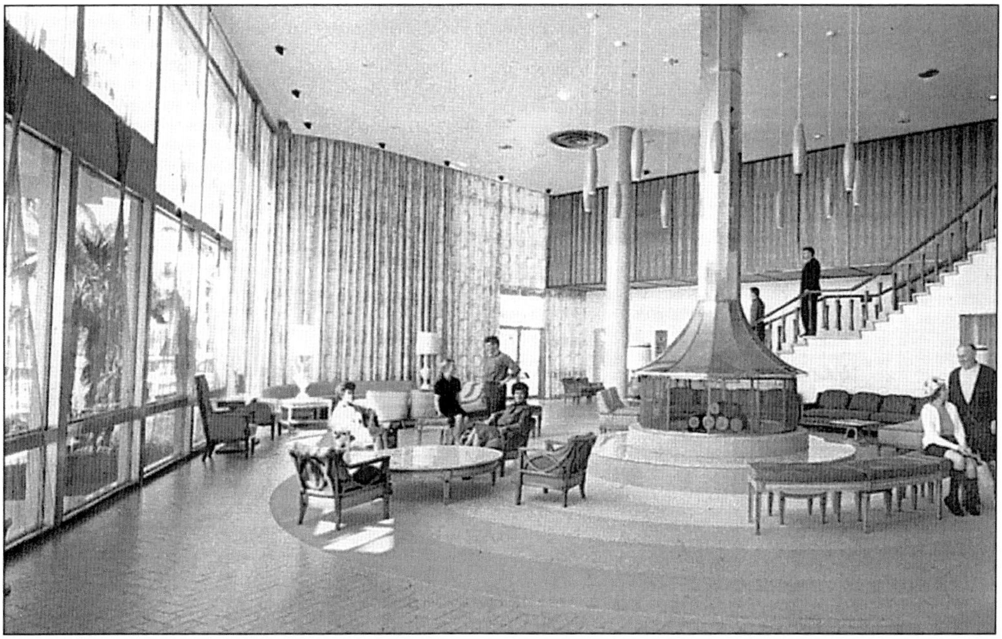

The Diplomat's distinctive lobby became a popular meeting place. Private golf courses, 19 tennis courts, and the Diplomat Country Club gave the resort a fashionable reputation.

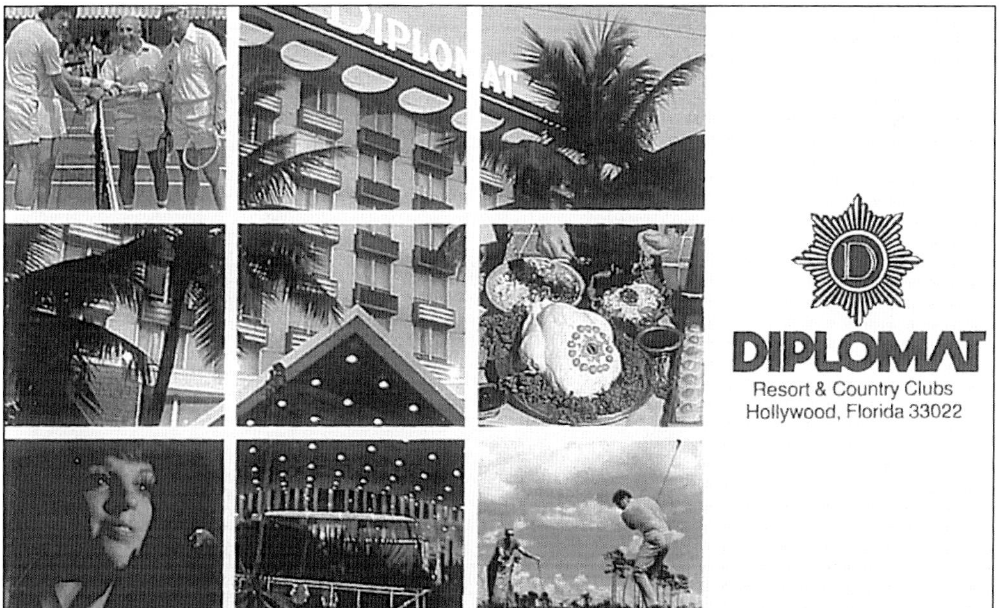

It was super-star entertainment, however, that became the Diplomat Resort's trademark over the years. Singer Tony Martin performed the hotel's first show. Liza Minelli was a frequent headliner. In 1963 a new convention hall was built; 1967 saw a 4-story addition with 150 rooms erected, and a tower with 330 rooms was added in 1969.

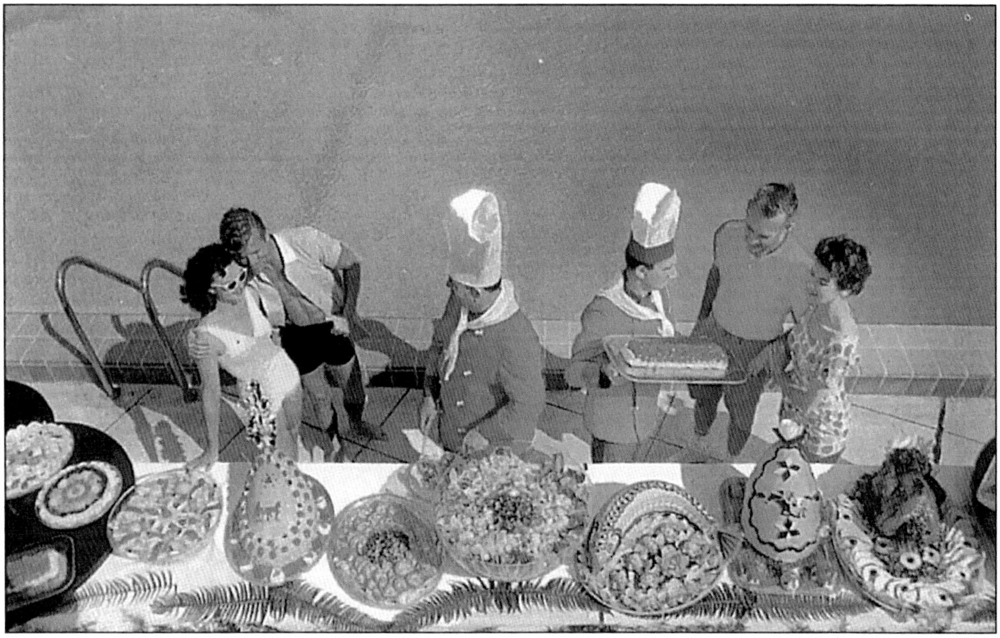

In its heyday, world-famous Diplomat chefs prepared cuisine for the rich and famous, including President Gerald Ford. The Diplomat had grown to a resort with 1,170 rooms and 2,000 employees. In 1978 the first hotel fire occurred. Later, fire consumed the room of Frank Fontaine, "Crazy Guggenheim" on Jackie Gleason's show.

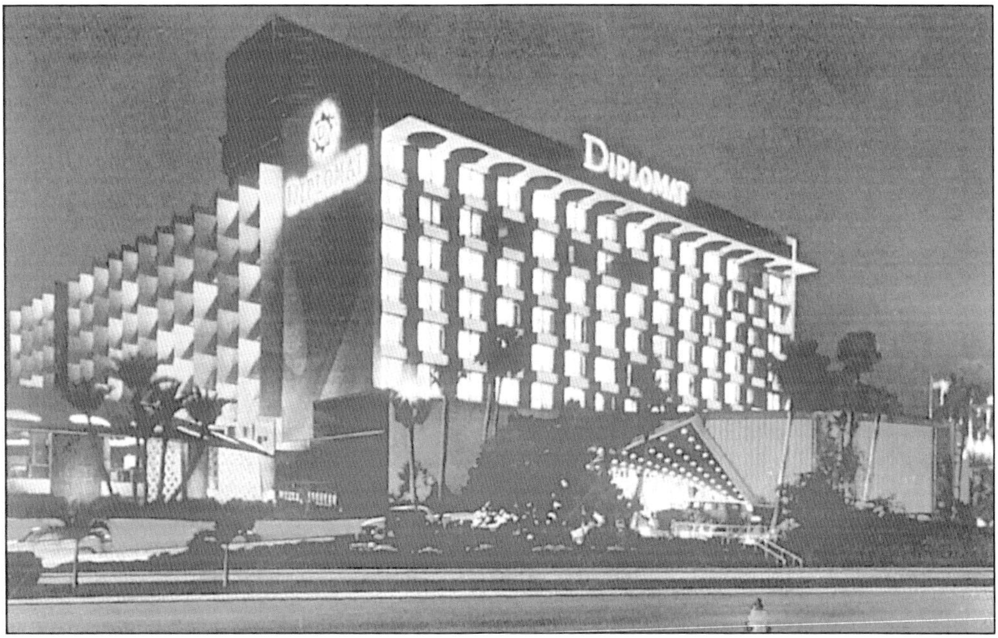

In 1983 there was a major fire from which the grand resort would never recover. Over 400 guests were evacuated and the main hotel closed for 13 months. After $5 million in damages and a loss of $20 million in revenue, the Diplomat never recovered financially and finally closed. The building was torn down in the 1990s.

Four

COMMUNITY LIFE

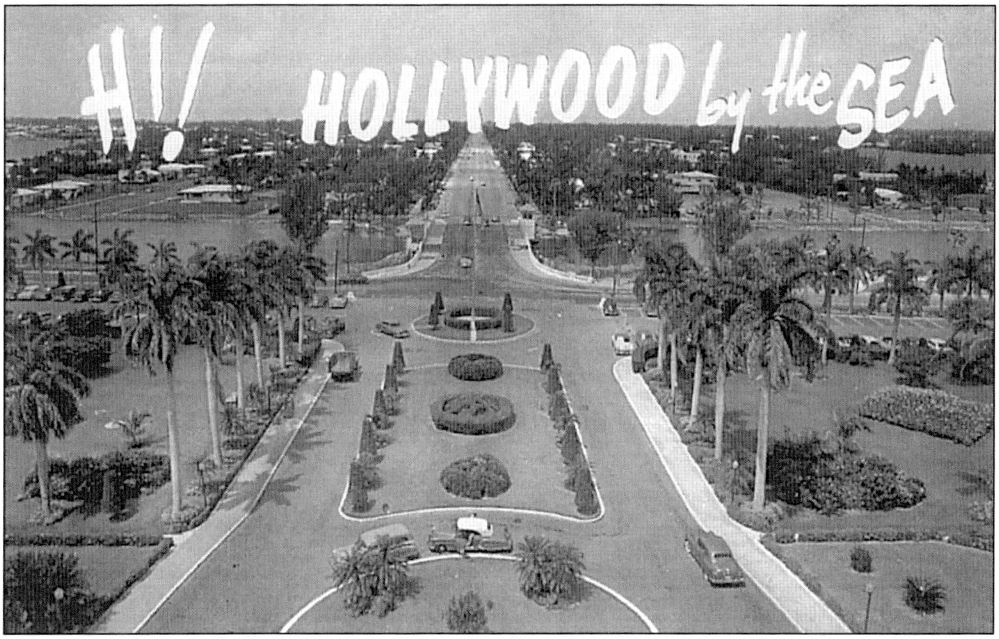

Hollywood, with its unique history, is comprised of strangers who came to enjoy its climate, scenery, and opportunities for new beginnings. The Depression, coming on the heels of the 1926 Hurricane, brought financial ruin to many, including the city's beloved Joseph Young. But WW II renewed the city's sense of purpose. Because of the coast's vulnerability, Port Everglades and Riverside Military Academy were used extensively by the U.S. Navy. Many military families stayed in the area after the war's end. Samuel Horvitz, founder of Hollywood Inc., continued to develop the area. In 1950 the census showed Hollywood as Broward County's second largest city with 14,351 people. In 1954 Orange Brook Golf Estates was developed and Hollywood Inc. went on to develop Emerald Hills and Hollywood Hills. During the 1960s the city expanded, through annexation, westward beyond its Fifty-Sixth Avenue boundary. An influx of people from Cuba, Haiti, and Nicaragua spilled over from Dade County to add variety to Hollywood's demographic profile. By 1997 Hollywood's jurisdiction had grown to 26.9 square miles, and its population had soared to 121,700.

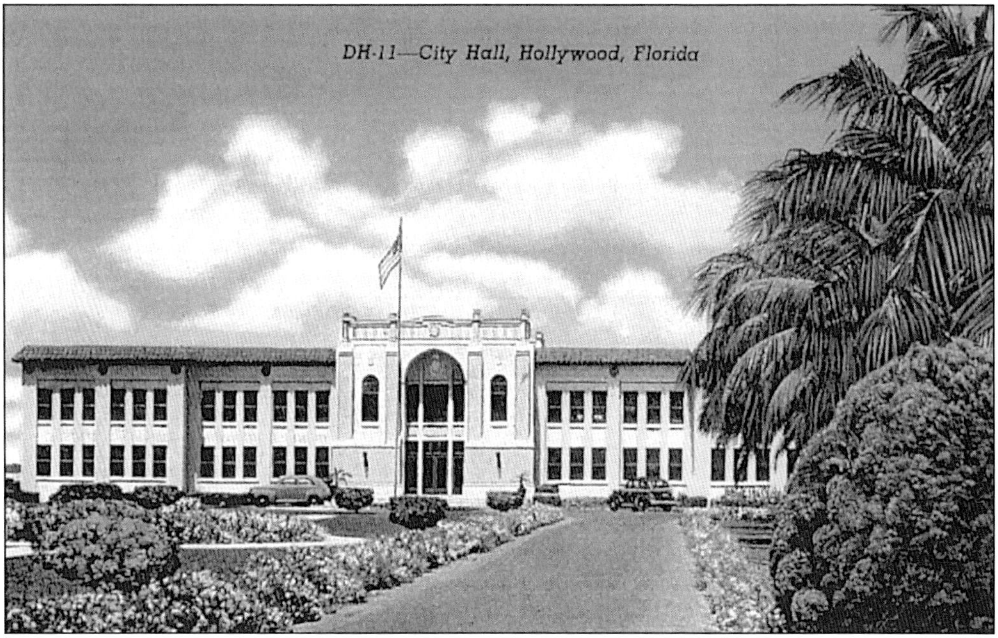

City Hall Circle was once a pineapple field, but it became the hub of the community when the first city hall was built there. For a time, until gambling was banned in 1948, there was a slot machine in the men's room at city hall. Today, though the building has been renovated and expanded, it still stands on its original site.

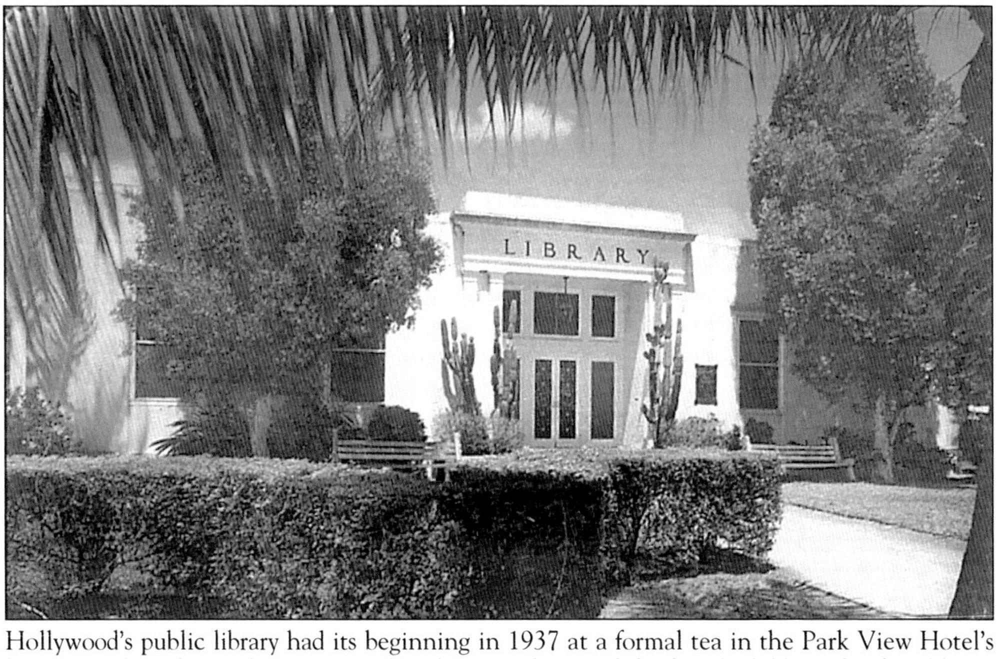

Hollywood's public library had its beginning in 1937 at a formal tea in the Park View Hotel's lounge, and its first volumes were placed in an alcove of the hotel's lobby. The first library building opened on Polk Street in June of 1942 with 9,000 books. This library building, still in use at Administrative Circle, was built in 1959.

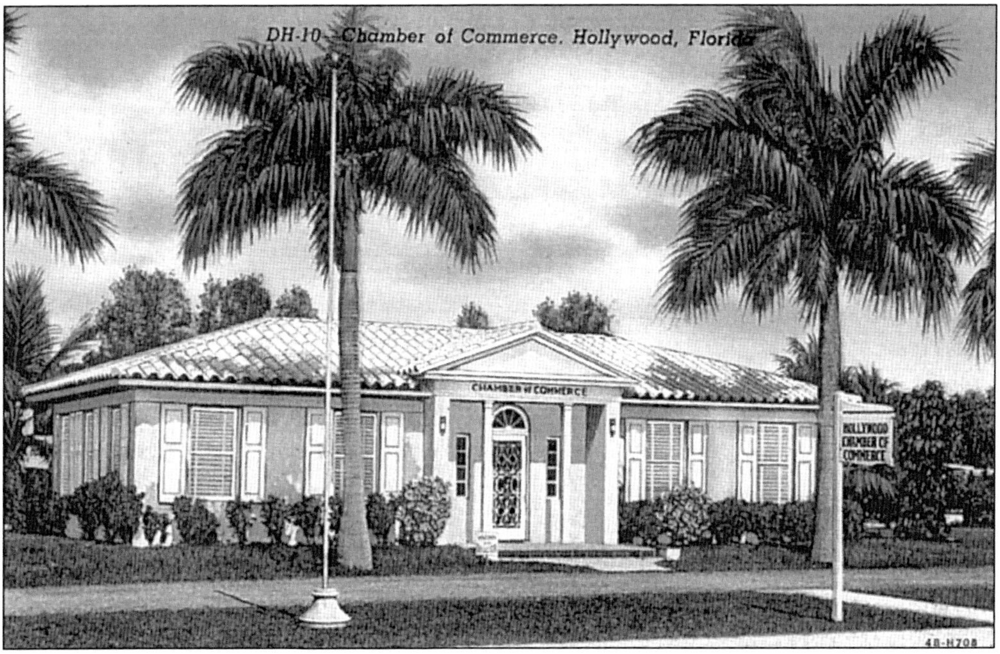

The Hollywood Chamber of Commerce was organized in 1923. In the early 1930s its first building, a small wood cottage, stood on the downtown circle. In 1941 the City donated two lots on Federal Highway between Polk and Tyler Streets, and this $8,000 Colonial-style building was constructed with donated time and materials.

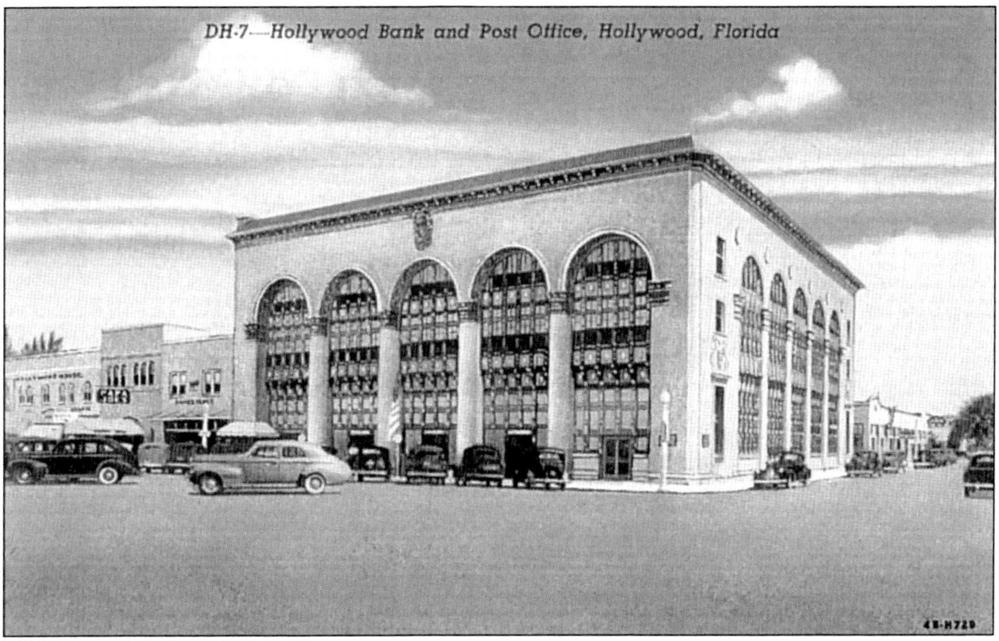

The Hollywood Bank, later the First National Bank, was built in 1924 on the north side of Hollywood Boulevard at the corner of Twentieth Avenue. The post office occupied a double-store space in the building from 1926 to 1950. This very distinctive Spanish/Moorish-style structure was a landmark for many years.

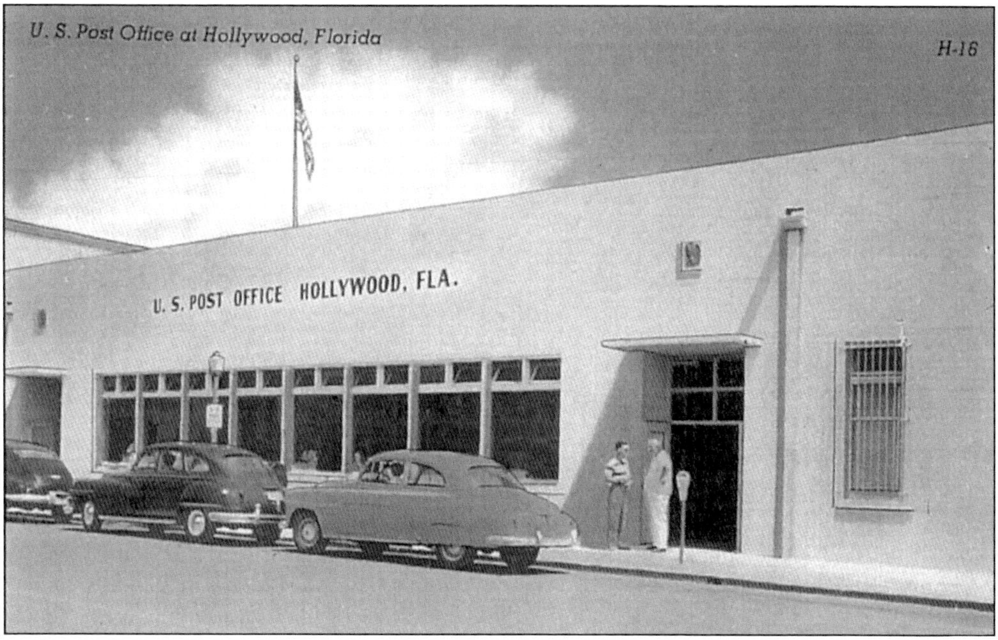

Hollywood's post office was established in August of 1922. Its first letter carrier was Albert Fritz. Its first building was a stucco structure on Harrison Street at Nineteenth Avenue, but that building was totally destroyed during the 1926 hurricane.

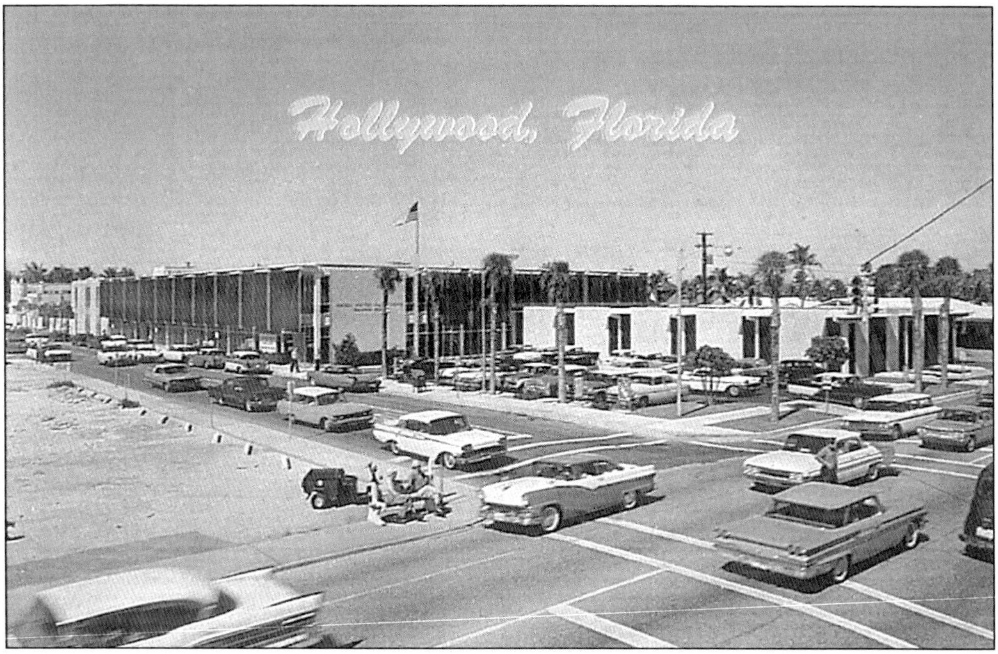

Between 1950 and 1960 the main post office was in the 2000 block of Harrison Street. During the spring of 1961 it moved to much larger quarters at the corner of Polk Street and Federal Highway. Of course, there are many branch post offices now.

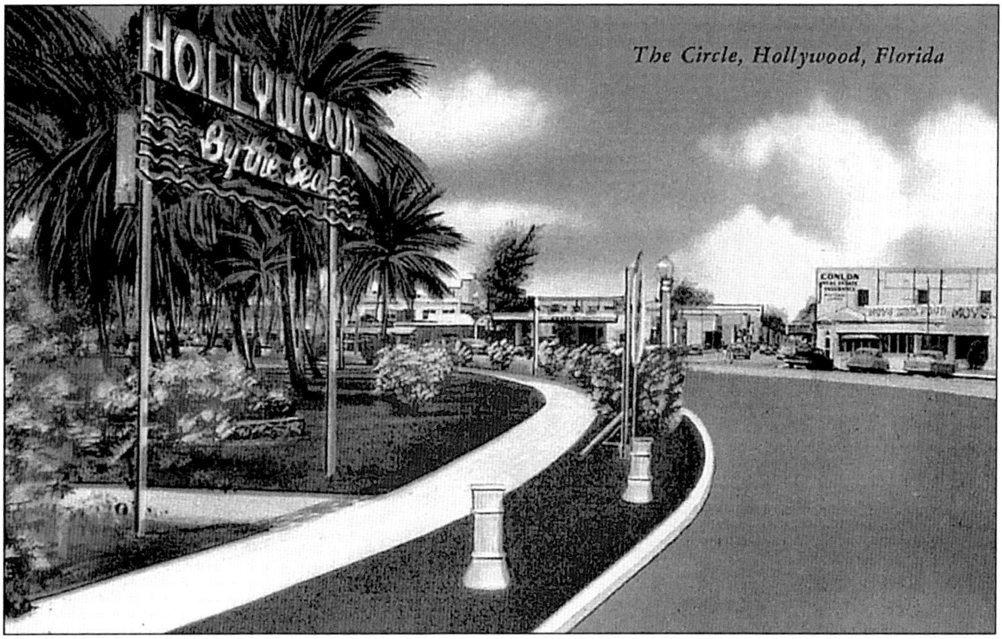

Young Circle remains the hub of the downtown area. In this 1940s view the town sign still reads "Hollywood By the Sea." This area was a park in 1923, but it wasn't until 1931 that Harding Circle, as it was then known, was officially designated a park, and a ban was placed on commercial activity there.

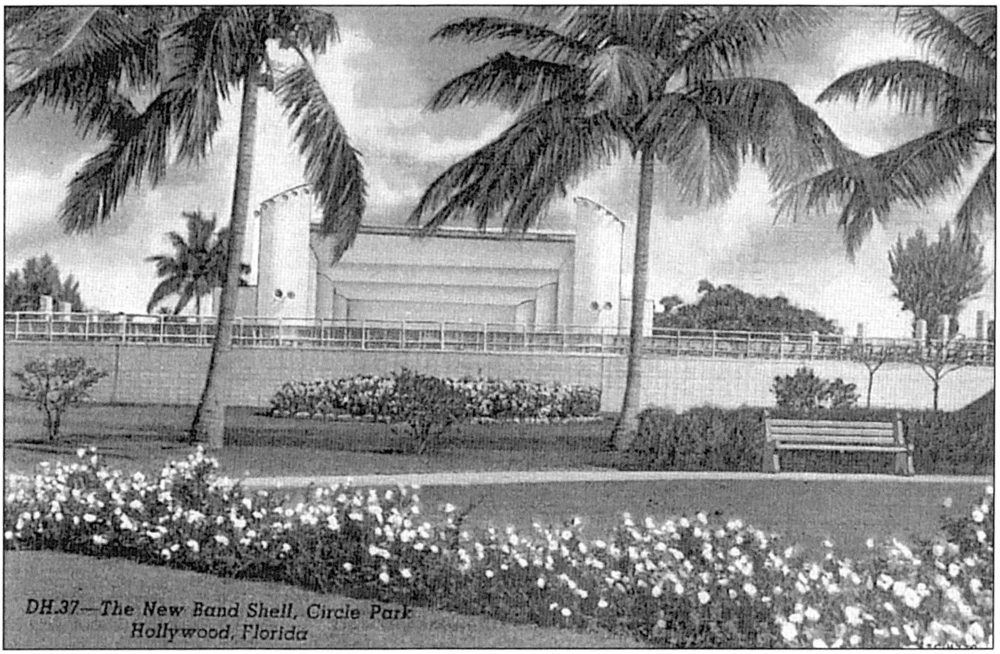

This new band shell, built in the 1940s, was the site of frequent events as well as free concerts in the balmy evenings. In 1955 Dad wrote to Charles in Connecticut, "This is the theatre where Howard 3rd and his class from school presented a Xmas show."

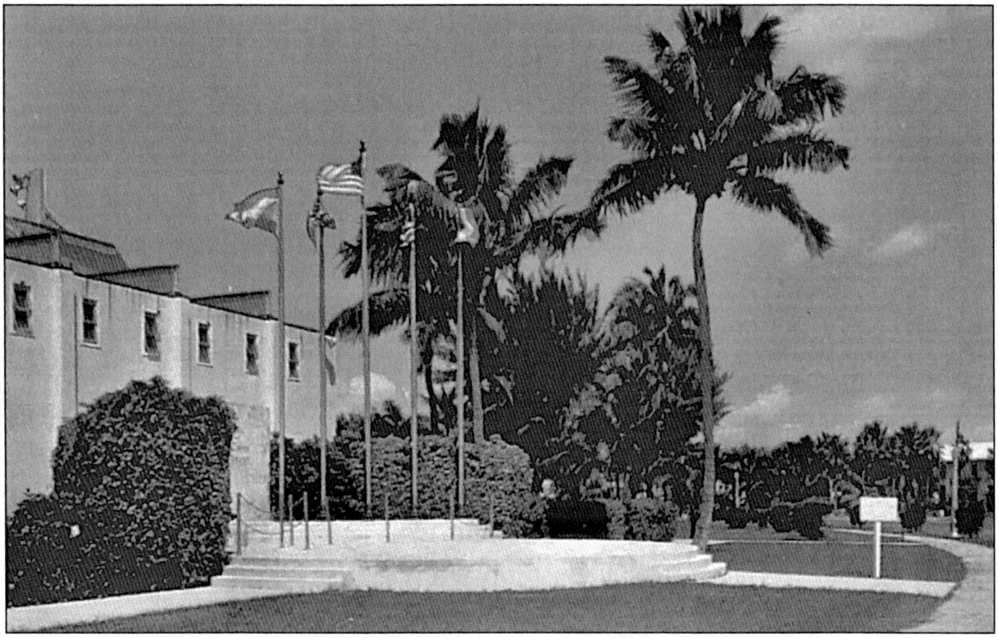

The War Memorial in Young Circle Park was erected to honor those who lost their lives during WW II. During the war, the park was the site of parades featuring U.S. Army and Navy vehicles, weapons, and marching units for war bond drives. Its five flying flags rouse patriotic feelings in the hearts of its many visitors.

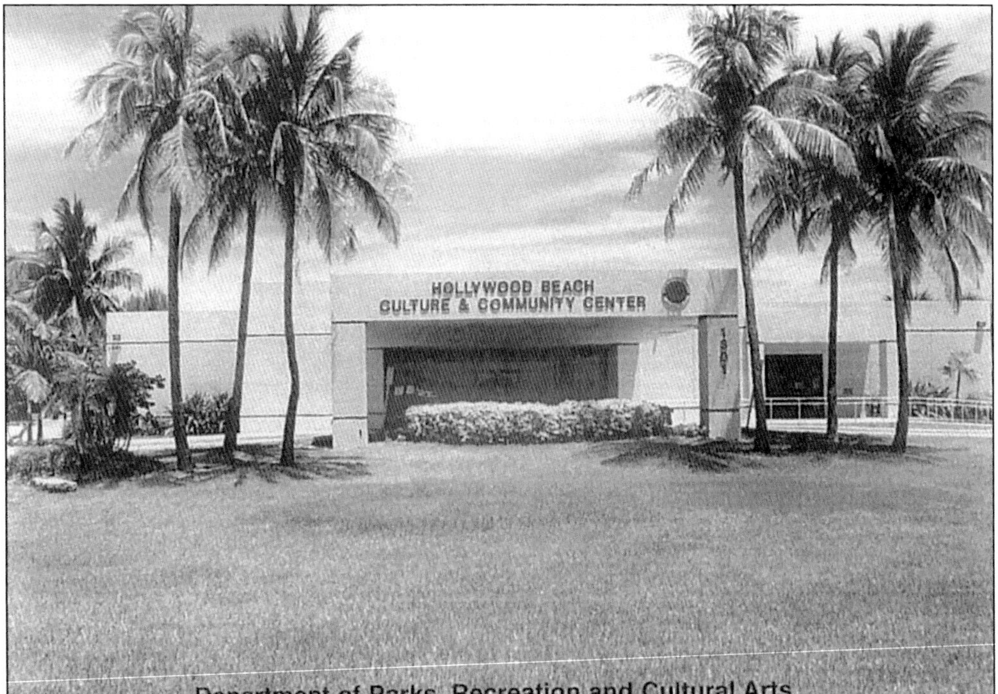

Located at 1301 South Ocean Drive, the Hollywood Beach Culture and Community Center is the site of many neighborhood programs and classes.

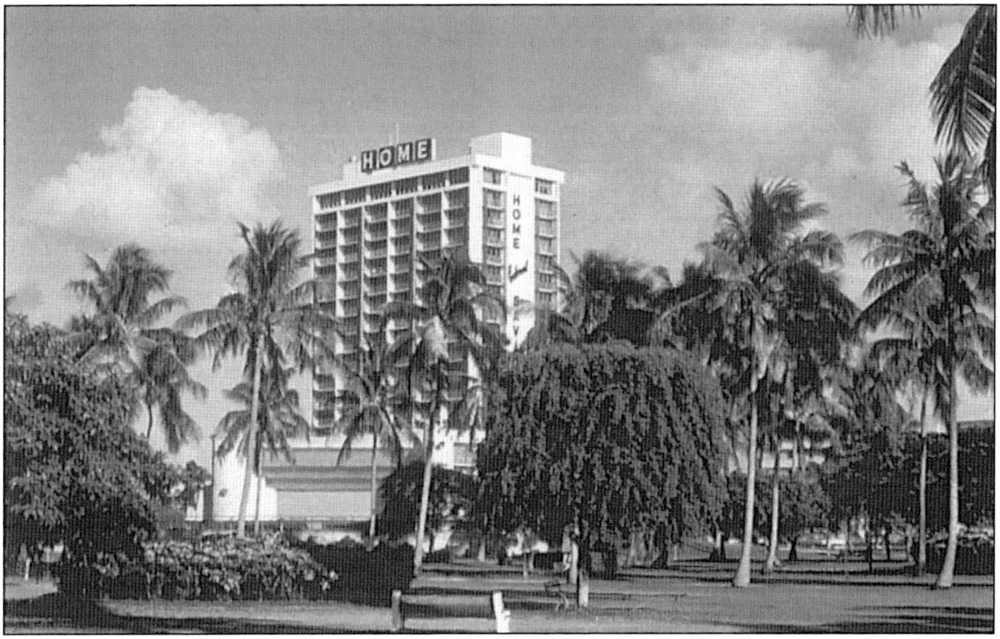

Rising above the band shell in Young Circle Park was the Home Federal Bank building. The "Top of the Home" restaurant, located on the building's highest level, had an excellent reputation. The elegant and expensive eating place was especially popular for special occasions such as anniversaries and Mother's Day.

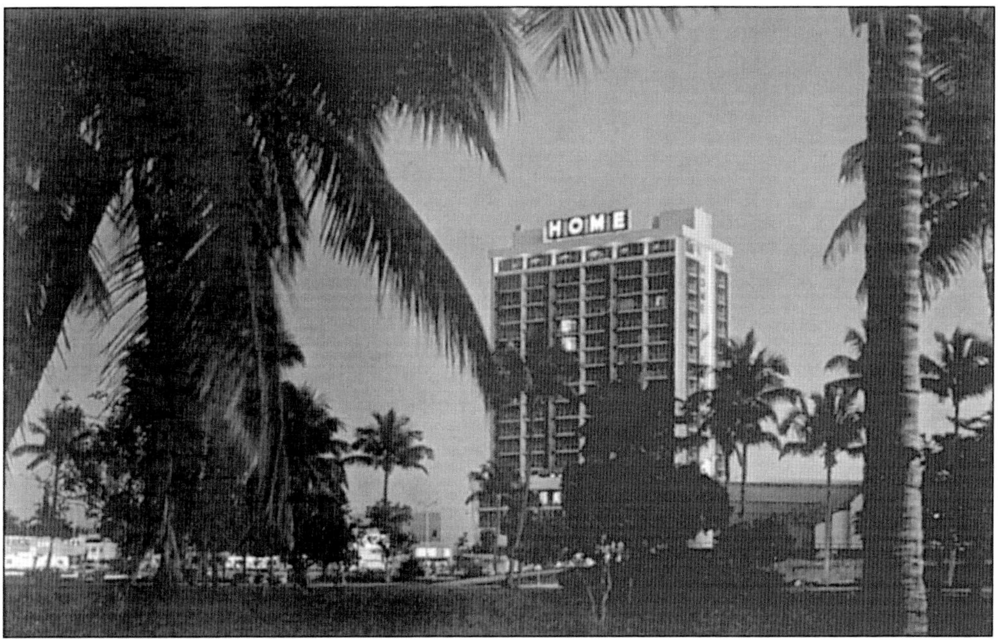

A landmark for many years, the building's familiar and comforting "Home" sign, which greeted returning residents and snowbirds as they drove into Hollywood, is gone. During the late 1990s, the building was being renovated to accommodate new offices and a different restaurant.

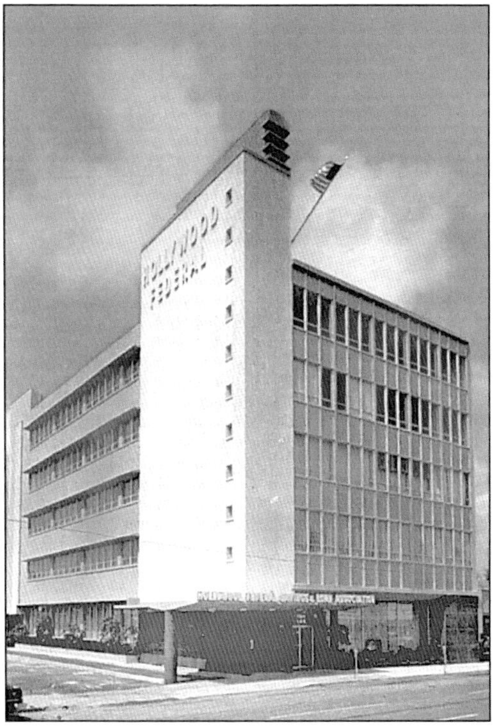

Hollywood Federal Savings and Loan opened in 1934 and moved to 1901 Tyler Street in 1946. In the 1970s it introduced the first "by-phone" telephone bill-paying service in the country. The bank pioneered self-service banking terminals inside grocery stores. By the early 1980s it had 560 employees and over $1.2 billion in assets.

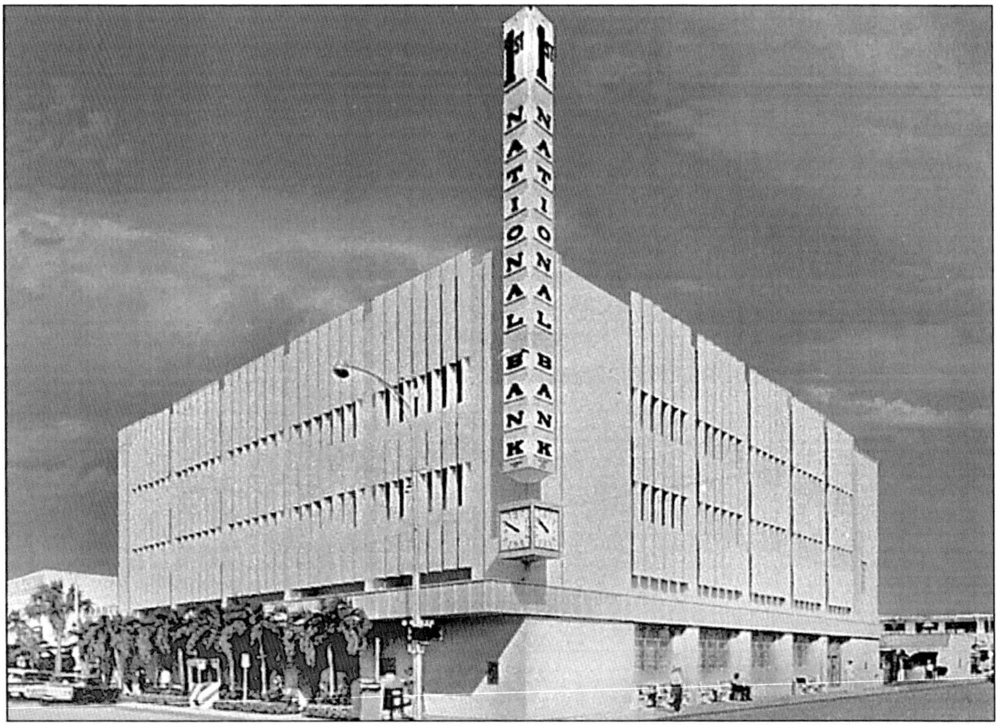

Located at 2001 Hollywood Boulevard, the First National Bank of Hollywood offered drive-through windows during the early 1960s. With expertise in trust facilities, the bank's slogan was "Broward County's Senior Bank."

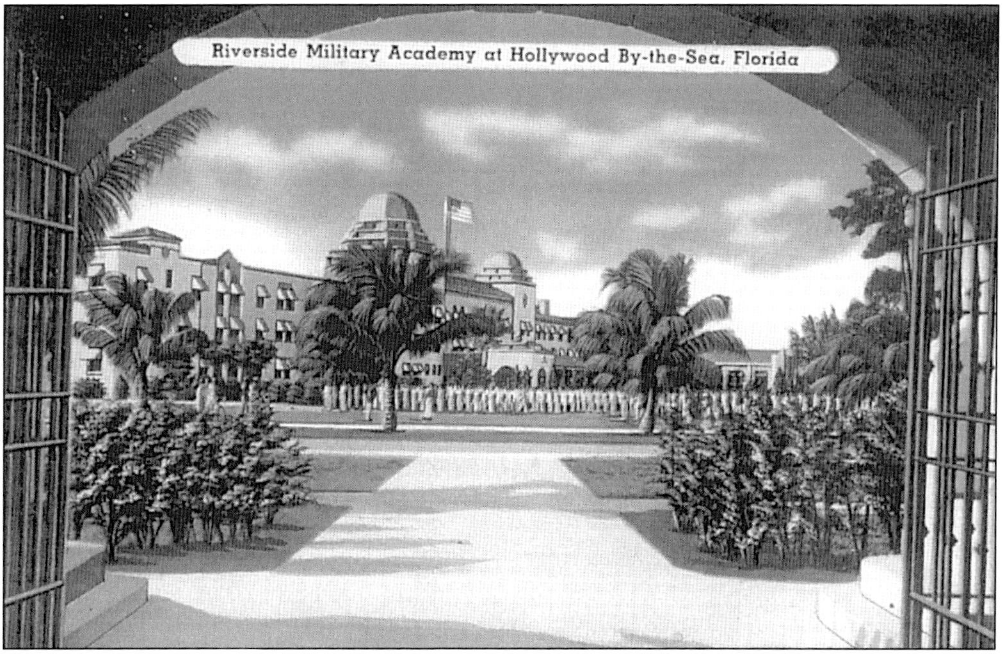

The Riverside Military Academy of Gainesville, Georgia, made Hollywood its winter home in 1932. With 600 students and 100 faculty members, not to mention visiting parents, the academy gave a boost to the local economy. Cadets arrived every January for a three-month stay.

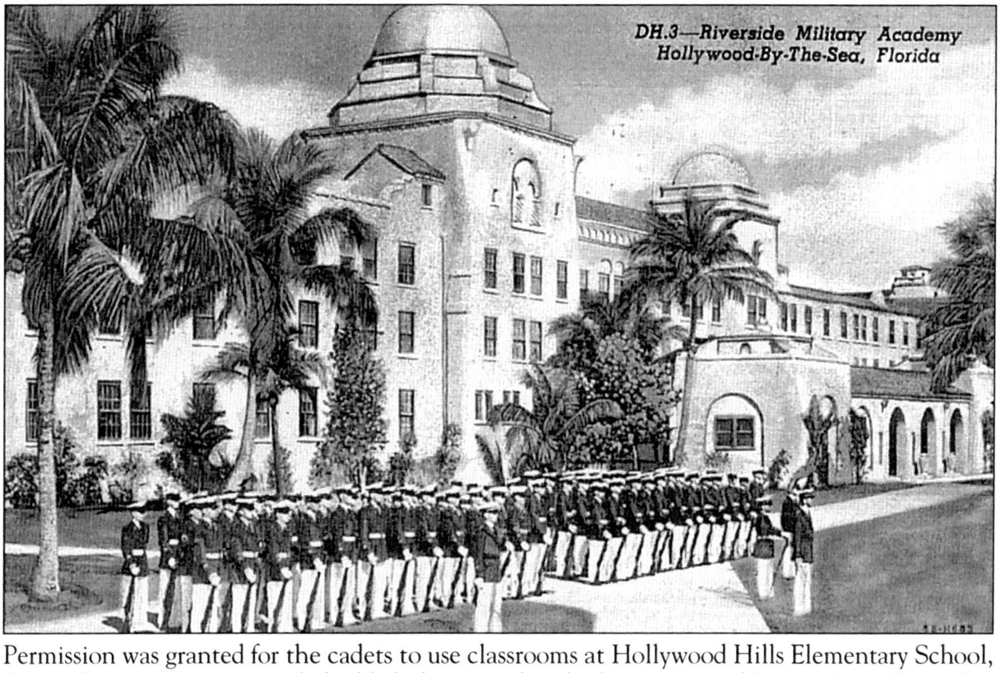

Permission was granted for the cadets to use classrooms at Hollywood Hills Elementary School, deserted since so many people had left the area after the hurricane and Depression. The cadets marched, in formation, the mile to and from the school on Taft Street and Thirty-Fifth Avenue until 1936, when the academy's own classrooms were built.

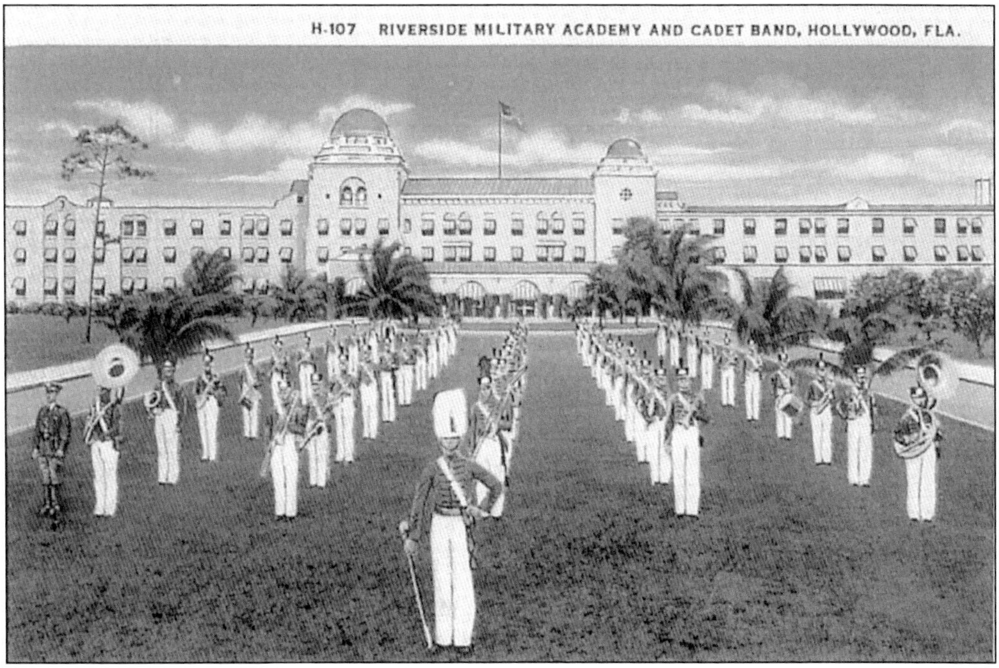

During WW II the U.S. Naval Air Gunners School took over the campus. Riverside Military Academy cadets stayed in Georgia for their full school terms, returning to Hollywood in 1947. In 1959 a dropped cigarette ignited a fire that destroyed one wing of the building, and an entirely new complex was built.

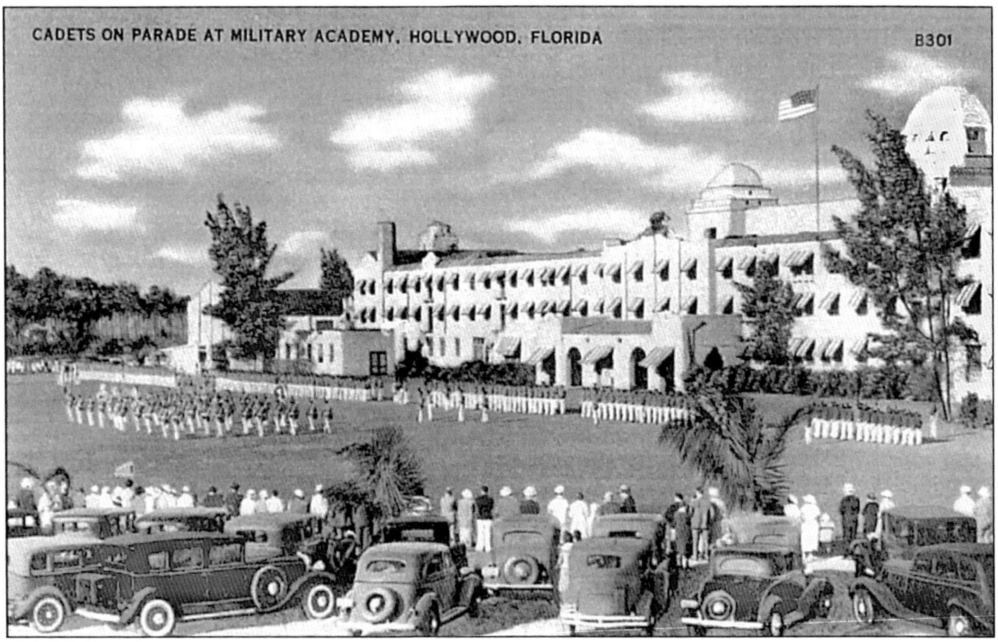

Affectionately dubbed the "River Rats," the cadets became part of the community. Sunday afternoon dress parades always drew large audiences. Riverside's athletes competed with local high school teams in basketball and track. Locals claimed they could always tell when the cadets were back in town by the increase in neighborhood pranks.

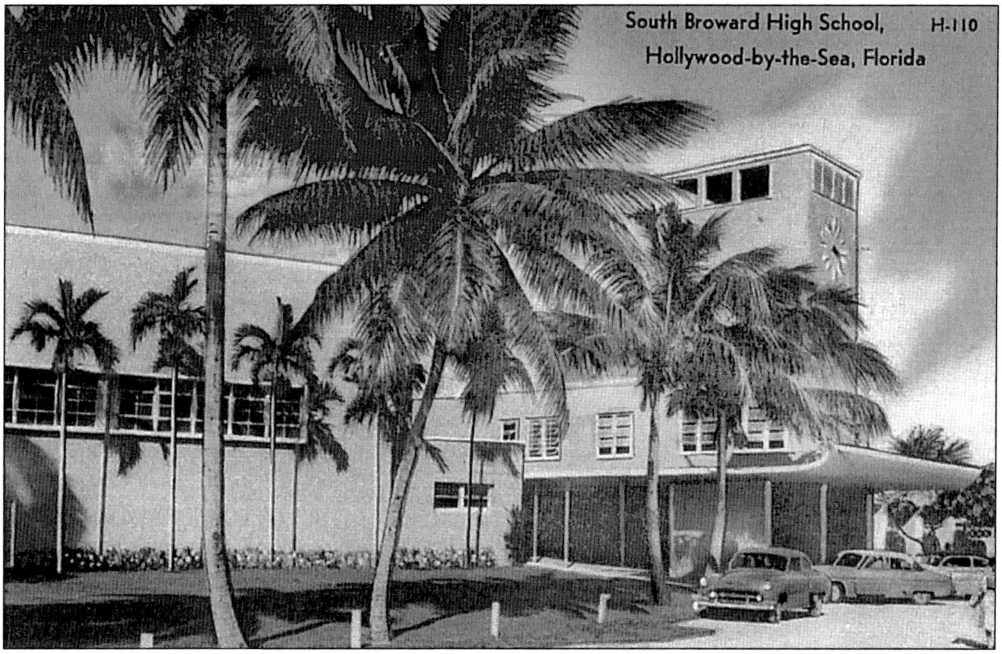

For many years the only accredited secondary school in southern Broward County was Dania High School, which was a few miles to the north. With the area's rapid growth following WW II, that school became hopelessly overcrowded. Hollywood proudly opened South Broward High School for the 1949 school year.

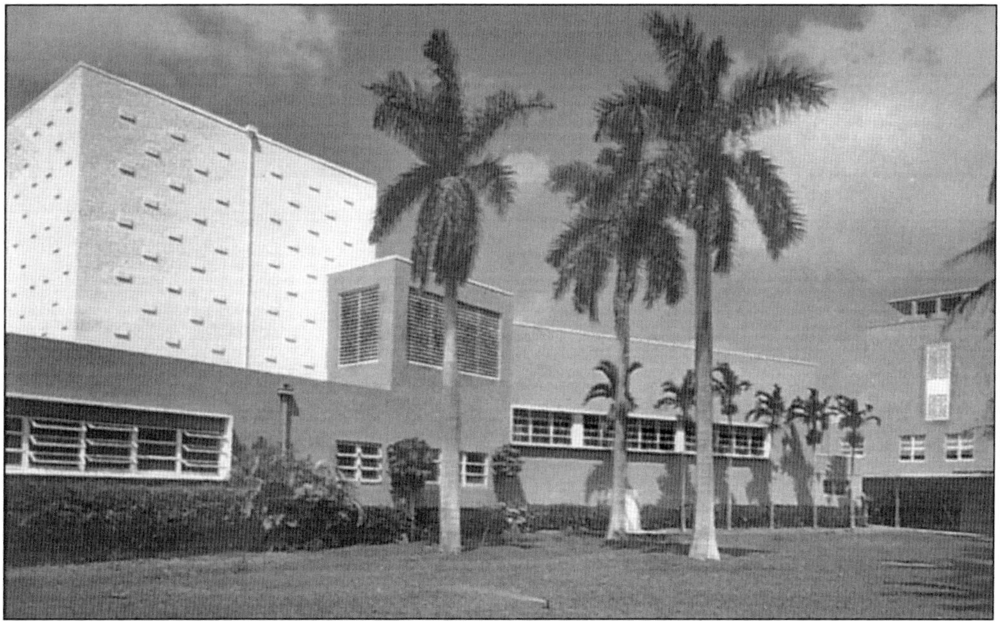

This school quickly became crowded as well. A large addition, as well as the familiar green color, were added in the 1950s. Today other area high schools include Hollywood Hills, McArthur, Nova, and Chaminade.

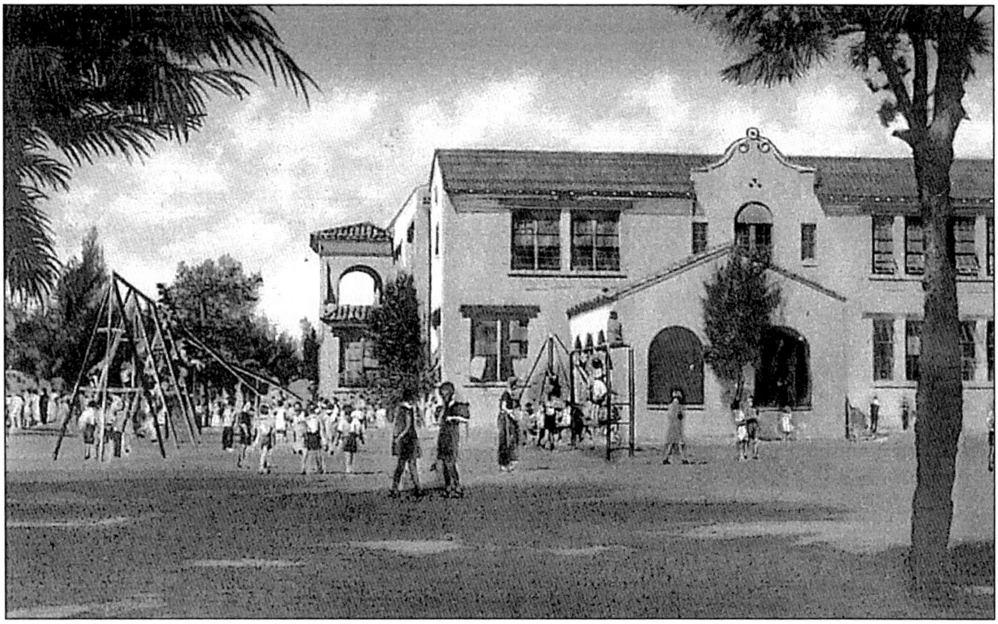

Hollywood Central Elementary School was built at Monroe Street and Seventeenth Avenue in 1925. Only one child in the first eighth-grade class had been born in Florida. The school was badly damaged during the 1926 hurricane and was rebuilt with some design changes around 1927. The school was destroyed by fire in 1968. Although this late-night blaze was the worst fire in Hollywood history, no one was injured.

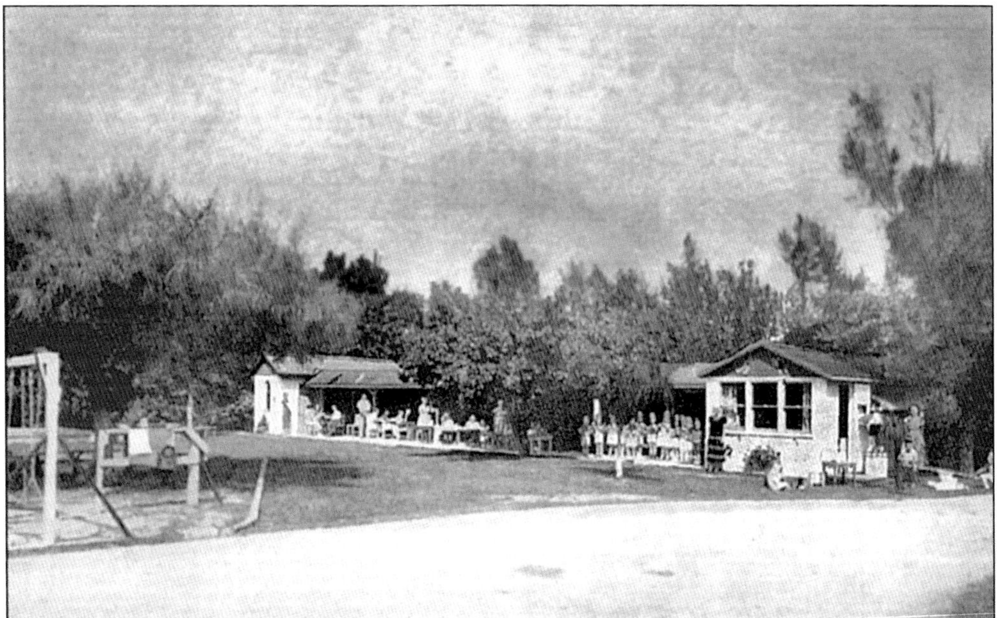

The Outdoor Private School at 2305 Polk Street and 2306 Taylor Street occupied three buildings on 1.5 acres of playground in the heart of town. It was founded by Lamora Mickelson in 1938 and emphasized sound academic principles, horseback riding, swimming, languages, and social dancing. The school closed in the 1970s.

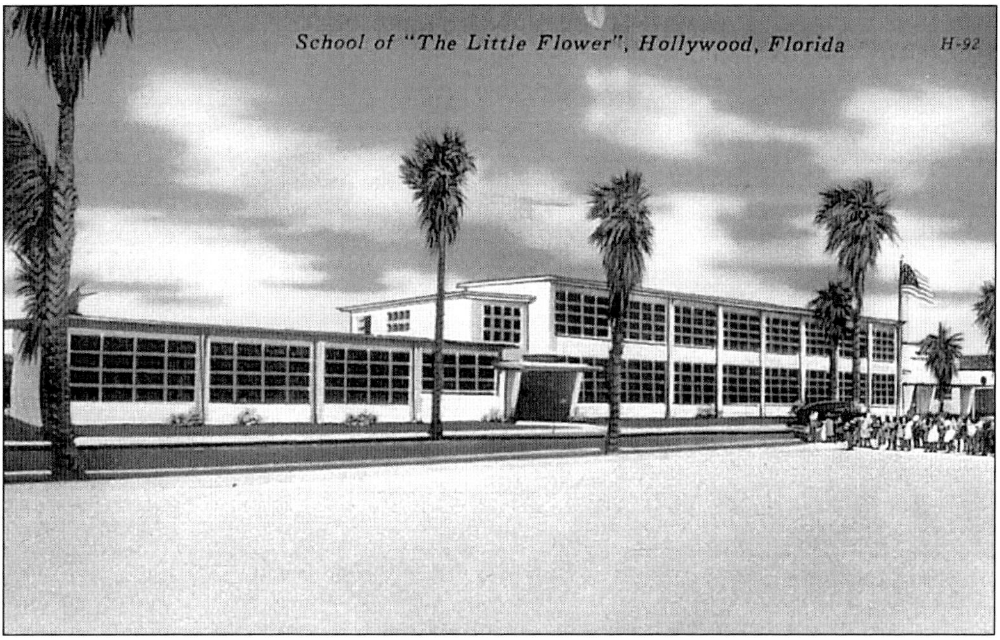

Other private schools included church-run establishments such as the School of the Little Flower. This school building and its auditorium were built just after WW II.

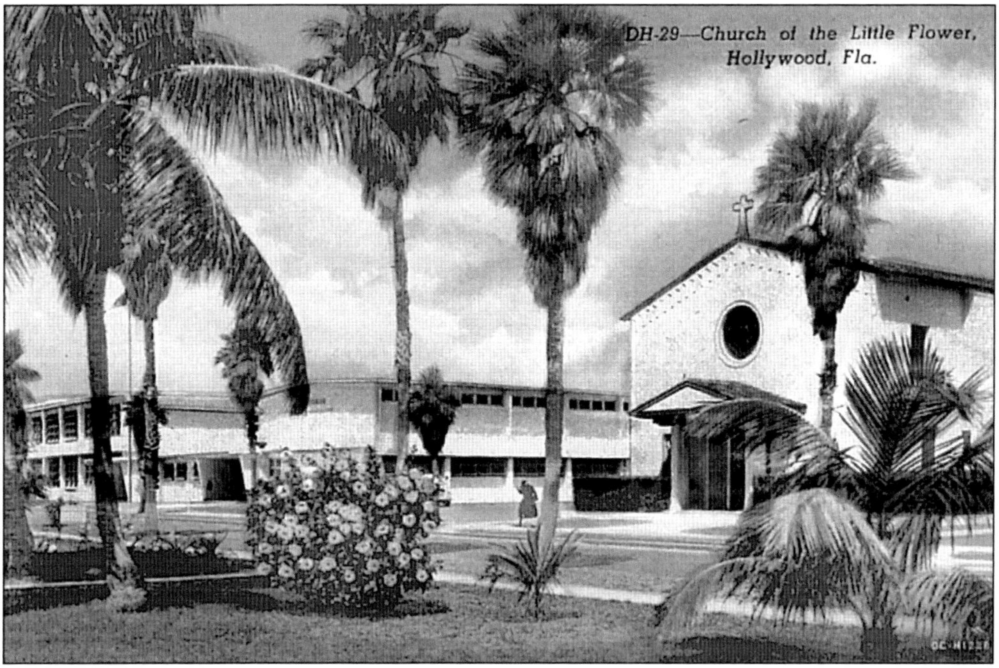

The Church of the Little Flower was Hollywood's first Catholic church and remained its only one until the mid-1950s. Organized in 1925, the church's first Mass was held inside the Hollywood Fire Station. A church and parish hall were built in 1926, at the corner of Van Buren Street and Twentieth Avenue.

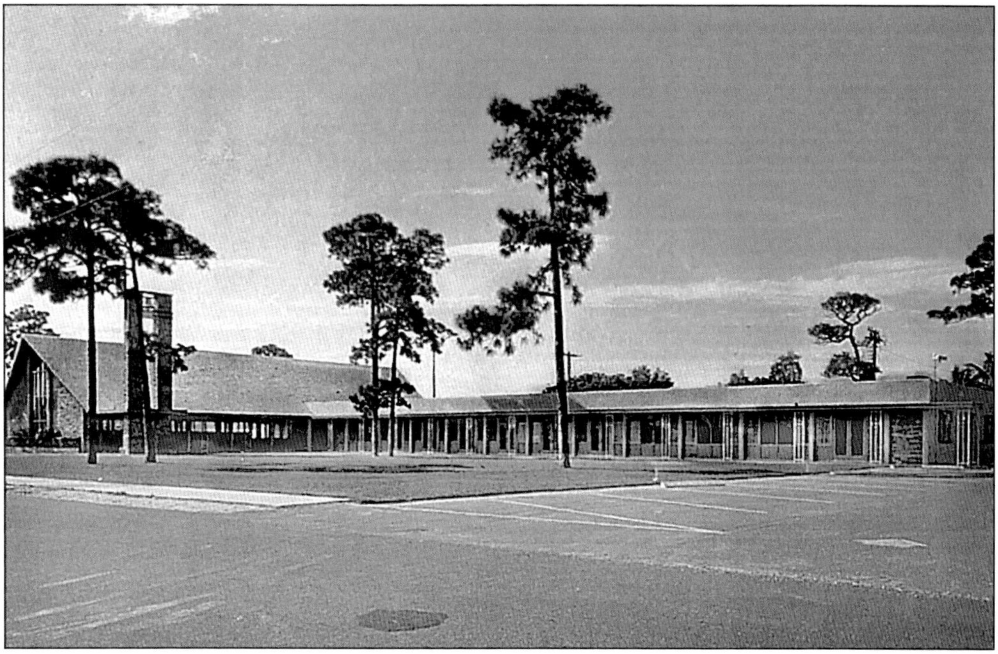

St. John's Evangelical Lutheran Church, located on Van Buren Street and State Road 9, was dedicated on December 8, 1957. Located close to Hollywood Boulevard, it was well-attended by both residents and tourists. Two worship services were held each Sunday, and many programs for families were begun.

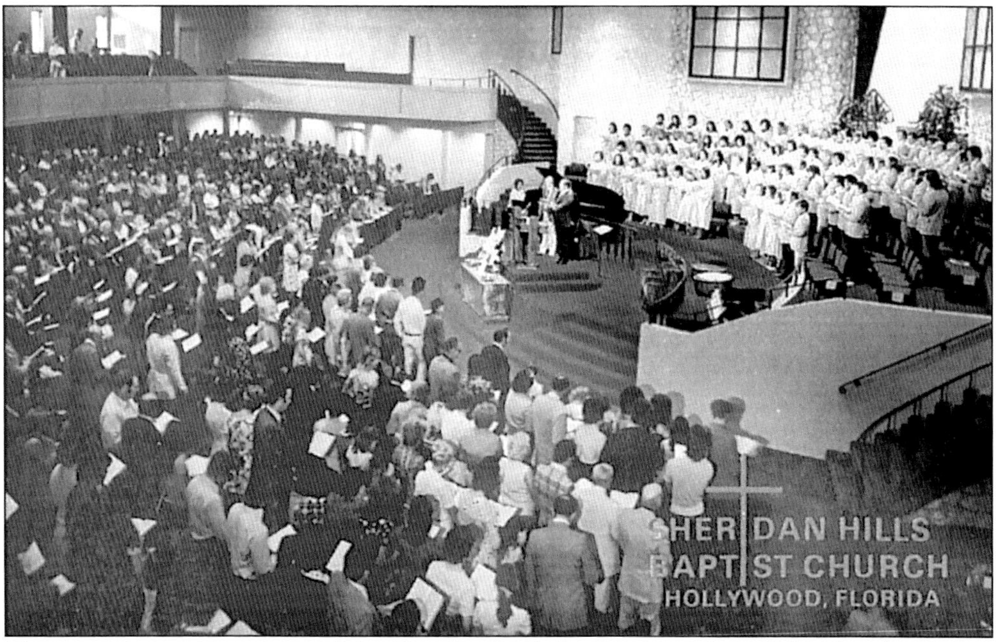

This view shows the interior of the Sheridan Hills Baptist Church at 3751 Sheridan Street. The the first church in Hollywood was the Methodist church on Van Buren Street and Federal Highway, constructed in 1923. Its cornerstone was laid on Easter Sunday of 1924, with William Jennings Bryan as the featured speaker.

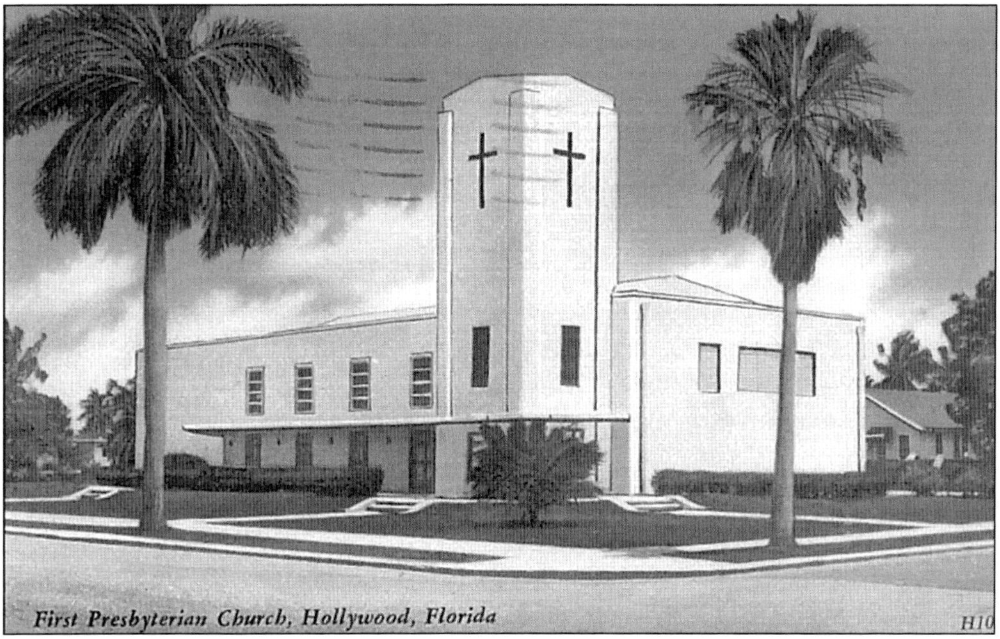

Many religious denominations have churches in Hollywood. This 1940s view shows the First Presbyterian Church, which held two services every Sunday.

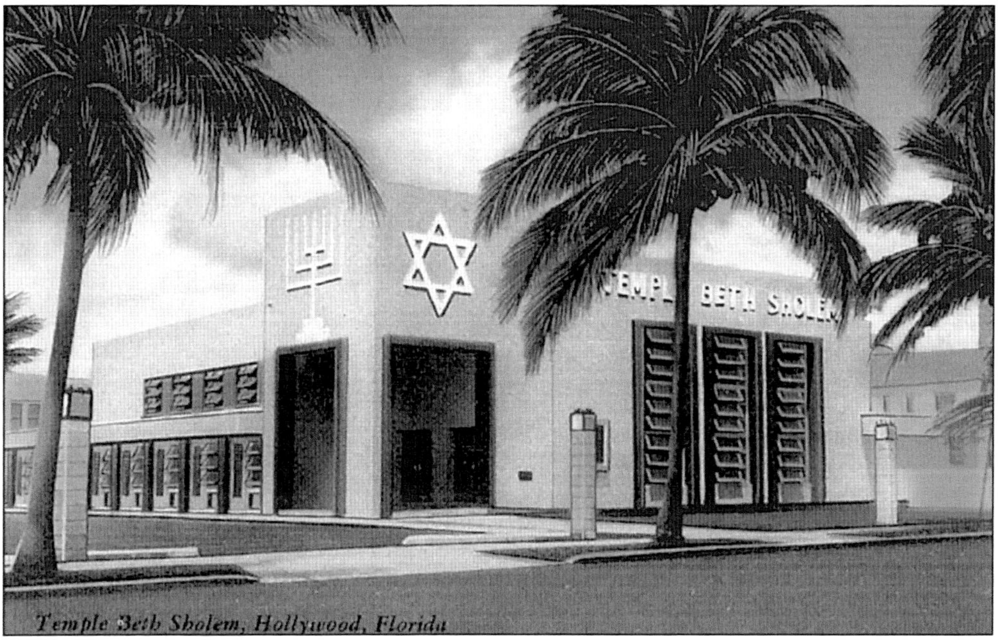

The 1930s were difficult years for Jewish residents, who battled anti-Semitism. Sam Lerner, founder of Lerner Stores, helped build Broward County's first synagogue, and the Jewish Community Center was formed in the early 1940s. Temple Beth Sholem, Hollywood's first synagogue, was built downtown after WW II.

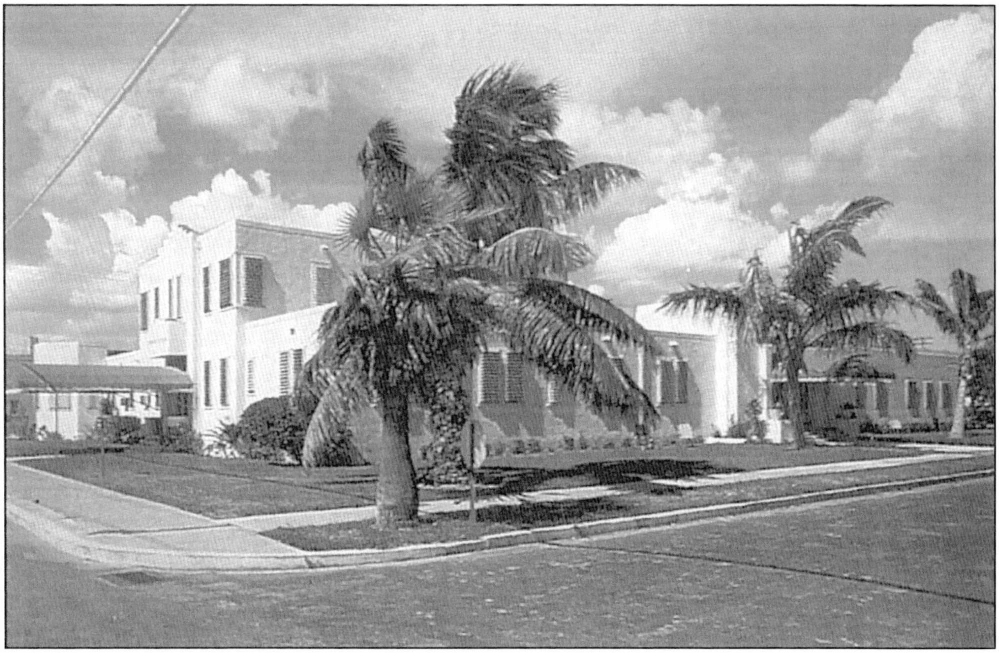

The city's first hospital began in 1925, in an apartment building on Indiana Street. It was run as Gulfstream Hospital by Dr. Harrison Walker, the Hollywood Beach Hotel's first resident physician. It closed in 1929 and Hollywood had no hospital until 1937. This view shows the Hollywood Hospital, which was founded that year.

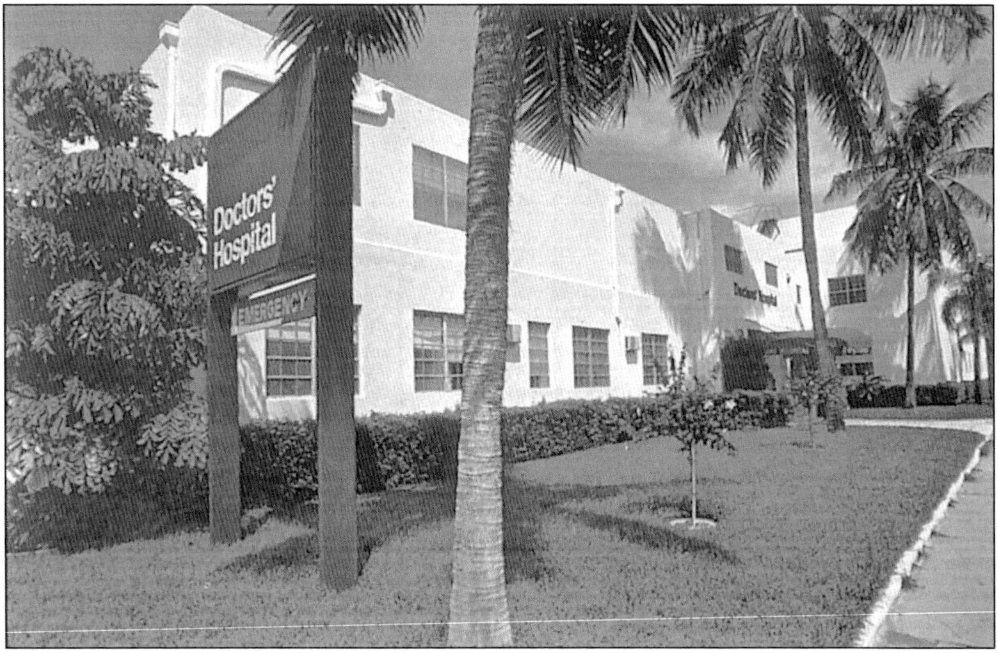

The Hollywood Hospital was renamed Doctor's Hospital of Hollywood. Still located at 1859 Van Buren Street, the building has been remodeled. In the 1960s this was an American Medicorp Hospital, with 124 beds and modern technology.

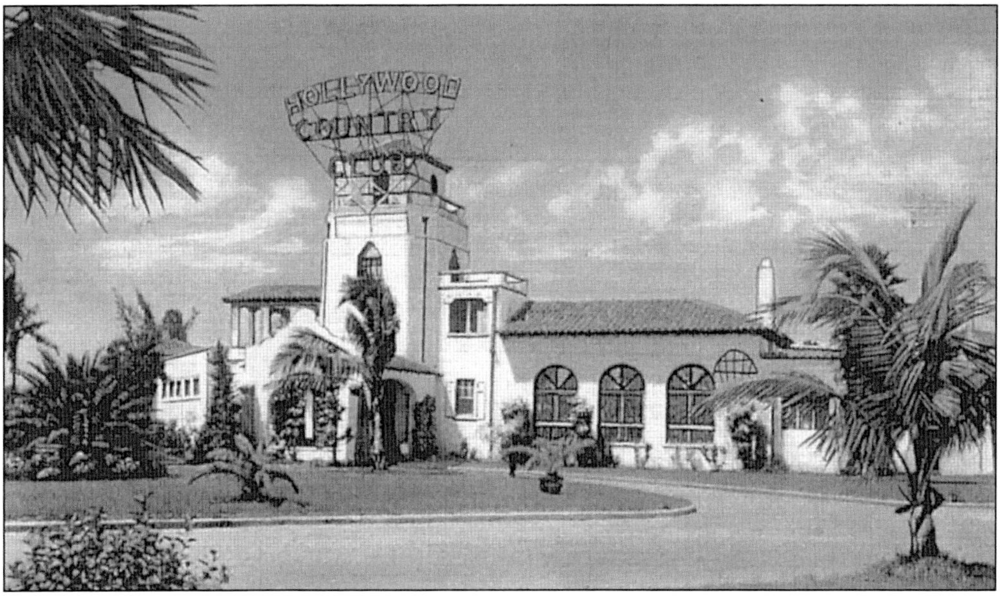

From 1929 to 1931 the Hollywood Golf and Country Club was a gambling casino leased by Chicago mobster Al Capone. It was operated extravagantly and local residents weren't admitted. During Prohibition, men carried their coats inside, in spite of the hot weather. Then they removed the liquor bottles from their hiding places in the sleeves and the club waiters served setups.

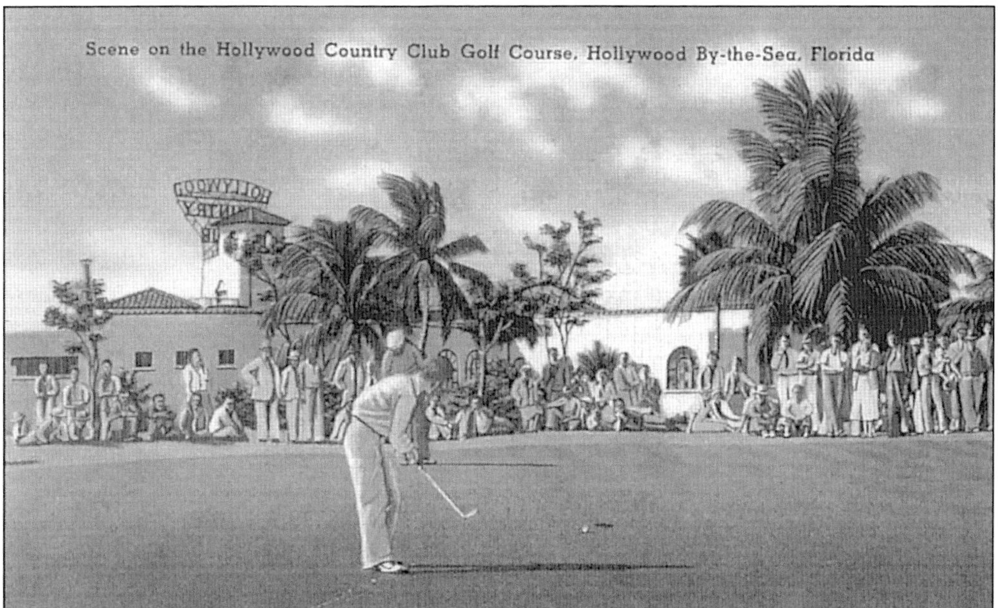

The golf course, which had nine holes open for play in 1922 (even before the clubhouse opened) was extremely popular. President Warren Harding, Gene Tunney, movie star Thomas Meighan, and Metropolitan Opera Tenor John McCormack were just a few of the celebrities who played this course.

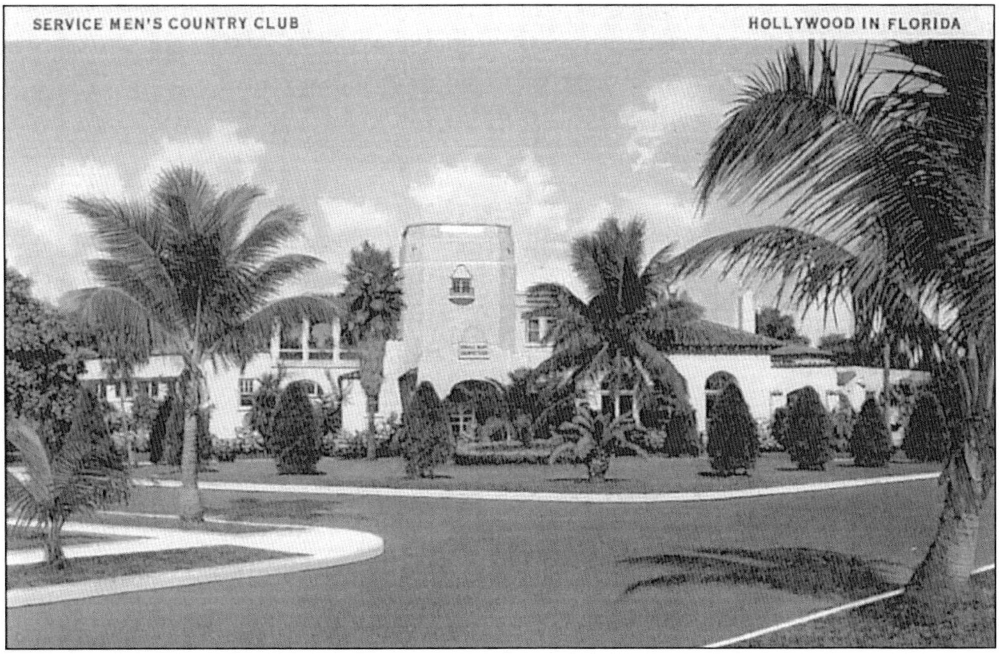

During WW II the Hollywood Golf and Country Club became the Service Men's Country Club. Between July and December of 1942 this club was sponsored by the Hollywood Chamber of Commerce. It was operated under the direction of the local USO unit.

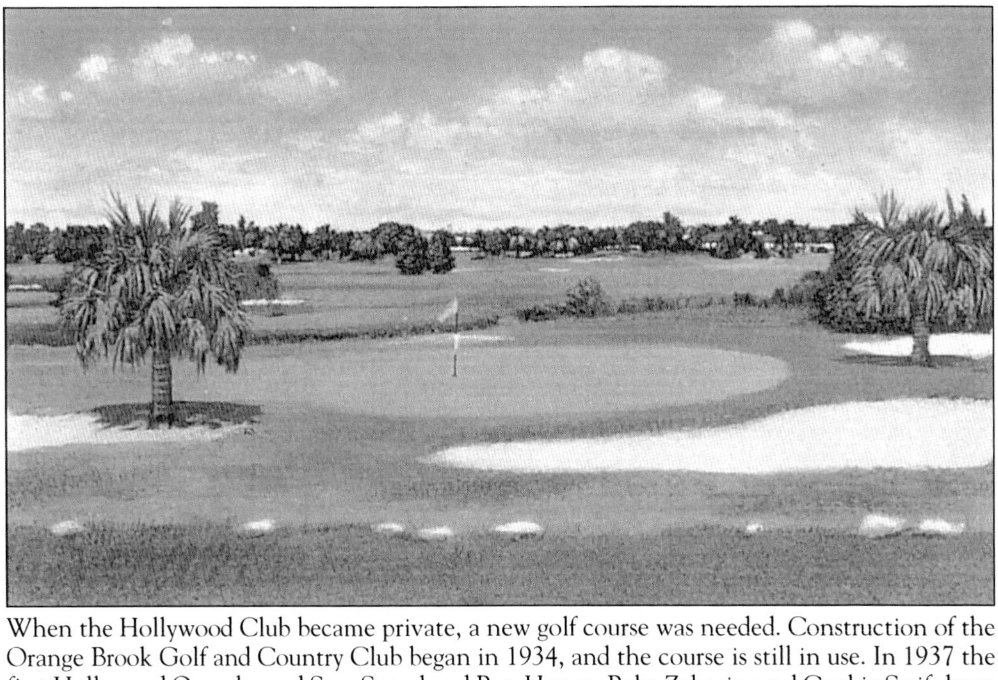

When the Hollywood Club became private, a new golf course was needed. Construction of the Orange Brook Golf and Country Club began in 1934, and the course is still in use. In 1937 the first Hollywood Open hosted Sam Snead and Ben Hogan. Babe Zaharias and Cookie Swift have also played there. By the mid-1960s the club was a social center with year-round activities and its course boasted 36 holes.

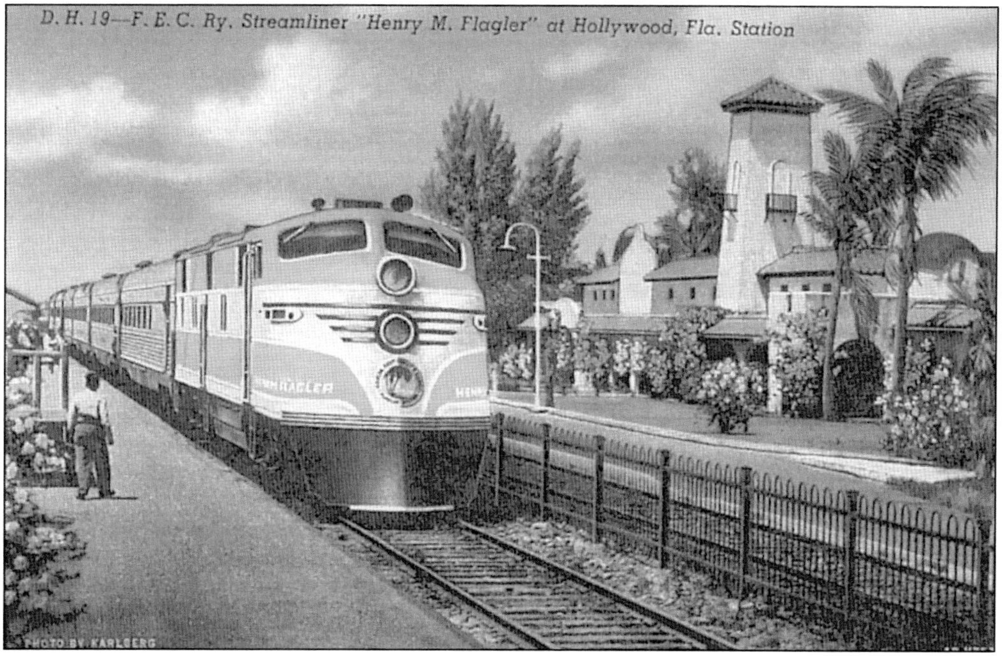

The train station, still in the same location, was originally 425-feet long and was built in the Spanish Mission style. Its plans had to be approved by Henry Flagler's Florida East Coast Railroad Company to be sure it could accommodate the single-track design. Shortly after, WW II steam locomotives were replaced by diesel engines.

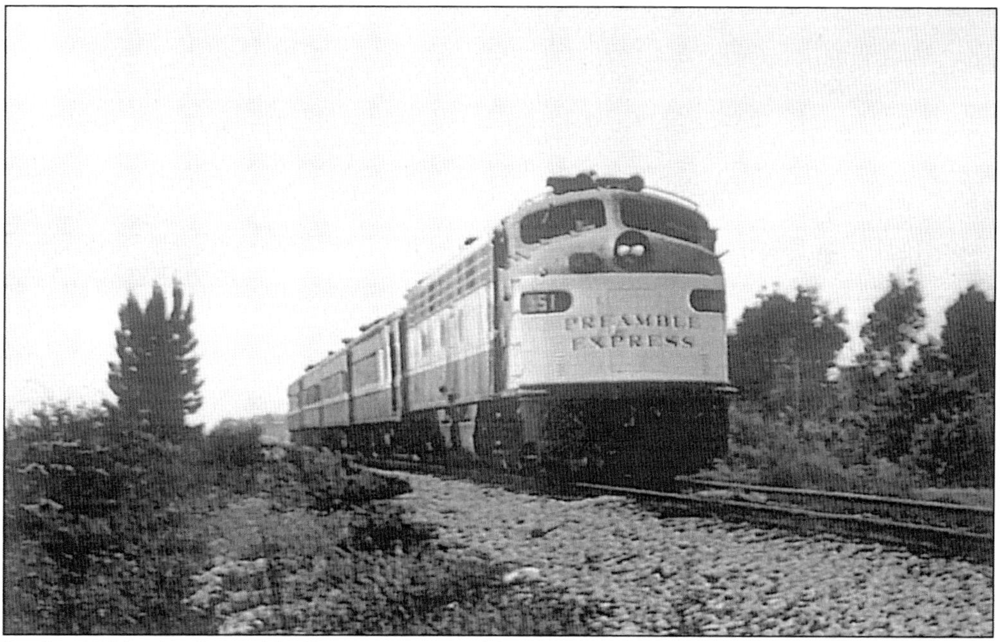

In the 1970s the Preamble Express, powered by Union Pacific Railroad's locomotive #951, headed through rural Hollywood on Seaboard Coast Line tracks. The Preamble Express was used to check security for the Freedom Train.

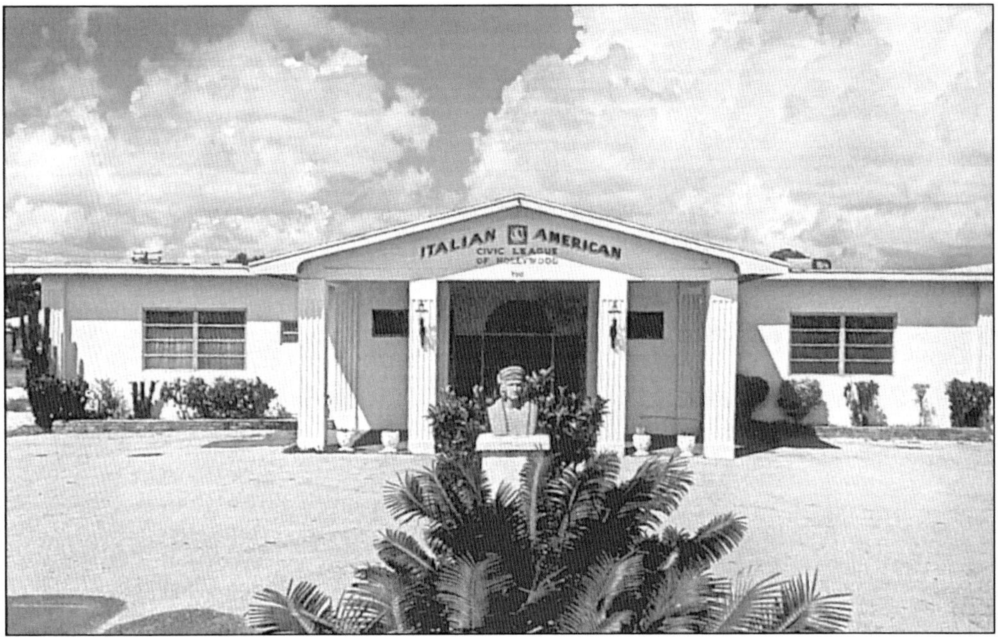

The Italian-American Club, located at 700 South Dixie Highway, illustrated the need for Hollywood's newcomers to talk to others from their former homes. Several such clubs formed, including many for people from specific states. This club was "Dedicated to the welfare of our people and for the good American Citizens."

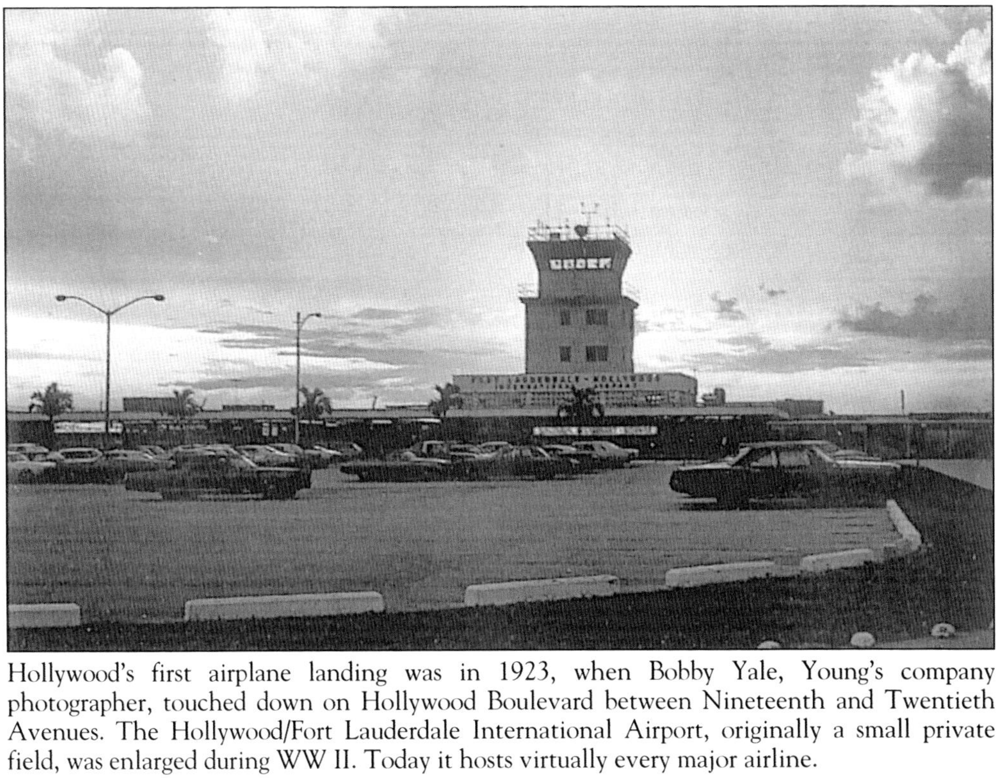

Hollywood's first airplane landing was in 1923, when Bobby Yale, Young's company photographer, touched down on Hollywood Boulevard between Nineteenth and Twentieth Avenues. The Hollywood/Fort Lauderdale International Airport, originally a small private field, was enlarged during WW II. Today it hosts virtually every major airline.

Five

SHOPPING AND RESTAURANTS

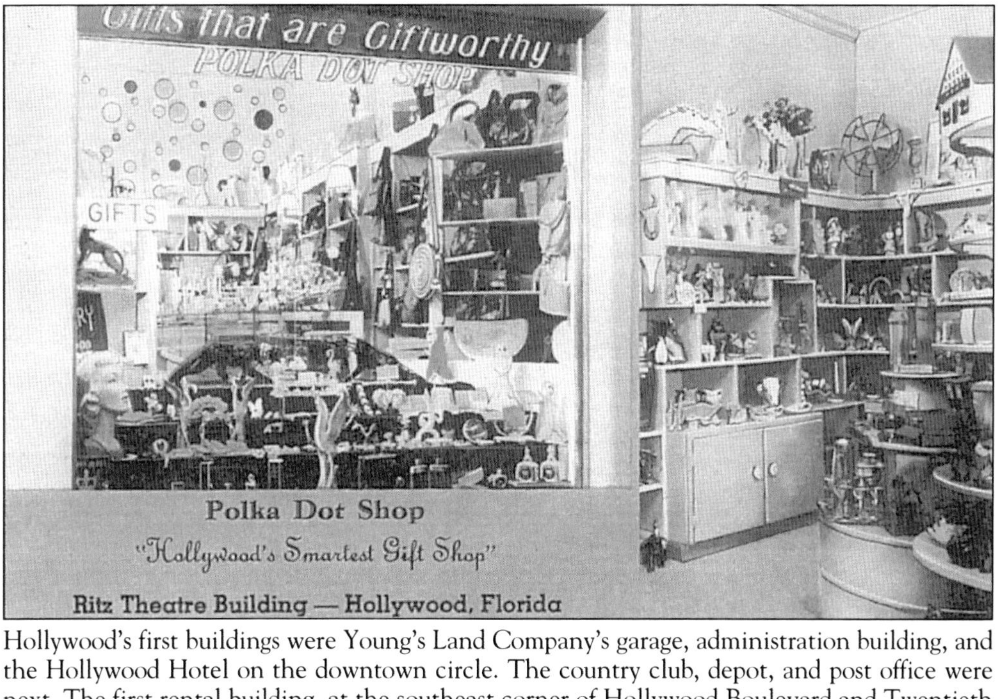

Hollywood's first buildings were Young's Land Company's garage, administration building, and the Hollywood Hotel on the downtown circle. The country club, depot, and post office were next. The first rental building, at the southeast corner of Hollywood Boulevard and Twentieth Avenue, leased its first storefront to Black's Drugstore, which also served as the Greyhound bus stop. The downtown area had begun to prosper. In spite of the Depression, Hollywood managed to thrive throughout the 1930s due, in large part, to tourist dollars. Samuel Horvitz and his Hollywood Inc. held firmly to his policy of high-quality development and he refused to build in any other way. Samuel died shortly after the opening of Hollywood Inc.'s Golf Estates in 1954, and his son William took over the company. In addition to residential development, Hollywood Inc. built shopping centers and light industrial parks. Hollywood's primary industry continues to be tourism, with light industry and retail businesses adding to the economy.

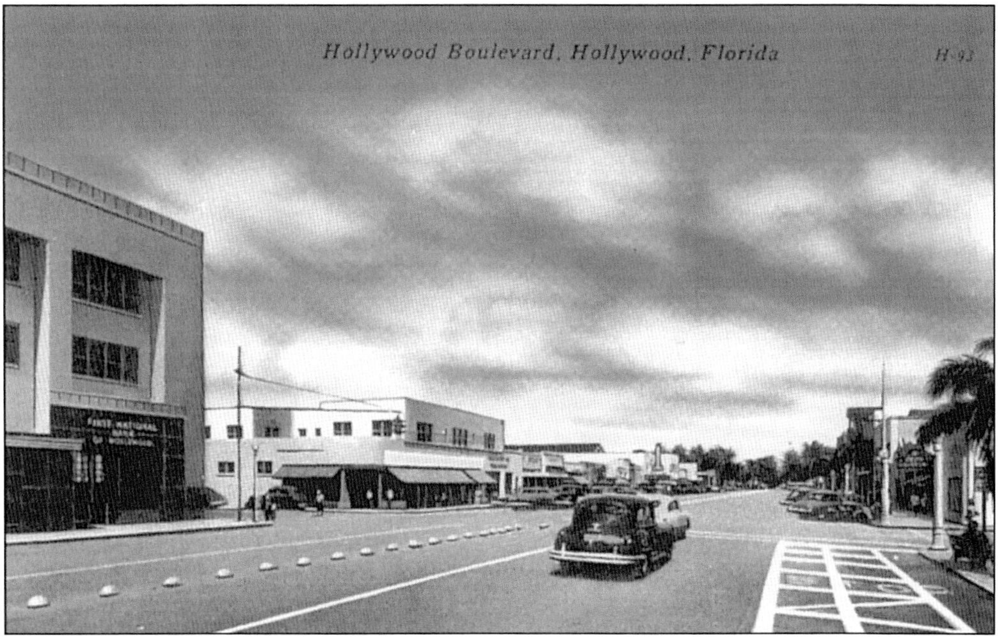

The downtown area has traditionally been the hub of Hollywood's business activity. Traveling east along Hollywood Boulevard from City Hall Circle in the early 1950s, the new First National Bank of Hollywood building could be seen on the left.

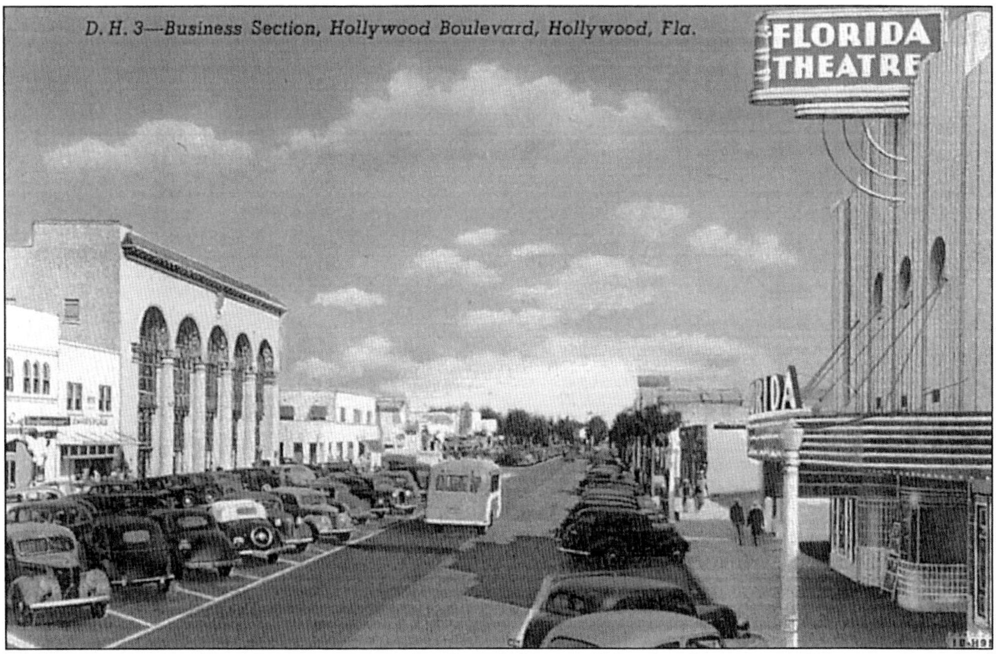

The First National Bank was previously the Hollywood Bank, sharing its distinctive arched and columned building (on the left) with the post office. Across the street, at 2016 Hollywood Boulevard, was the Florida Theatre, built in 1939. Fire destroyed the theatre in January of 1964, just one hour after patrons left its final show.

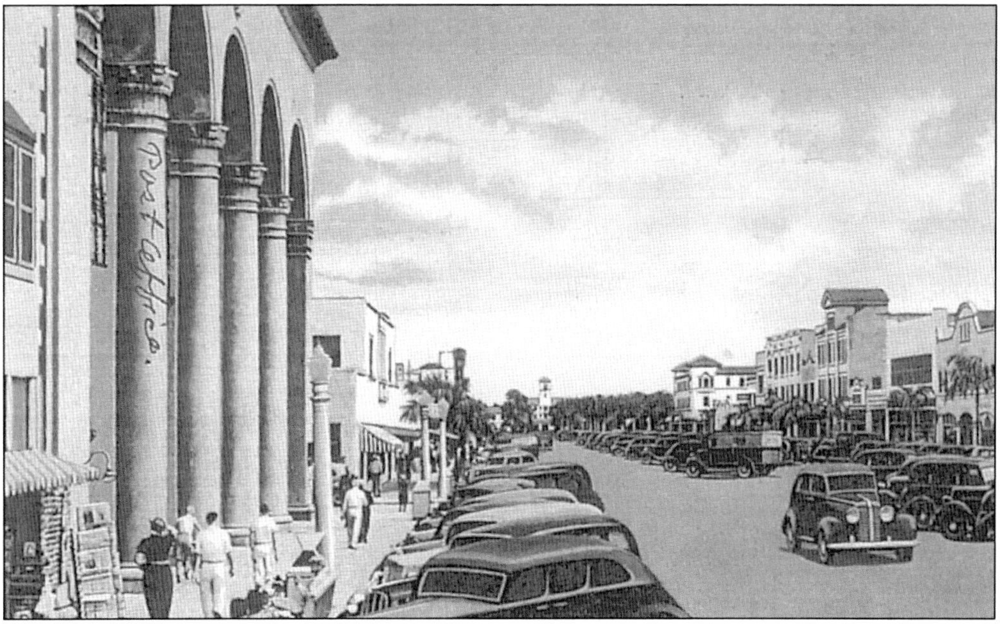

Looking east, the newsstand and Hollywood Bank/Post Office are on the left. The Park View Hotel stands at the far end, across from Harding (now Young) Circle Park. In 1999 an area embracing 45 buildings along Hollywood Boulevard, from Dixie Highway to Young Circle, was added to the National Register of Historic Places.

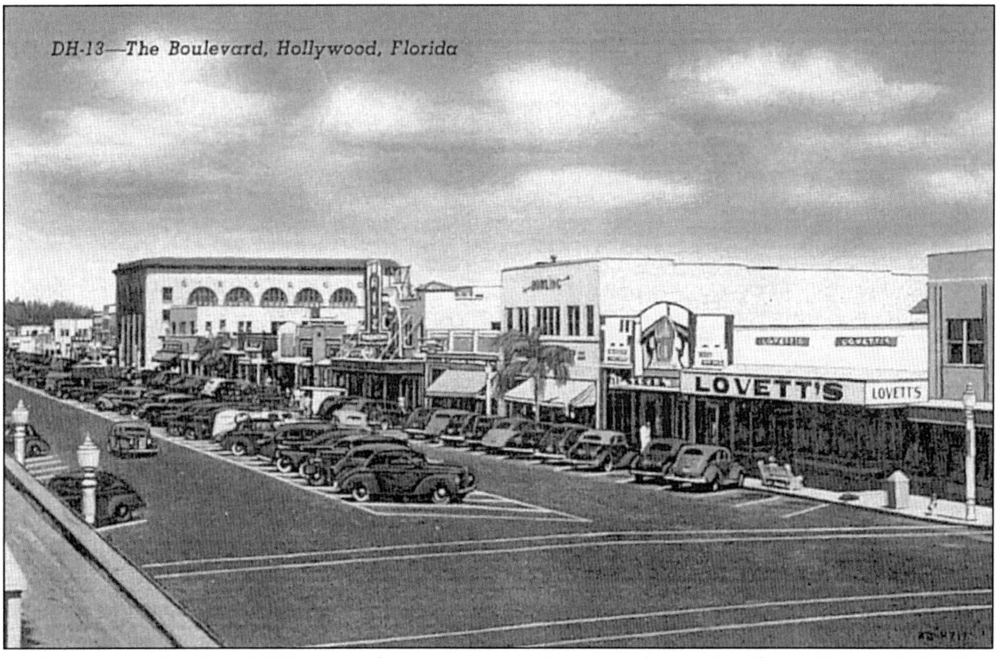

Looking west, this late 1930s view shows Lovett's, the second-story bowling alley, and the Ritz Theatre building. Originally called the Hollywood Theater, Hollywood's first movie house was renamed the Ritz in 1926. Its ushers used "the gun," a dispenser filled with mosquito repellent, to spray each patron at the entrance.

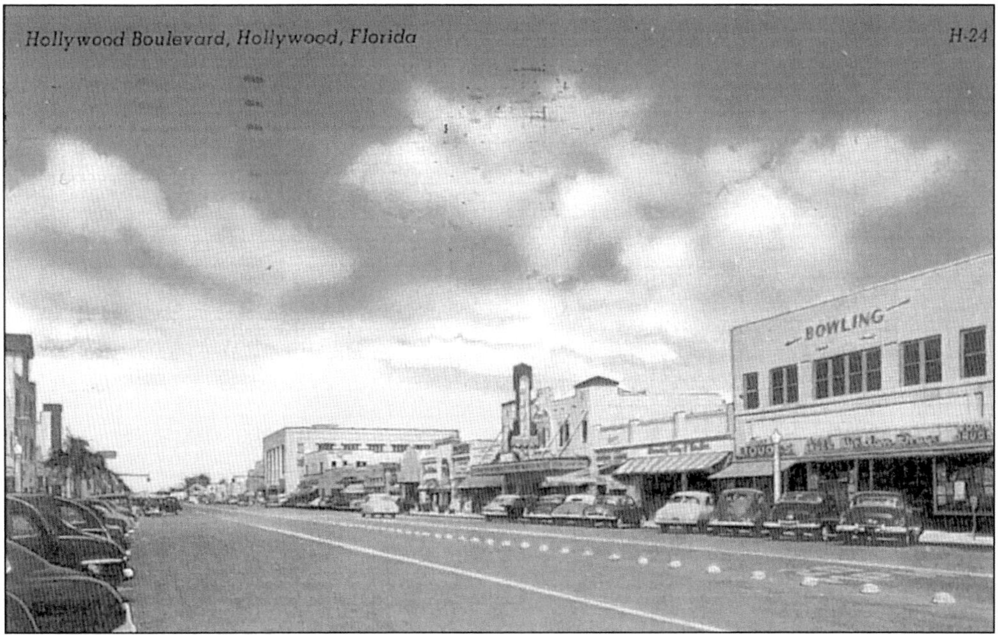

In 1946 parking meters were installed and middle-of-the-street parking was discontinued. It has since been reinstated. Below the Bowling Alley stood Whelan's Drugs (with its soda fountain) and a liquor store. The former Ritz Theatre building now houses Irving Berlin's Men's Apparel.

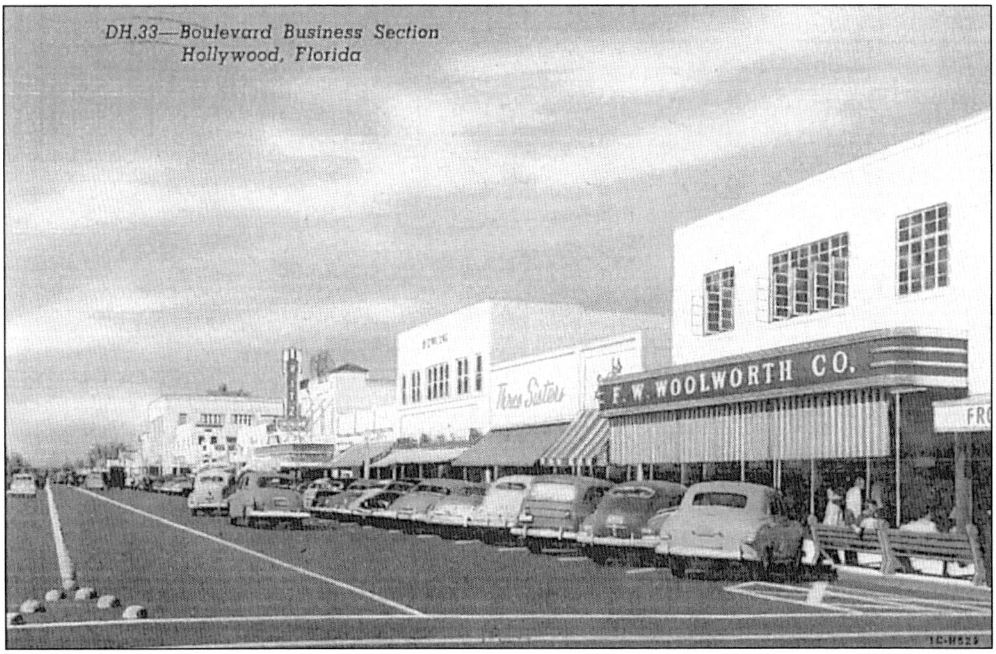

Backing up but still looking west along Hollywood Boulevard, this view shows the Three Sisters dress shop, which was formerly the Rainbo Grill and is now the Rainbo Cafe. The striped awning next to it is now Trader John's Books. F.W. Woolworth became Poland's Department Store and is now O'Hara's Night Club.

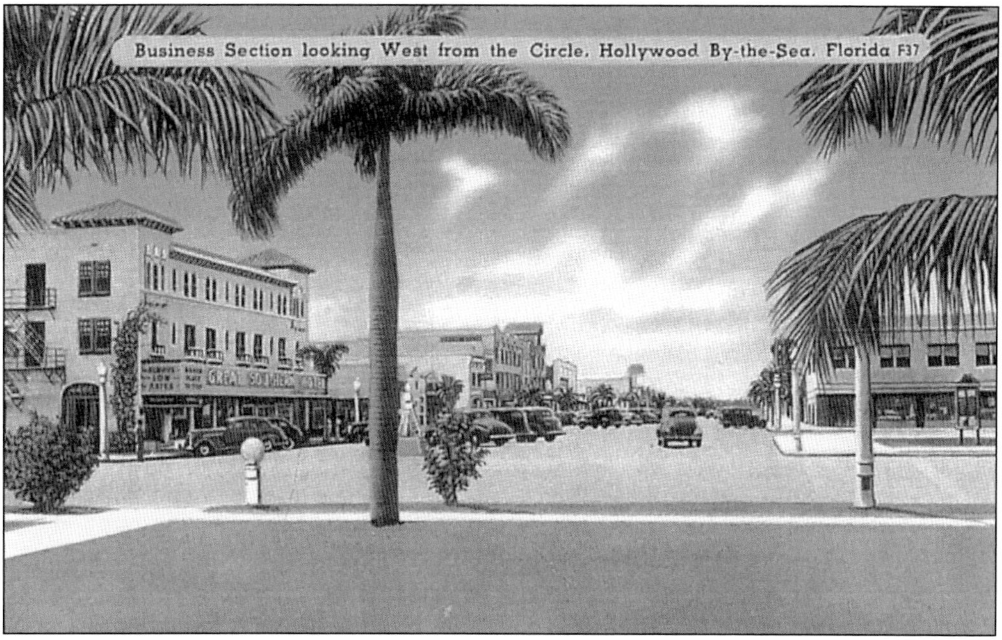

Looking west from the downtown circle, the Great Southern Hotel is on the left. This historic hotel, with an original capacity of 100 guests, is still in use today. One morning in July of 1940, firefighters responded to a call and found the entire building engulfed in smoke and flames. Forty percent of the structure was damaged, but it was repaired.

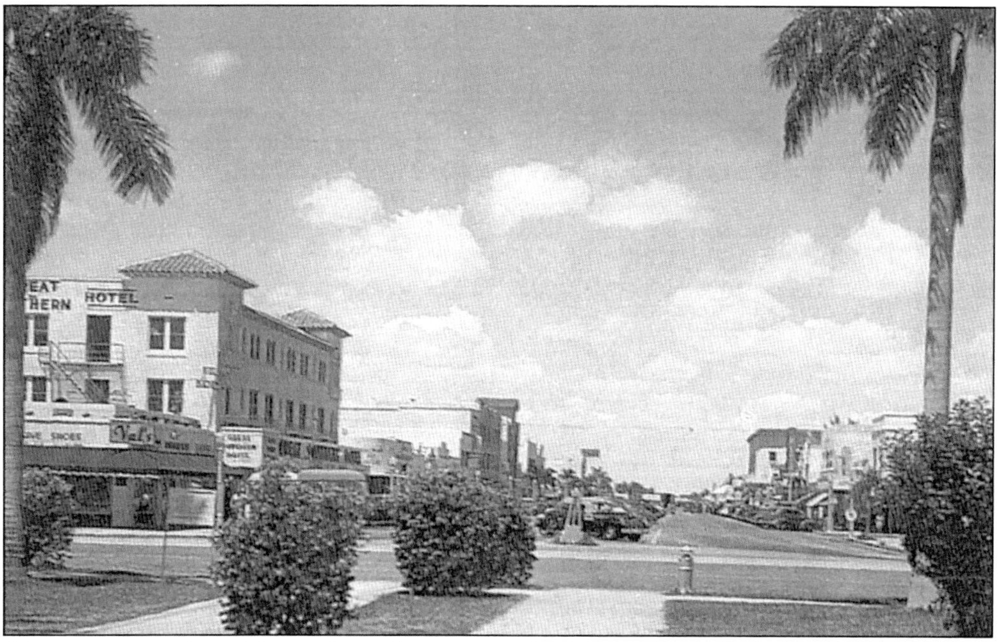

This same view, about 30 years later, shows some changes. Today the stores on the ground level of the Great Southern Hotel include a consignment boutique as well as jewelry and gift shops. The hotel was purchased in 1999 and is being restored.

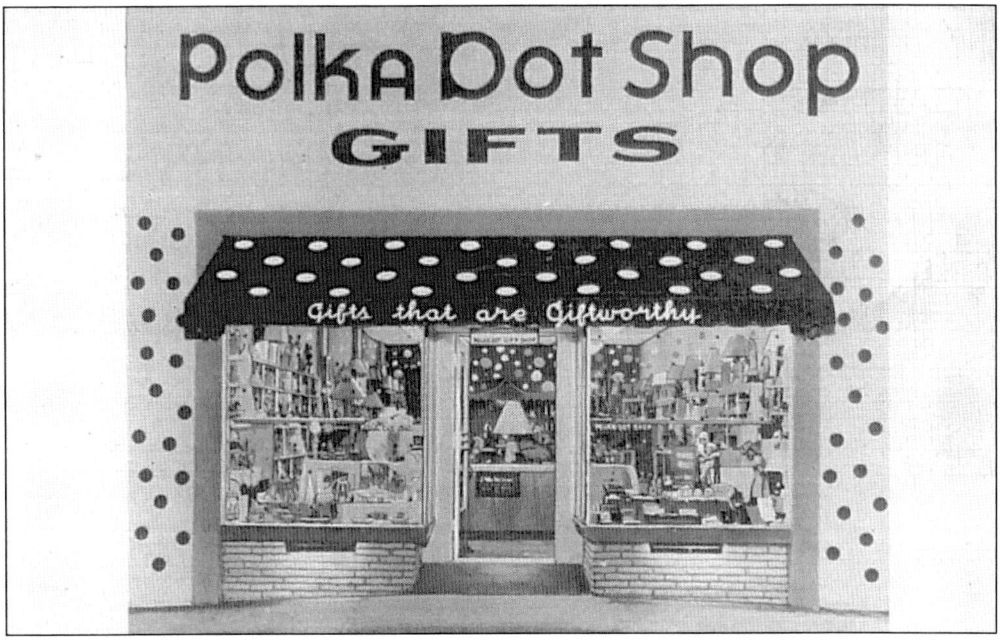

The Polka Dot Gift Shop opened in the Ritz Theatre Building. Proprietor Joe Williams called it Hollywood's finest gift shop. Featured items included ceramics, perfumes, alligator bags and shoes, as well as costume jewelry with a tropical motif.

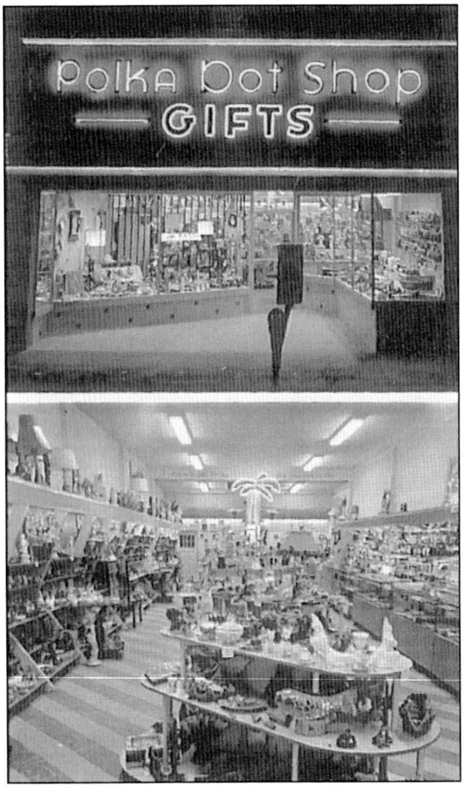

By the early 1960s the Polka Dot had moved across the street to 2012 Hollywood Boulevard. "Gifts that are giftworthy" was its new slogan. Today the storefront is occupied by Monarch Properties and attorney Evan Frankel.

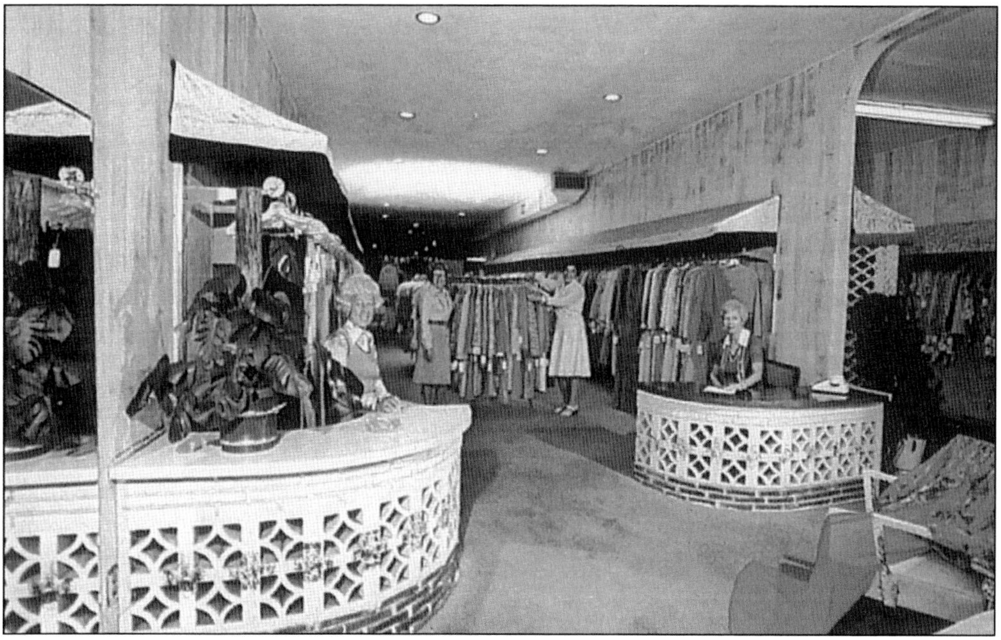

In the early 1960s, these four friendly saleswomen were always available to help customers of the Fashion Shop at 1918 Hollywood Boulevard. The shop was formerly called Perry's. Today Italiano Imports occupies this space and the 1918 address no longer exists.

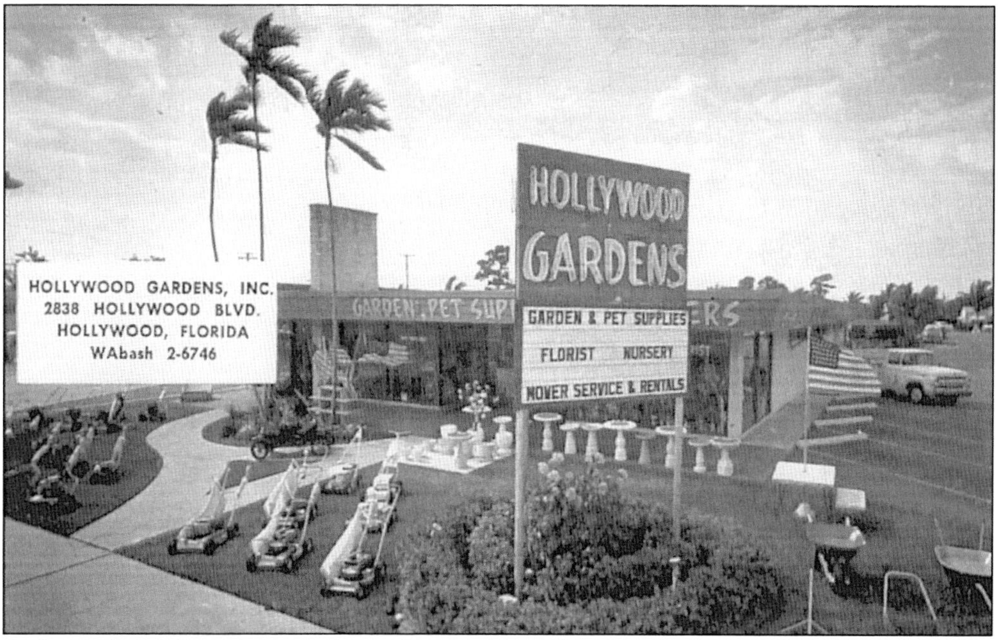

Hollywood Gardens Inc. was located at 2838 Hollywood Boulevard and had a Wabash-2 telephone exchange. The florist and nursery offered prompt delivery of "floral arrangements of love and sympathy," as well as fertilizer, insecticides, and plants for the house and garden. Today a U-Haul facility occupies this site.

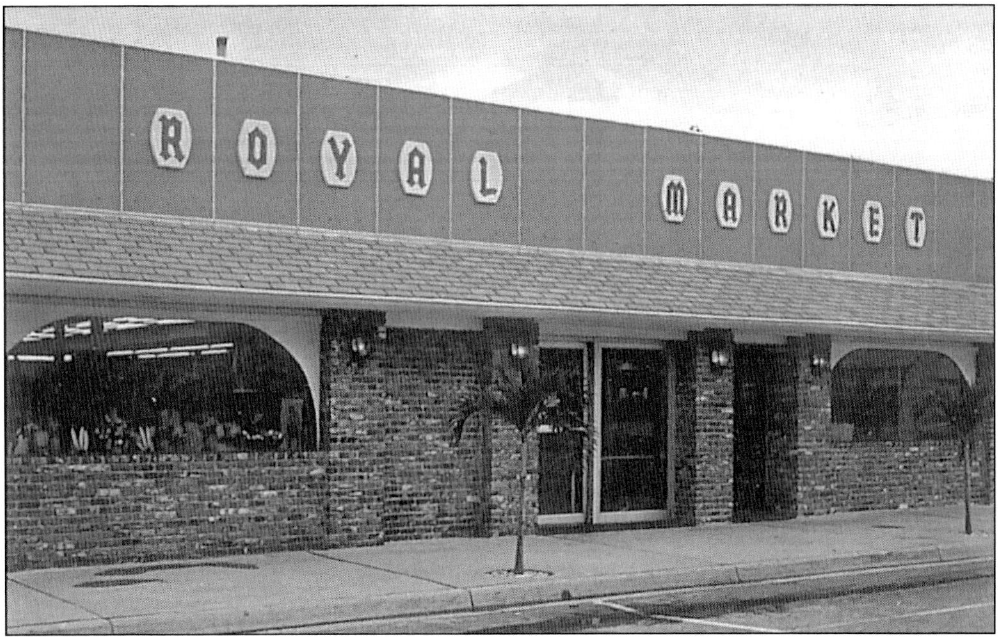

Owners Carl and John Perone personally managed the Royal Market, located at 1946 Harrison Street. Now gone, the grocery store was known as Florida's most unusual market.

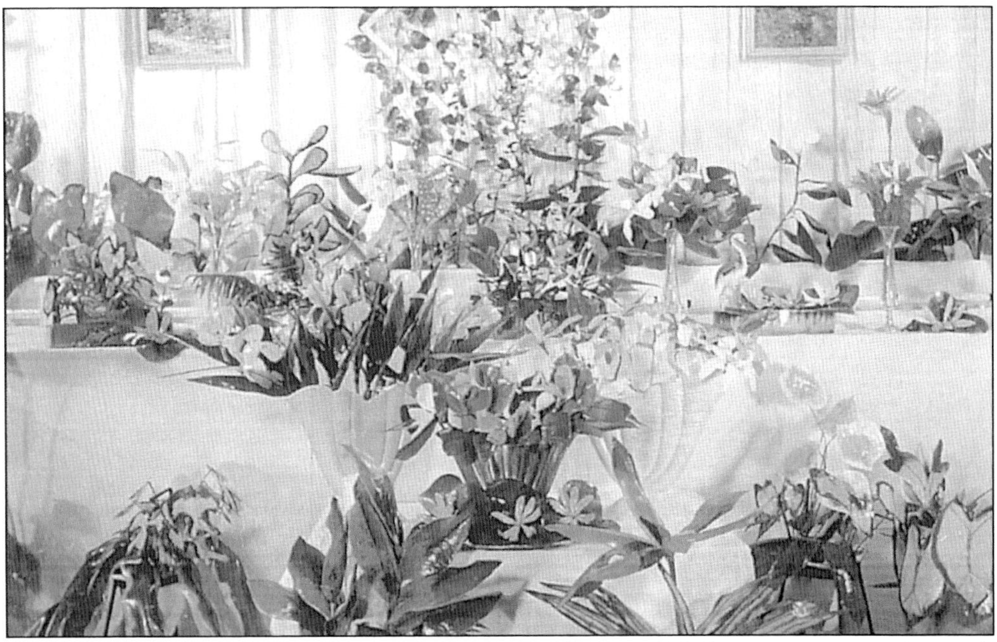

Employees of the A to Z Company at 530 North Dixie Highway were manufacturer's representatives for these plastic tropical plants. The colorful foliage was made of synthetic resins by a secret process. The plants were not affected by light, heat or cold, fire, steam, humidity, air-conditioning, water, insects, alcohol, or smoke fumes.

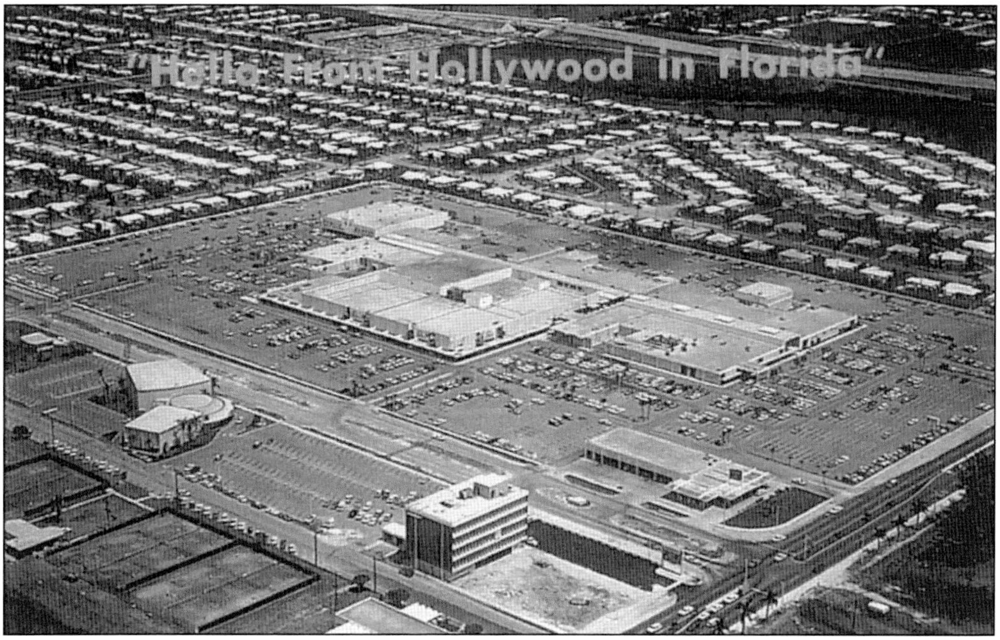

Hollywood Mall, located at 3251 Hollywood Boulevard, was the city's first enclosed shopping center. During the 1960s it was a favorite hang-out for the high school set. Its Sears Store, now replaced by Target, became infamous as the place from which little Adam Walsh, son of *America's Most Wanted*'s host John Walsh, was kidnapped.

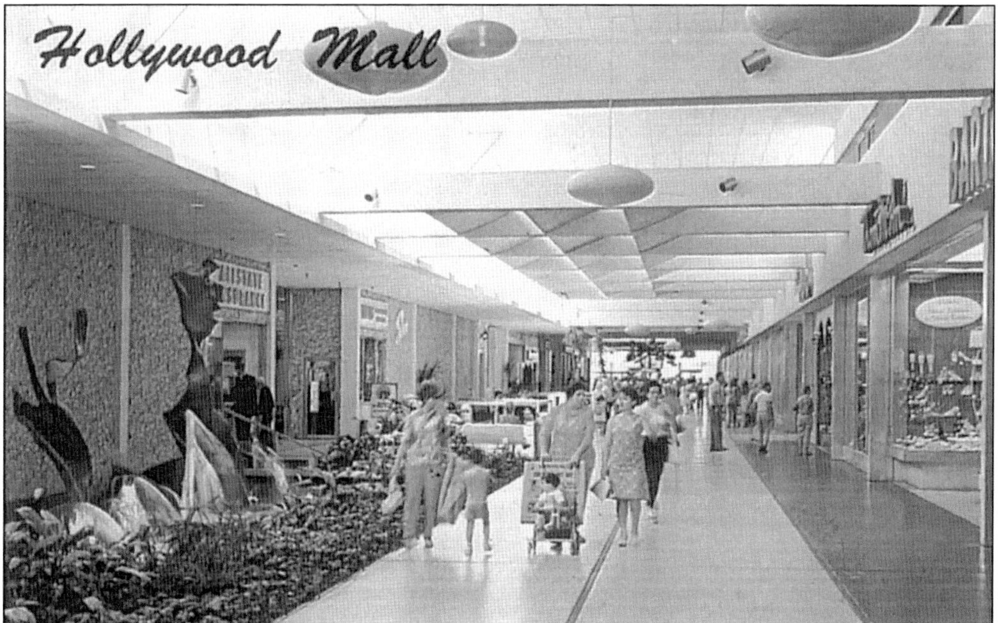

Mall stores in this view include Bartons and Thom McAn Shoes. Many thought the newer Fashion Center at Route 441 would cause the downfall of Hollywood Mall, but the Fashion Center is gone and the mall thrives today, after extensive remodeling. The movie theatres across the street are gone and have been replaced by fast-food shops.

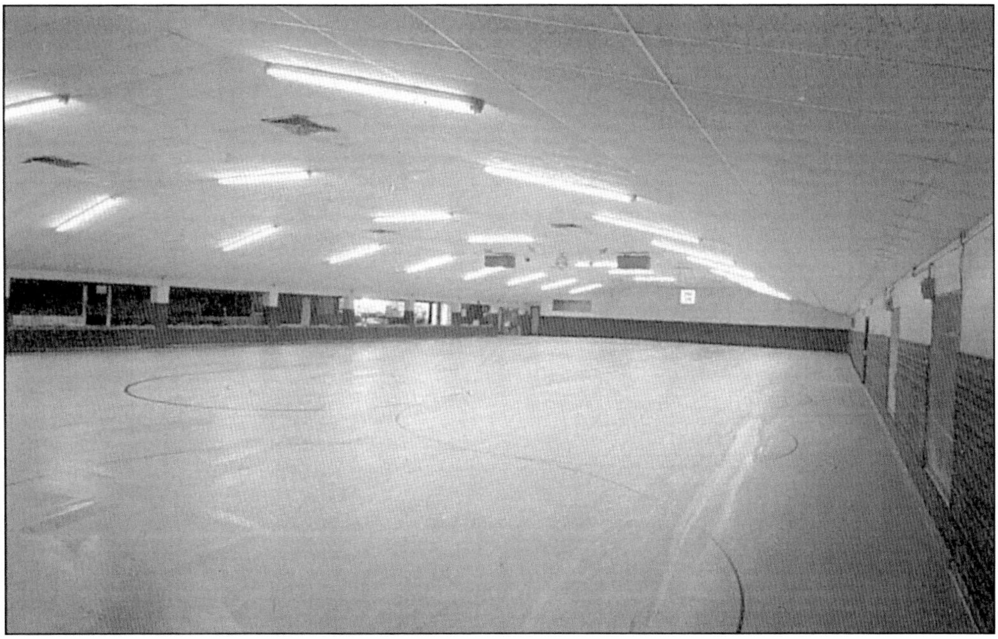

The Hollywood Skating Center, located at 2144 Johnson Street, offered a new and exciting family activity. Open evenings Wednesday through Sunday and weekend afternoons, the center's advertising emphasized that it was well-organized and well-supervised.

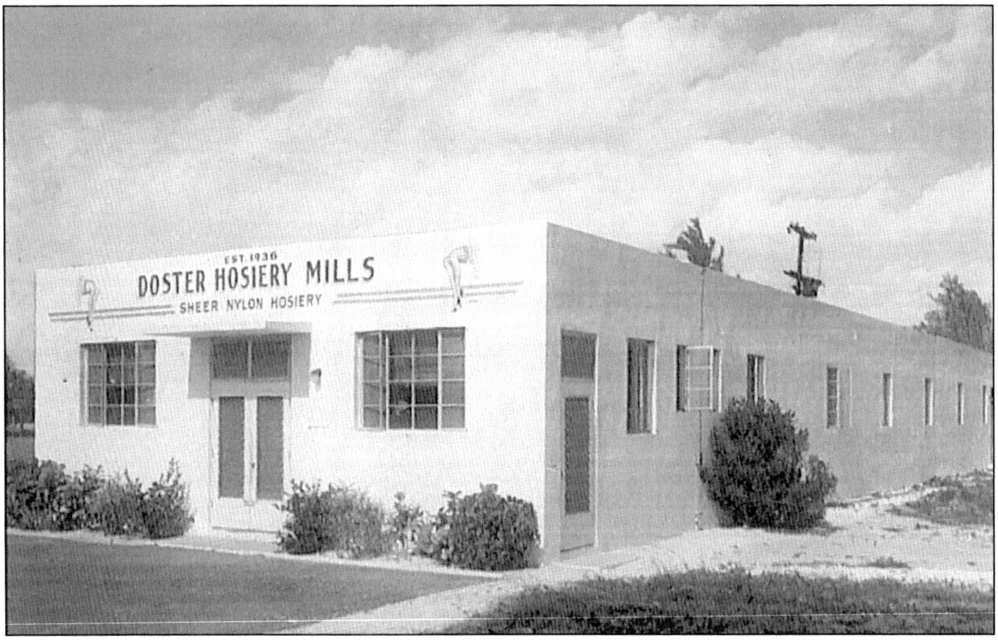

Doster Hosiery Mills, located at 2021 Coolidge Street, was typical of the kind of light industry Hollywood successfully attracted. Established in 1936, Doster manufactured ladies' sheer nylon hosiery.

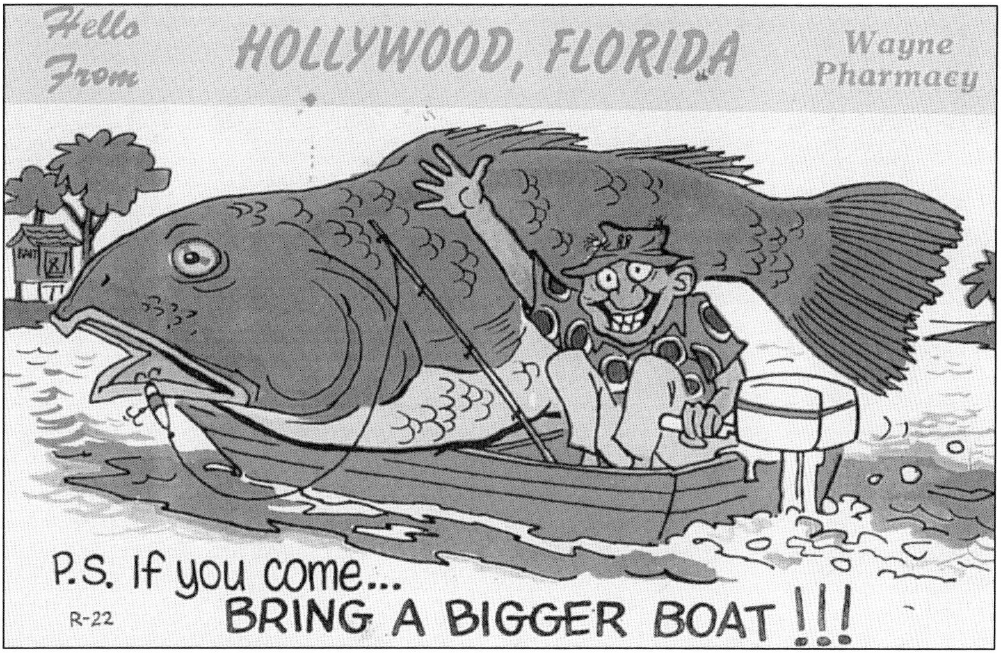

The Wayne Pharmacy chose to advertise in a humorous way. Schotzie, writing home to Garfield, New Jersey, wrote, "Just think of what we could have caught with a bigger boat!"

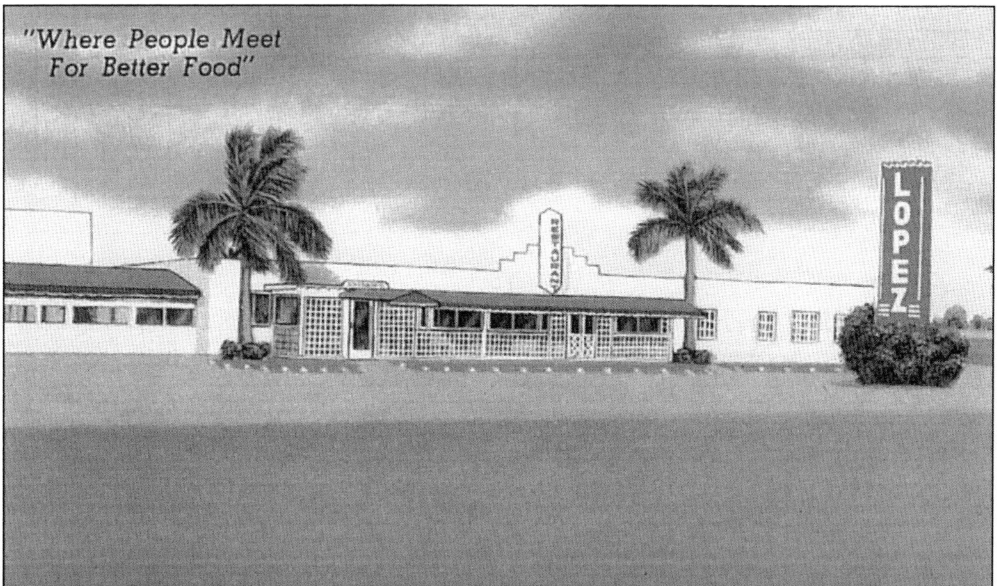

The Lopez Restaurant and Cocktail Room on South Federal Highway was the place for a high time in the 1940s. In 1948 a civil injunction was filed against the Lopez, as well as other area establishments, for gambling on the premises. Boasting good food and the choicest of imported and domestic liquors, its slogan was "Where people meet for better food."

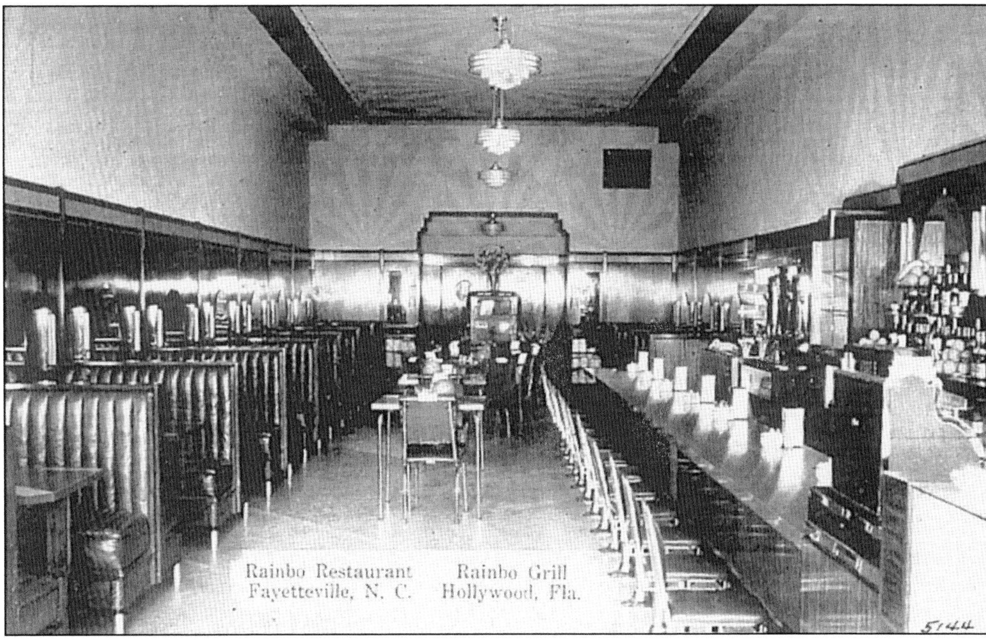

The Rainbo Restaurant in Fayetteville, North Carolina, and the Rainbo Grill at 1907 Hollywood Boulevard were owned by brothers Jesse and M.B. Wellons. Specialties of the house included seafood, steak, and chops.

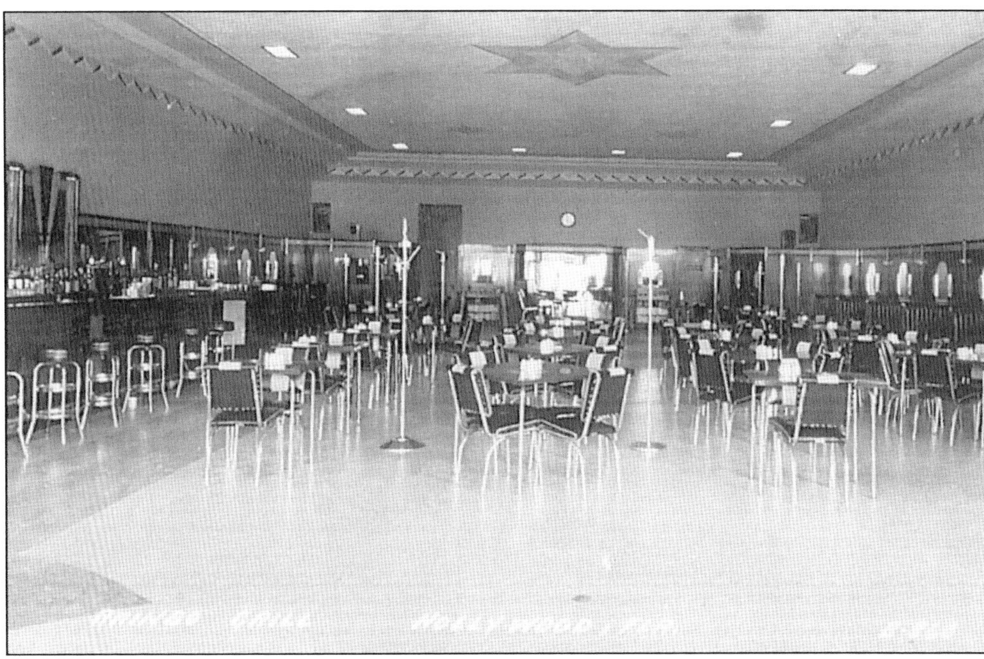

The Rainbo Grill was one of the first cocktail lounges to re-open after Prohibition was repealed in the spring of 1933. Today the Rainbo Cafe serves customers at 1909 Hollywood Boulevard and displays memorabilia from the old Rainbo Grill. The cafe has a second location at 1200 South Federal Highway in Dania.

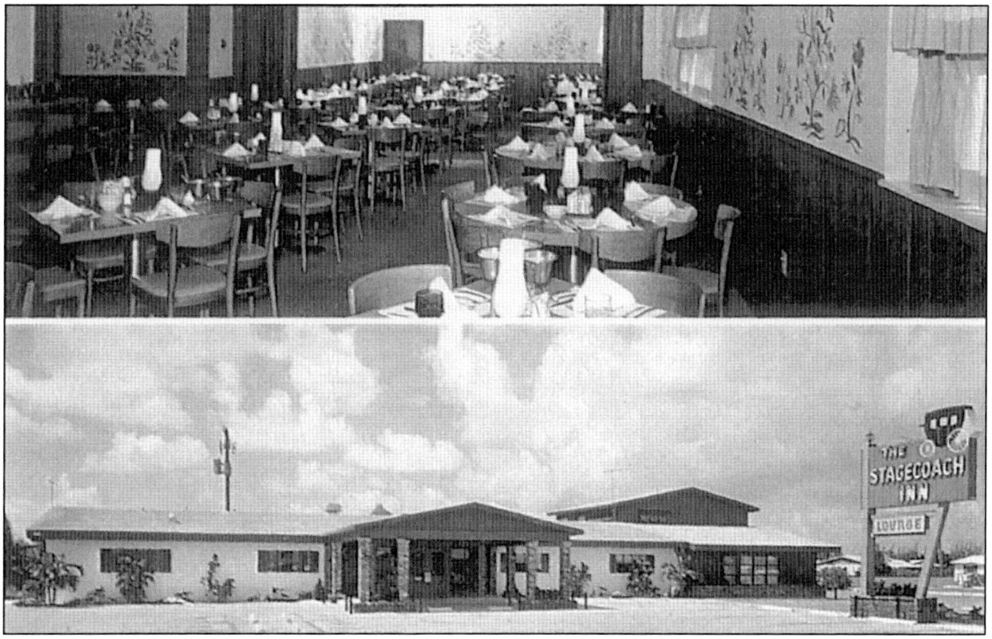

The Stagecoach Inn Restaurant and Lounge, 4520 West Hallandale Beach Boulevard, sported a Yukon-3 telephone exchange. Known for its international cuisine and famous for daily specials, the lounge also featured live music. The Stagecoach is gone, and a restaurant featuring ribs stands in its place.

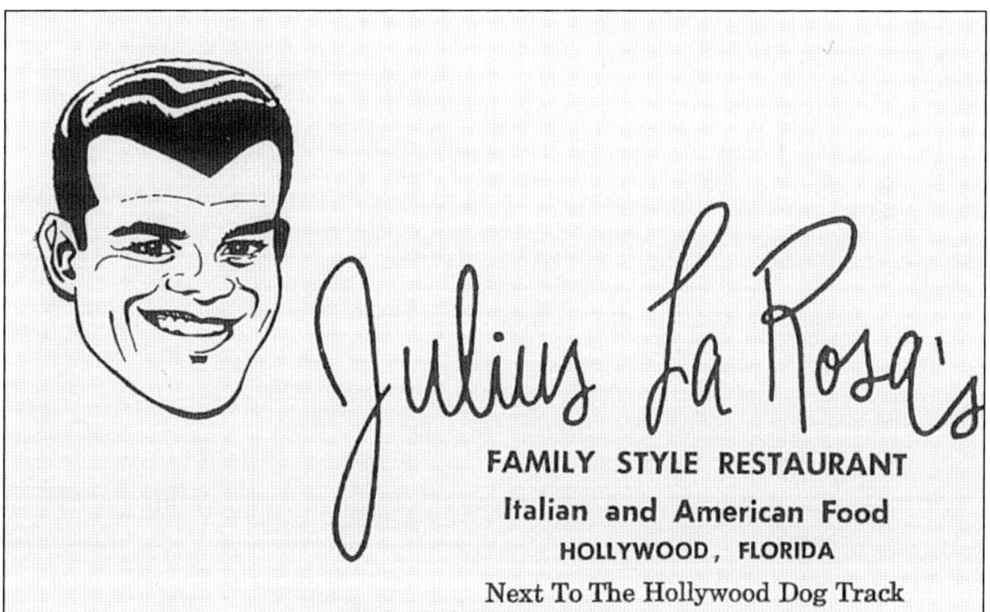

Julius La Rosa's, featuring Italian and American food, was located at 1945 Moffett Street, beside the Hollywood Dog Track. Mike and Amy Richel hosted restaurant patrons.

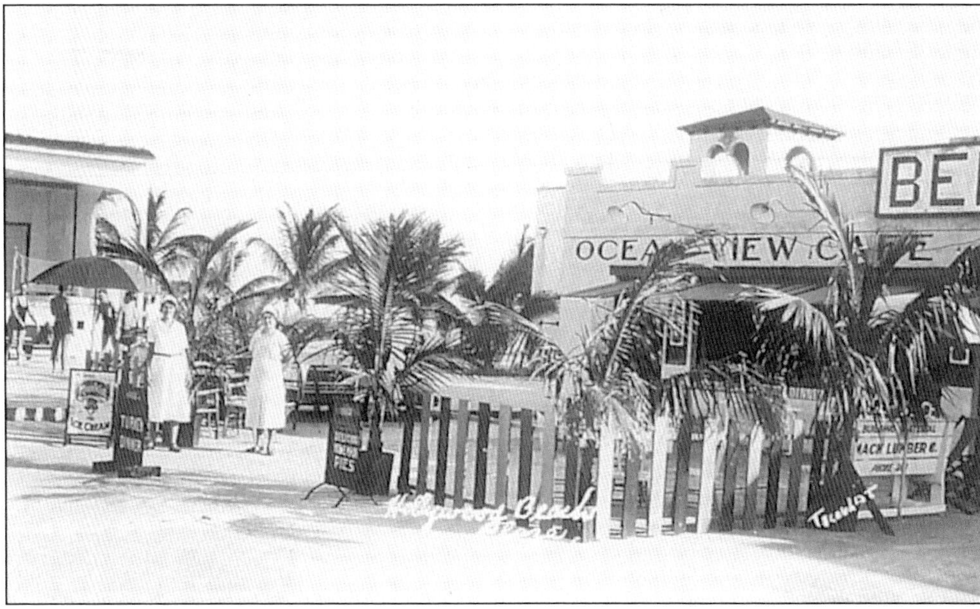

The Ocean View Cafe at the corner of the Broadwalk and Johnson Street was operated by sisters Mrs. William Knaebel and Mrs. Matthew Renn. It began when the rabbits that the Knaebels raised commercially, multiplied faster than the market would bear. Cafe specialties were rabbit stew and rabbit pot pies. The cafe was destroyed by the 1935 Labor Day Hurricane.

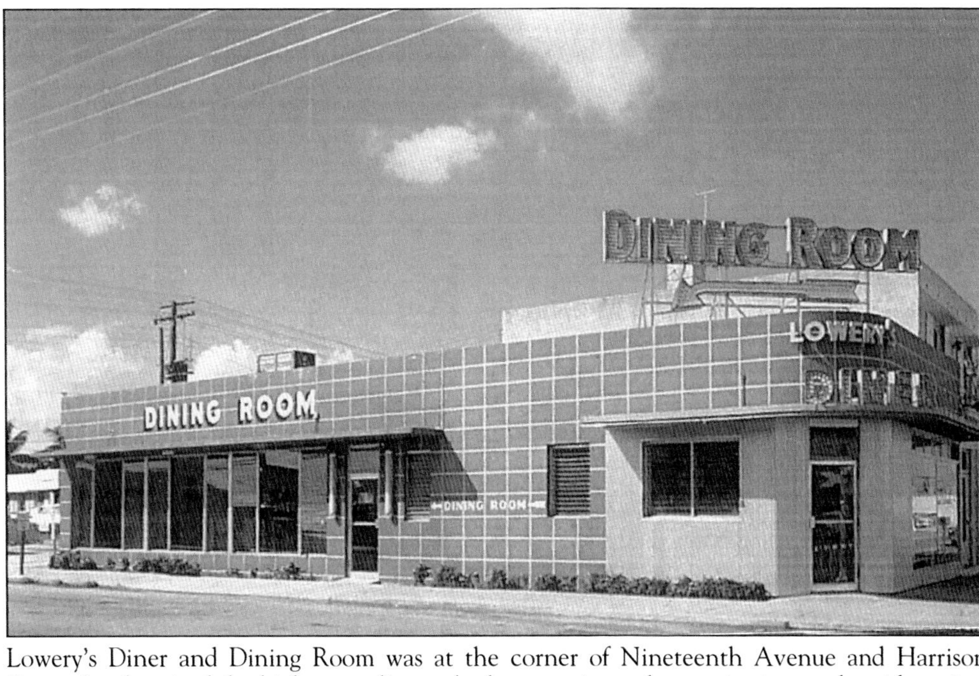

Lowery's Diner and Dining Room was at the corner of Nineteenth Avenue and Harrison Street. It advertised the highest quality at the lowest prices, ultra sanitation, and rapid service. Although the building still stands, the 1950s blue-tile exterior has been replaced with more modern siding.

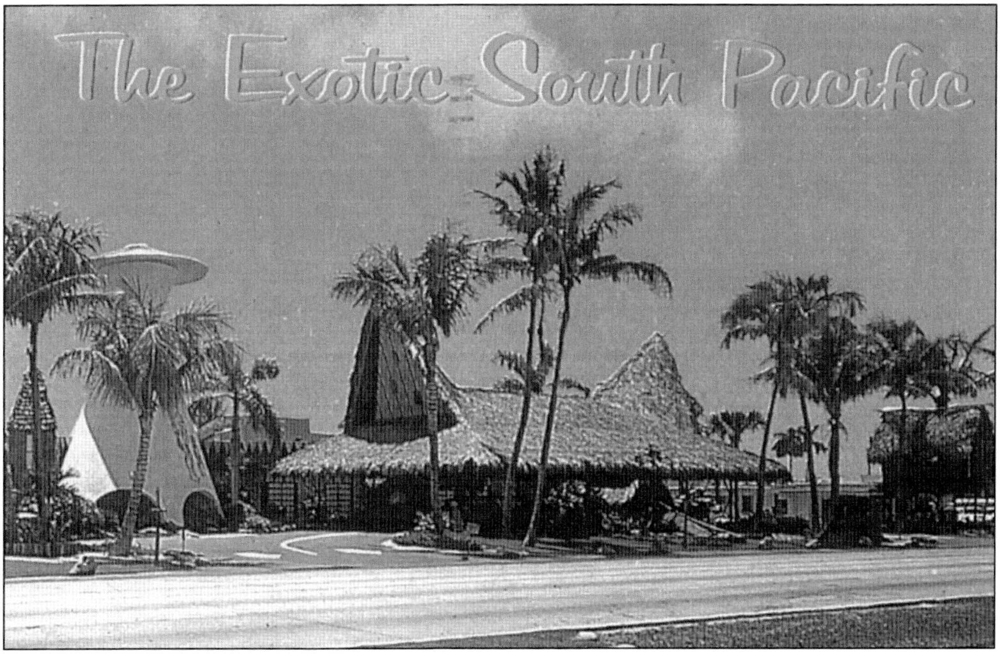

The South Pacific Polynesian Restaurant was located at the southern tip of Hollywood. Its tiki-hut motif blended well with its palm tree-dotted landscape and attracted customers who enjoyed its casual beach atmosphere.

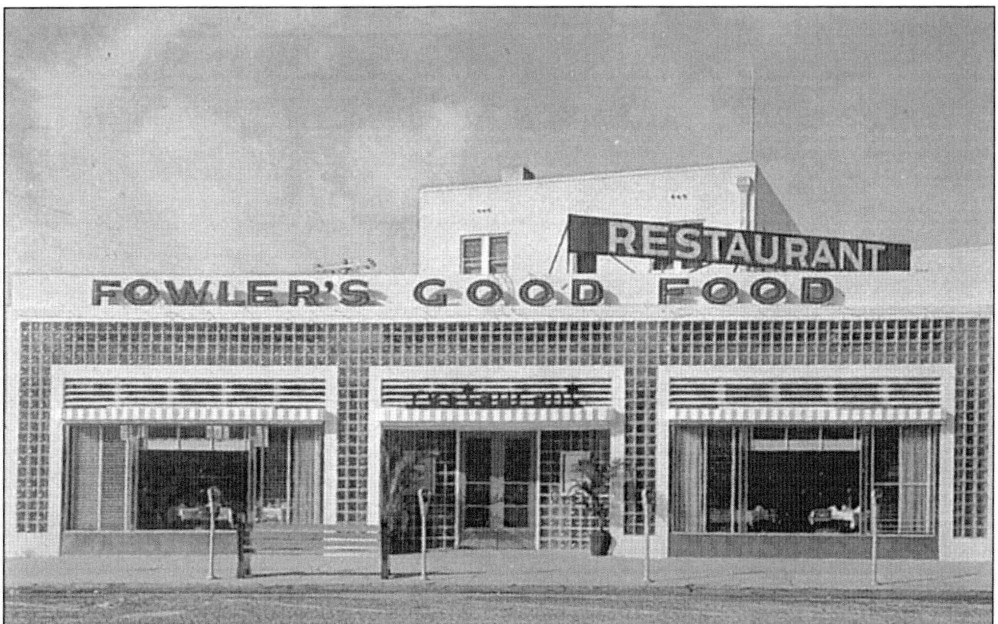

Fowler's Good Food Restaurant was located on the downtown circle. Its postcard boasts that it was "known from coast to coast for its food." The building is no longer there.

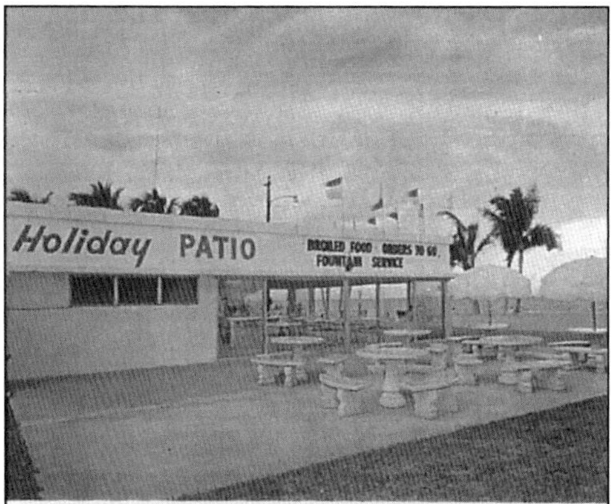

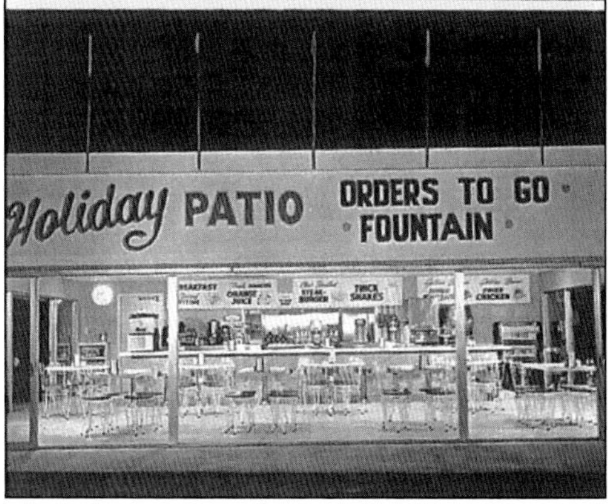

Holiday Patio, located at 200 Garfield Street, offered dine-in service with an ocean view as well as complete fountain service and take-out food. Its pastries were homemade and breakfast was served anytime. Menu items included fresh-squeezed orange juice, char-broiled steak burgers, thick shakes, and fried chicken.

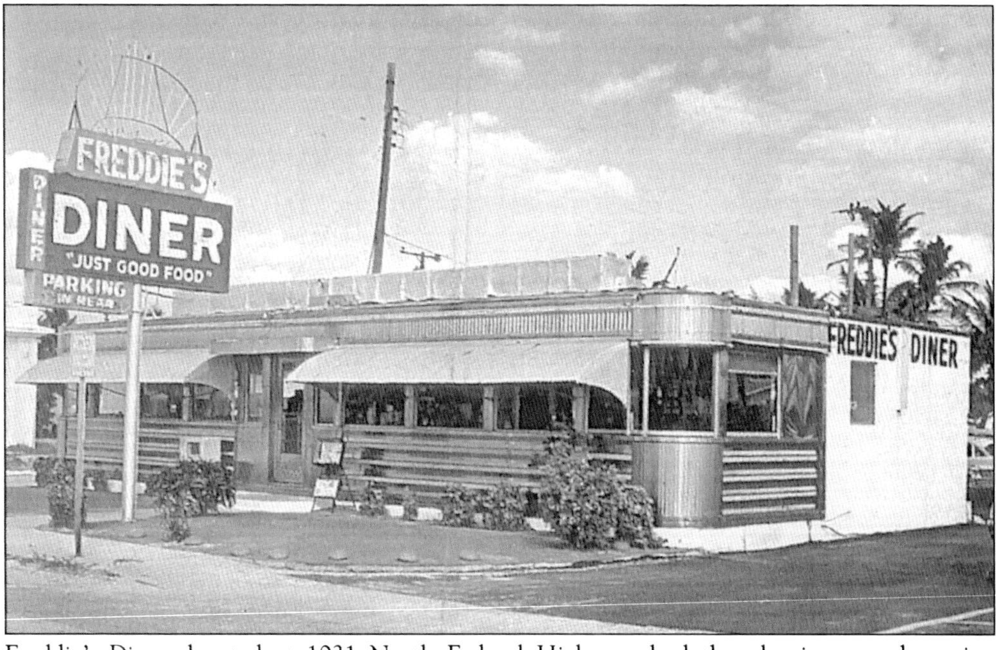

Freddie's Diner, located at 1031 North Federal Highway, had the aluminum and awning facade of a stereotypical diner and a concrete block rear section. "Just Good Food" was its claim to fame.

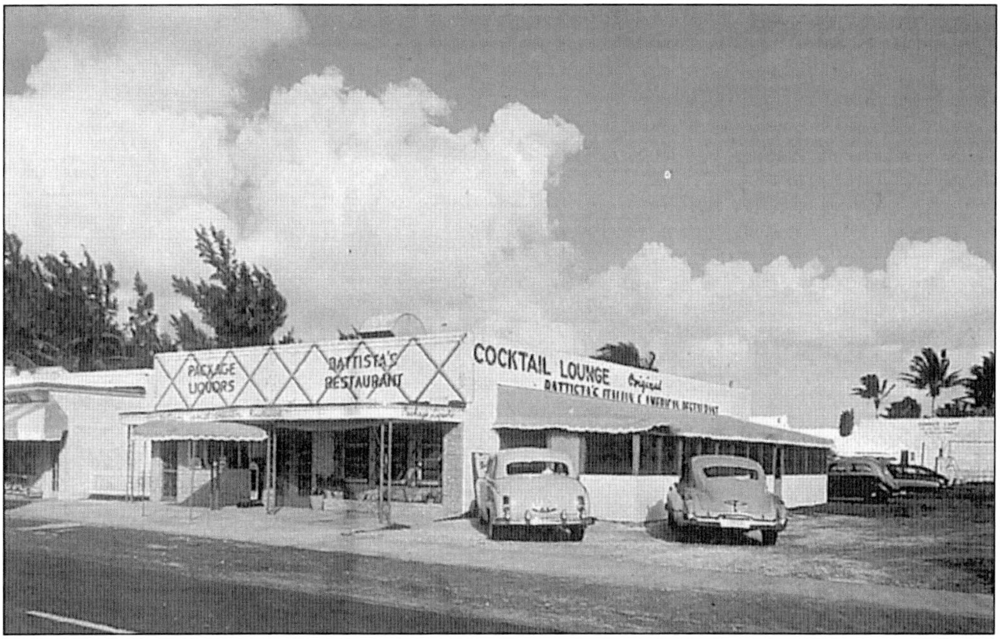

This early 1950s view shows the original Battista's Restaurant, Cocktail Lounge and Package Liquors. The Italian-American restaurant relocated from Miami and Coral Gables to this location at 1205 North Ocean Drive.

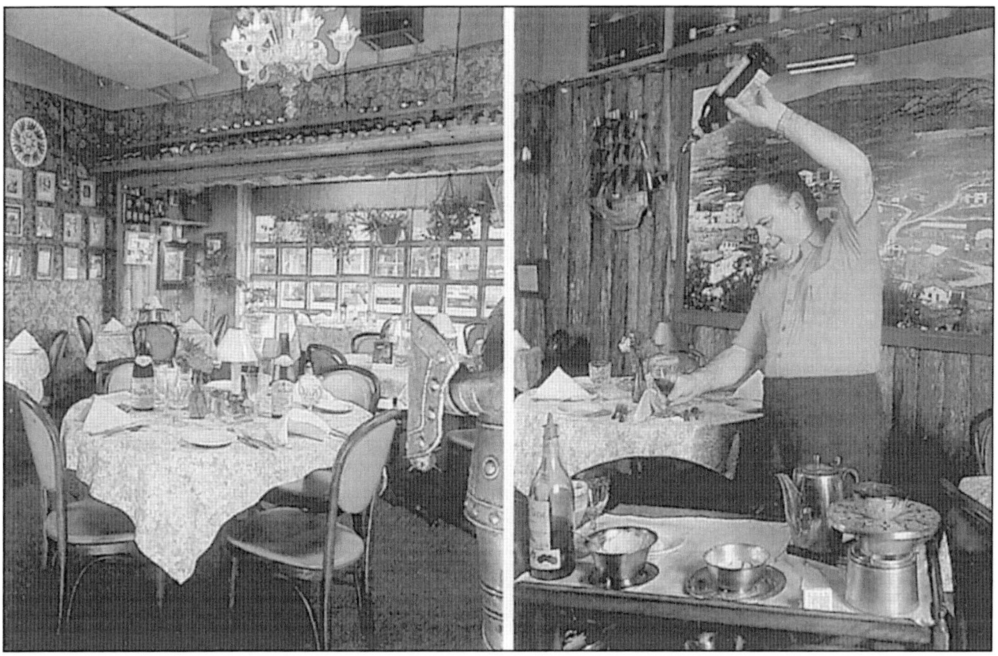

The Old Spain Restaurant and Lounge was well known as one of the best and most expensive restaurants in Hollywood. Its location at 2333 Hollywood Boulevard is now occupied by One Night Stan's Jazz Club.

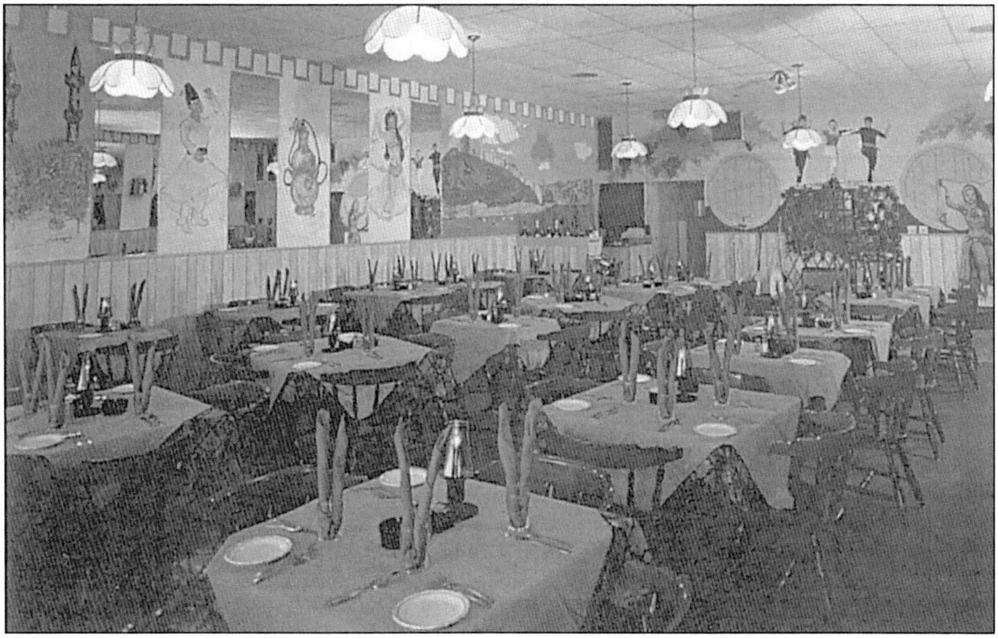

The Istanbul Restaurant, shown here in its original location at 2316 Hollywood Boulevard, later relocated to 707 North Broadwalk. Hosts Ali and Rita offered specialties such as flaming shish kebabs, moussaka, stuffed grape leaves, and roast lamb. Belly dancing provided entertainment with a middle eastern flavor.

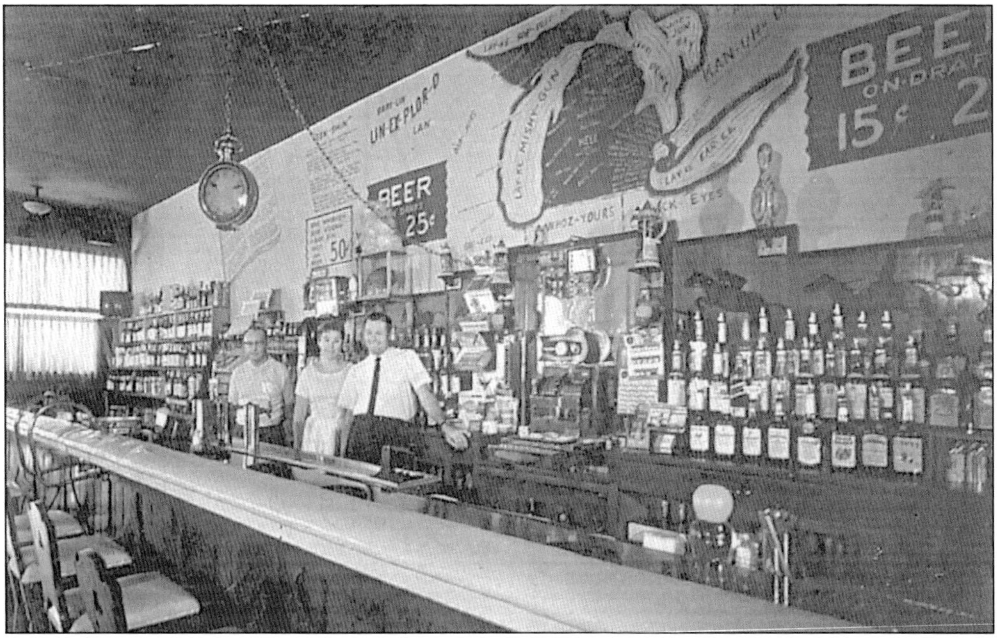

The Tally-Ho Bar, located at 112 South Twentieth Avenue, proclaimed itself the Michigan headquarters of South Florida and had the map on the wall to prove it. Opened in 1937 by Eddie and Helena Frank, the Tally-Ho was hosted by Paul Trussel and Ray Speed in the early 1960s. Beer on draft came in 15¢- and 25¢-sizes.

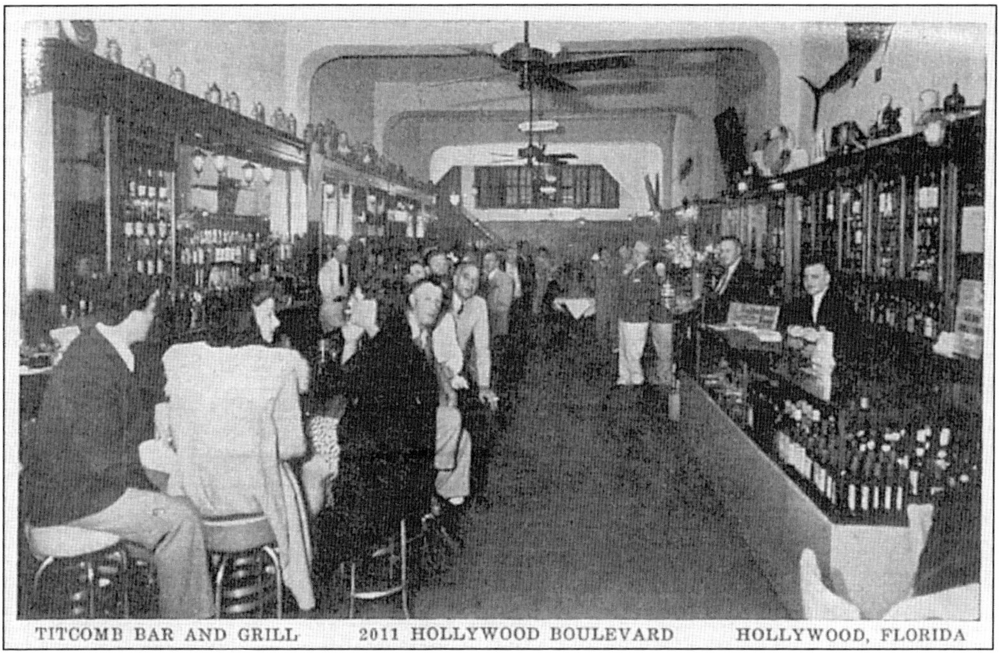

The Titcomb Bar and Grill, located at 2011 Hollywood Boulevard, boasted the largest bar of its kind in the country. The 65-foot-long bar was constructed of Italian marble and Philippine mahogany. L.B. Titcomb was president of the enterprise, while his wife, Elizabeth, was its secretary-treasurer.

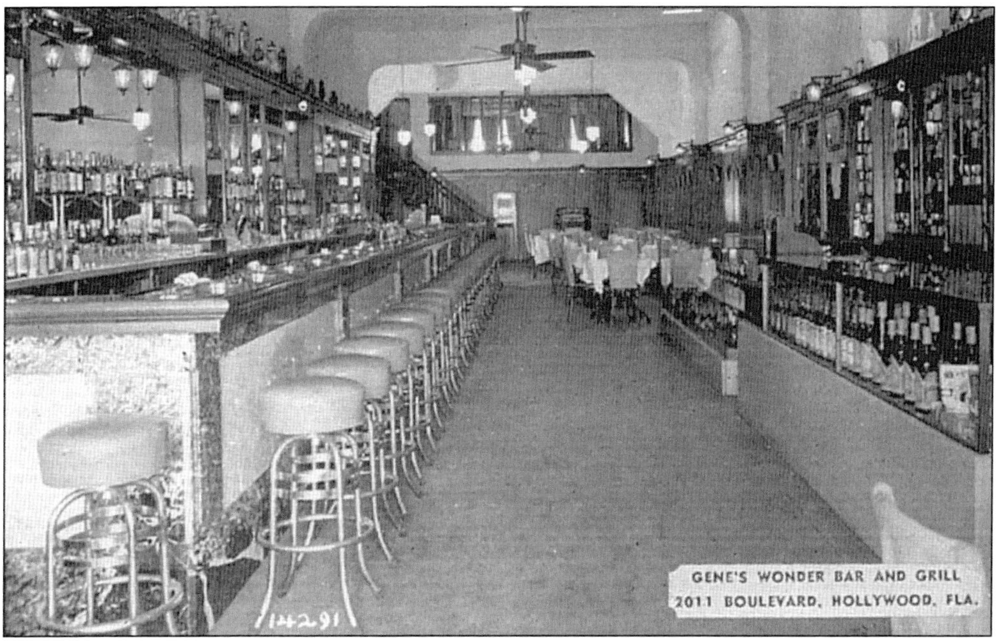

In later years Gene Smith took over this establishment, renaming it Gene's Wonder Bar and Grill. The famous bar remained intact. Today this site is a parking lot next to the Suntrust Bank building.

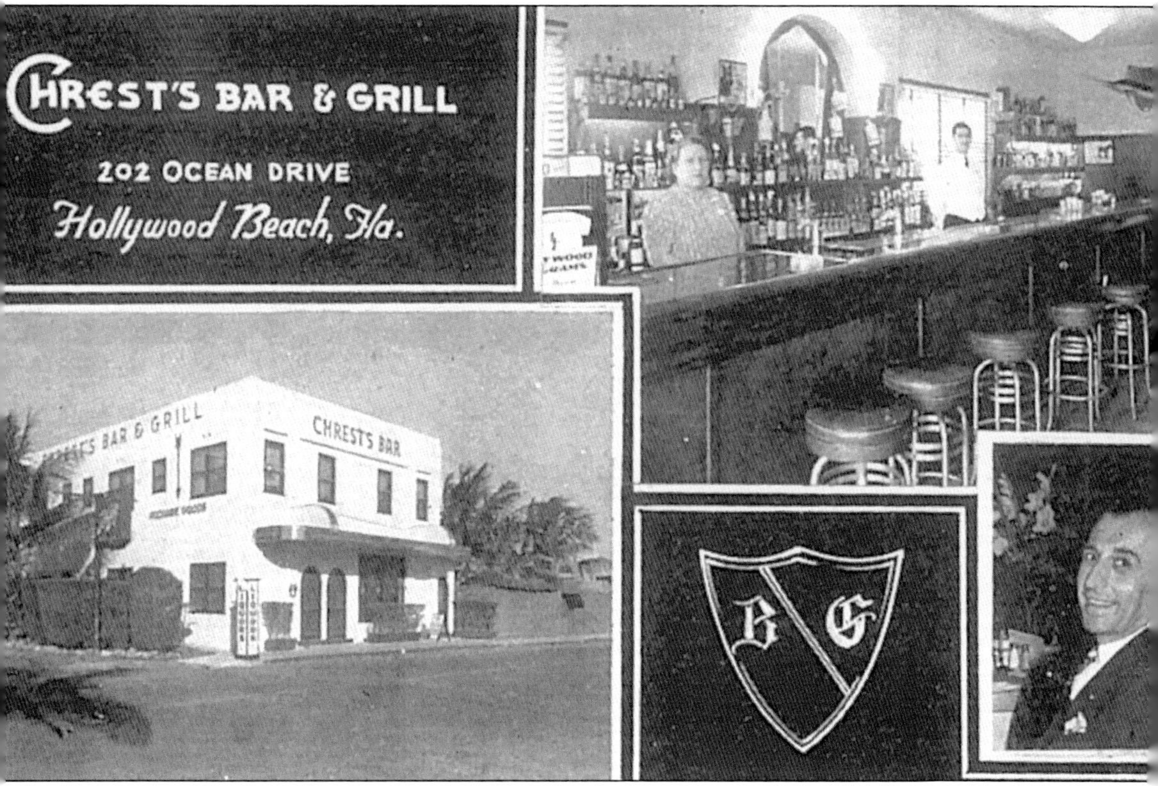

Mike Chrest managed the Tangerine Tea Room on Hollywood Beach until the 1926 hurricane destroyed it. He opened his own "Hotel Grill" in 1927 and remained in the restaurant business for over 20 years. During WW II Chrest's Bar and Grill at 202 Ocean Drive was a favorite of men in every branch of the armed forces. It was conveniently located just across the street from the Hollywood Beach Hotel, which had been taken over as a Naval Officers Indoctrination school. Mike won the respect and gratitude of the all-night Coast Guard sentry patrols by carrying urns of hot coffee to them each night through the unlit beach streets during the entire war period. He later estimated that he had served 10,000 servicemen. The walls of two rooms in his restaurant were covered with the scrawled and printed names of 3,500 customers, and some had even drawn war ships, planes, and class insignia. Servicemen saluted him as one of Hollywood's unsung wartime heroes.

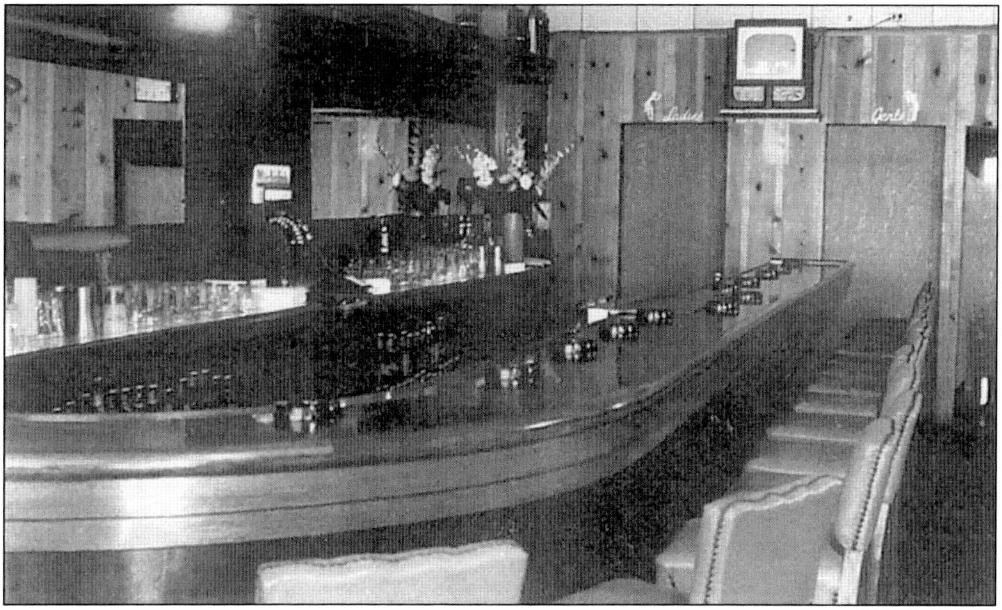

Charlie's Bar, located at 1934 Harrison Street near the downtown circle, invited guests to "meet your Jersey friends" here. Sports results and television were the main attractions in what hosts Doris and Charlie Sylvestre called "the friendliest bar in Hollywood."

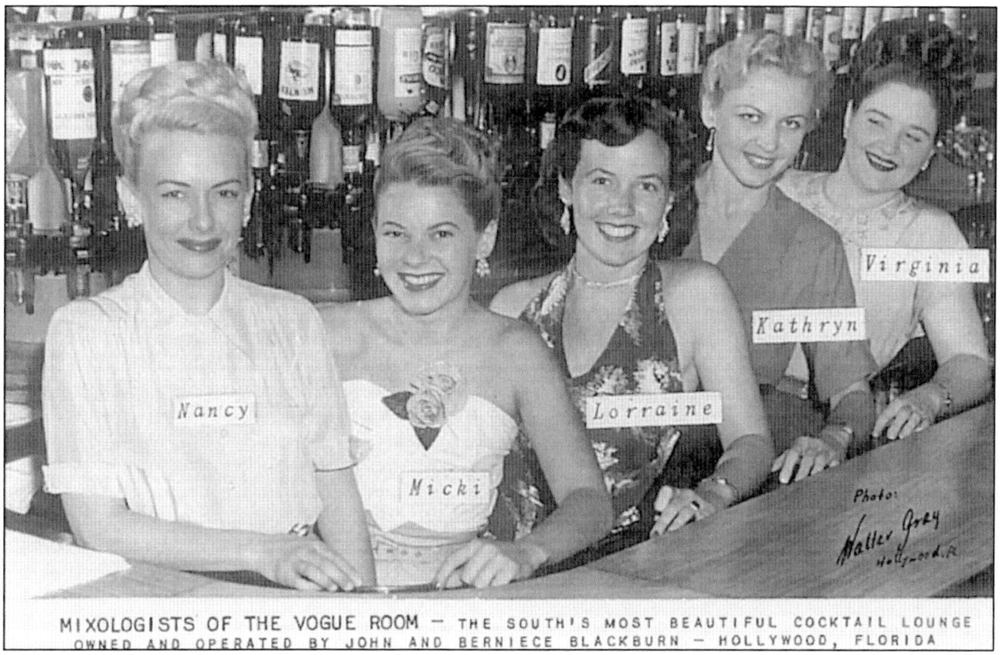

The lovely mixologists of the Vogue Room—Nancy, Micki, Lorraine, Kathryn, and Virginia—graced its beautiful cocktail lounge. John and Berniece Blackburn owned and operated this Hollywood establishment.

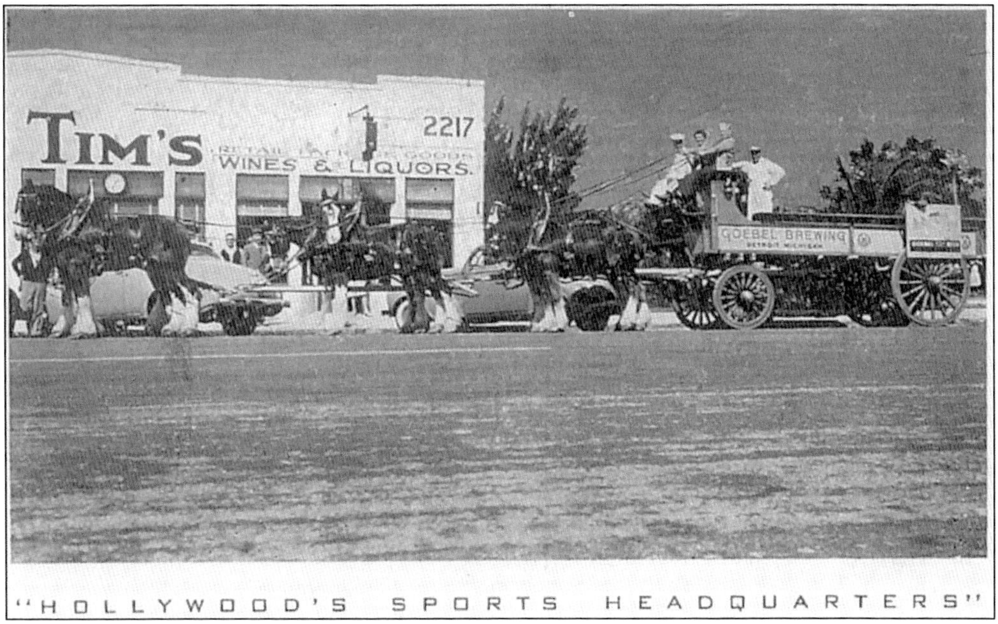

Tim's Bar and Grill at 2217 Hollywood Boulevard was a wine and liquor package store as well. Known as Hollywood's friendliest spot, it was opened by Tim and Emma Eagan right after Prohibition's repeal in 1933. The horse-drawn Goebel Brewing Company's beer wagon is shown here making a delivery.

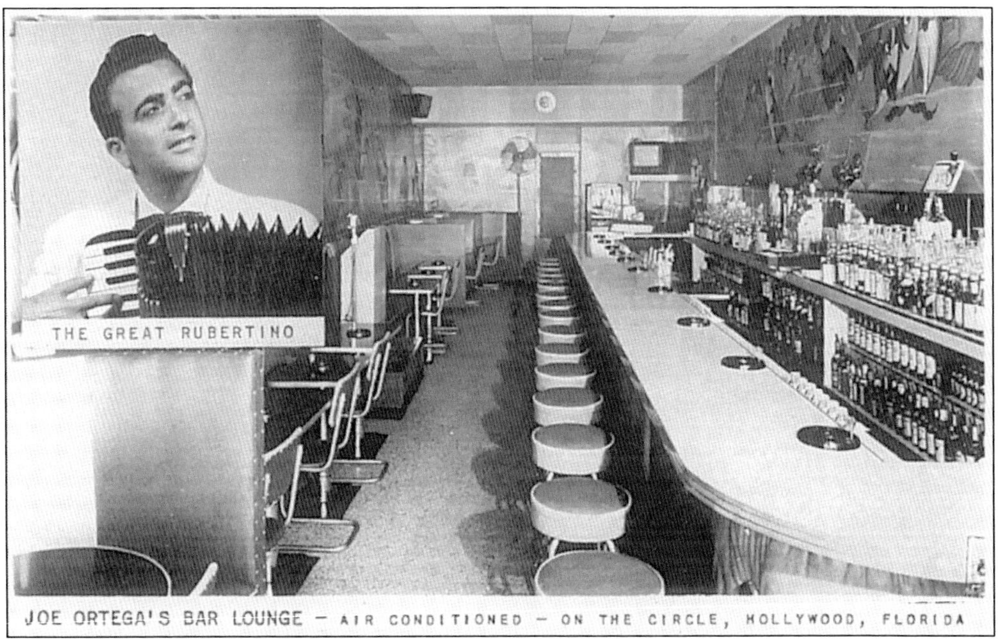

Joe Ortega's Bar Lounge was a popular spot near the downtown circle. Its air-conditioned booths and bar stools offered a welcome respite from the day's heat. The Great Rubertino entertained guests with accordion tunes.

Six

Recreation and Tourism

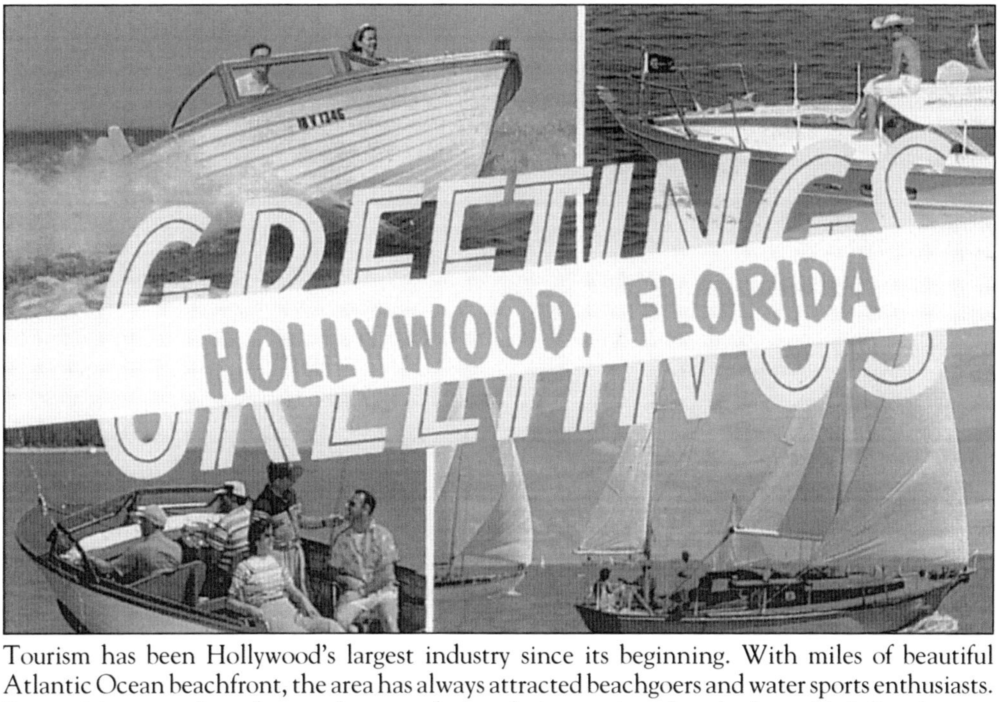

Tourism has been Hollywood's largest industry since its beginning. With miles of beautiful Atlantic Ocean beachfront, the area has always attracted beachgoers and water sports enthusiasts. Some visitors stay for only a week or two during their vacations, but the "snowbirds," as they are known, return year after year for the entire winter season. Hollywood has always been a favorite spot for French Canadians, and there are many apartment-motels, trailer courts, shops, and restaurants that announce French-speaking employees, hired to make these visitors feel right at home. There have never been any huge amusement parks in Hollywood, but the city is close to attractions in Miami and Fort Lauderdale. In fact, it is the secluded and homey nature of this small city that has endeared it to travelers over the years. Residents and sight-seers alike utilize the same recreation facilities.

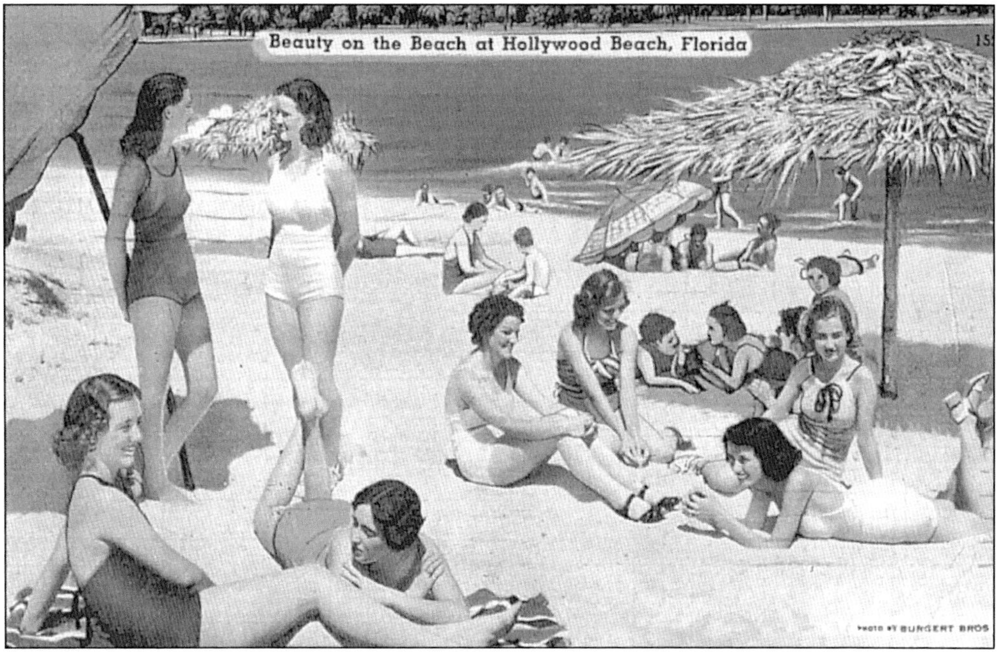

Beauty abounds on the beaches of Hollywood. Bathing suit fashions certainly have changed since this 1940s view! Many of these lovely ladies enjoyed wearing their summer sandals in the sand. This postcard touts the sugary sand gleaming in the mild February sun.

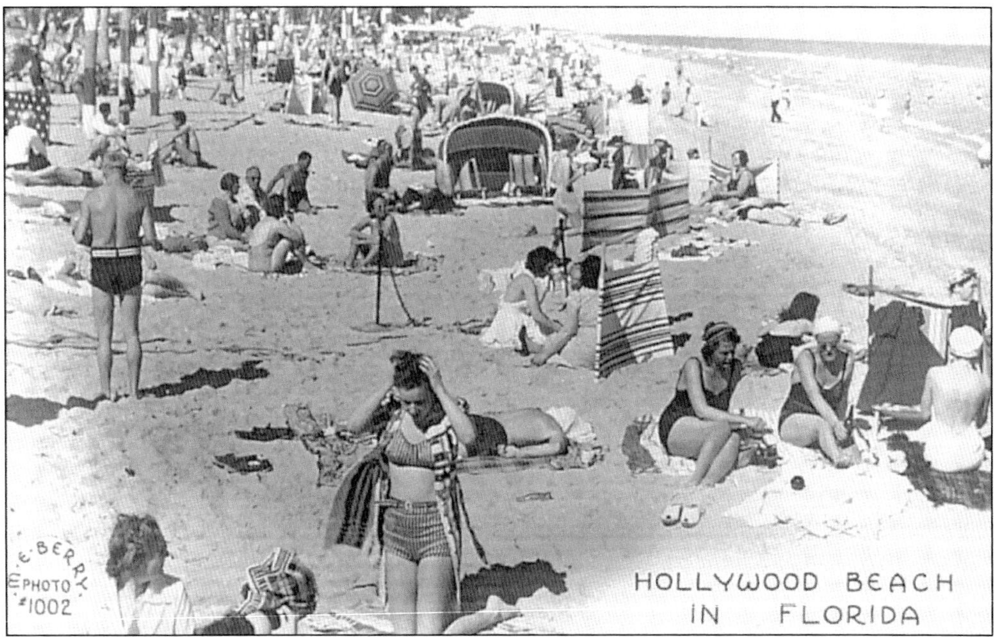

A few years later, the thatched umbrellas were replaced by canvas cabana chairs, which could be taken inside to protect them from hurricane winds. Two-piece bathing suits made their debut, and the public beaches became much more crowded.

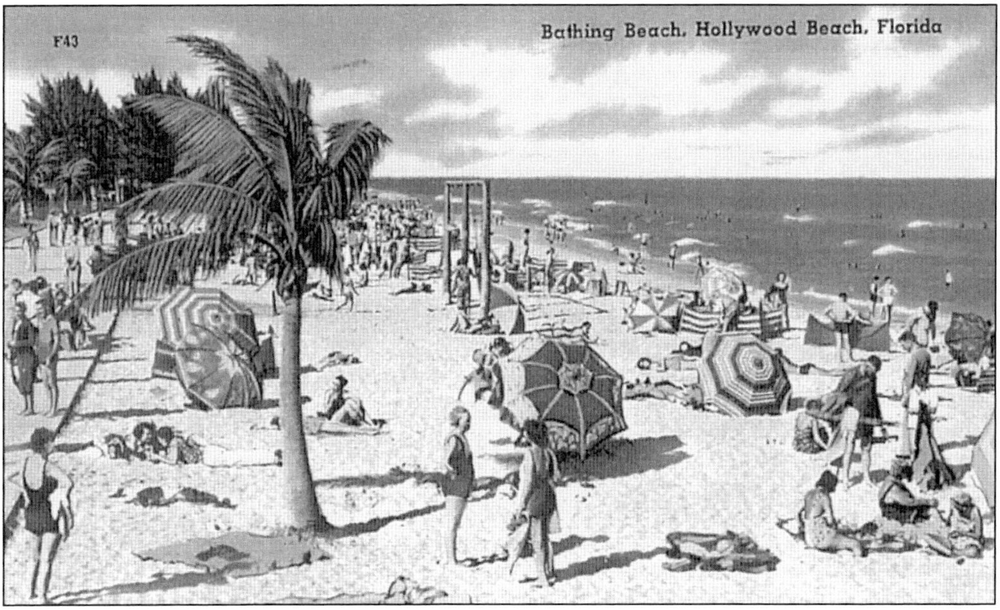

The wide, concrete Broadwalk can be seen at the far left in this 1940s scene. Unlike many beaches that have wooden boardwalks, Hollywood has always had a more formal strolling area, known as the Broadwalk.

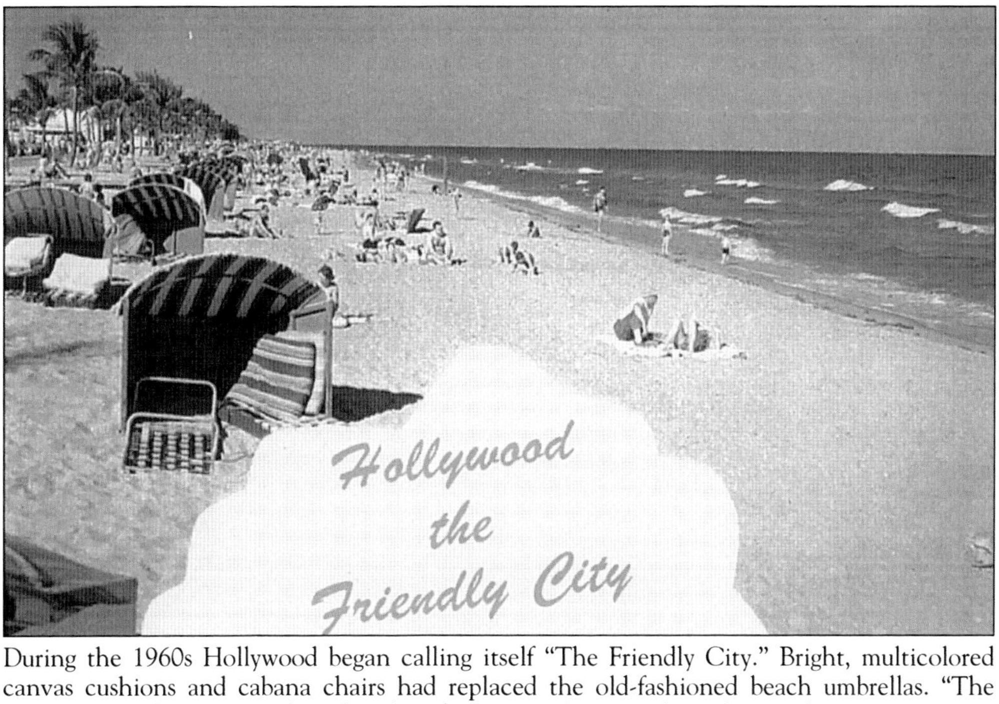

During the 1960s Hollywood began calling itself "The Friendly City." Bright, multicolored canvas cushions and cabana chairs had replaced the old-fashioned beach umbrellas. "The beach is grand," wrote Beth to her friend in Massachusetts, "but what sunburns you can get down here!"

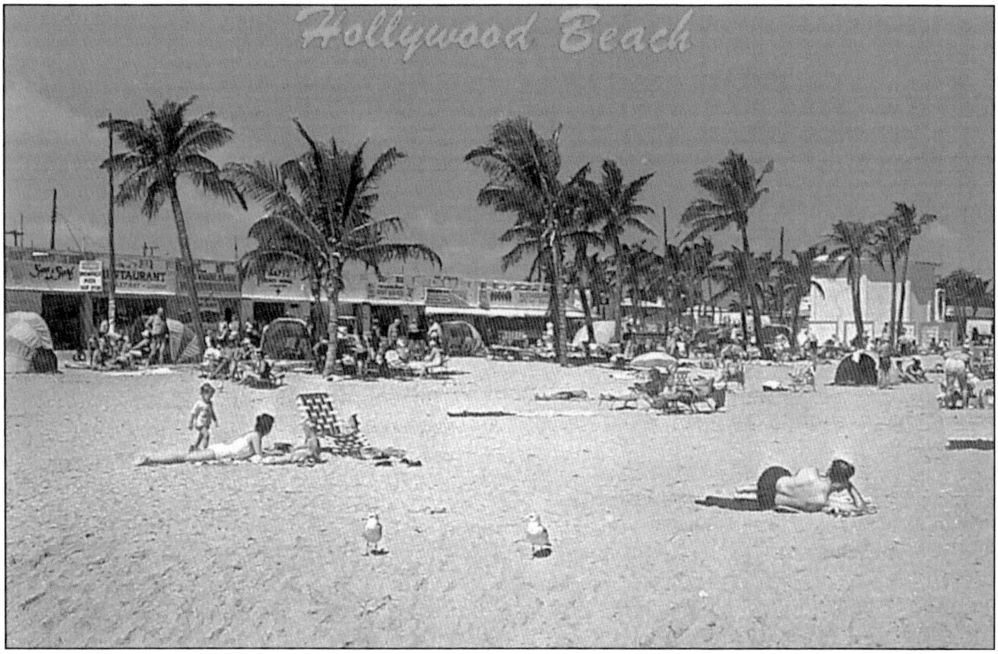

In the 1960s the shops along the Broadwalk began to be almost as popular as the beach itself. The Sun and Surf Shop and several sand-side eateries can be seen in the background. While residents knew better than to feed the seagulls, the birds were thrilled with tourists, who offered delicacies such as french fries and popcorn.

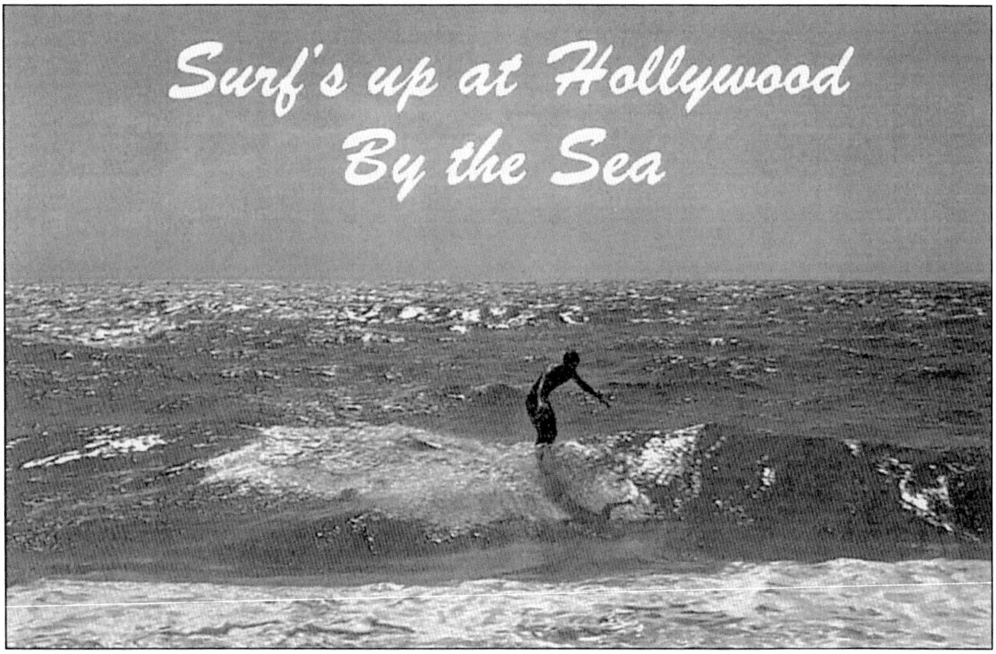

Some hardy visitors tried their luck at surfing, though the waves along Hollywood Beach were often too small for an exciting ride.

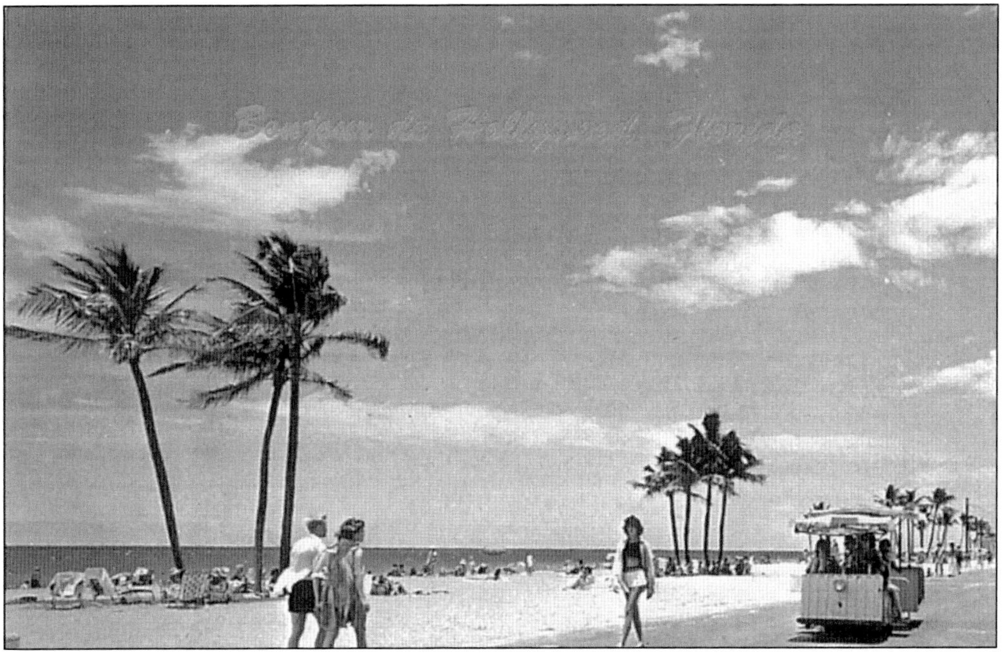

Small carts were handy for transporting tired beachgoers from one end of the Broadwalk to the other. "Bonjour de Hollywood, Florida, la place prefere des Canadiens" (Hello from Hollywood, Florida, the place preferred by Canadians) proclaims this postcard.

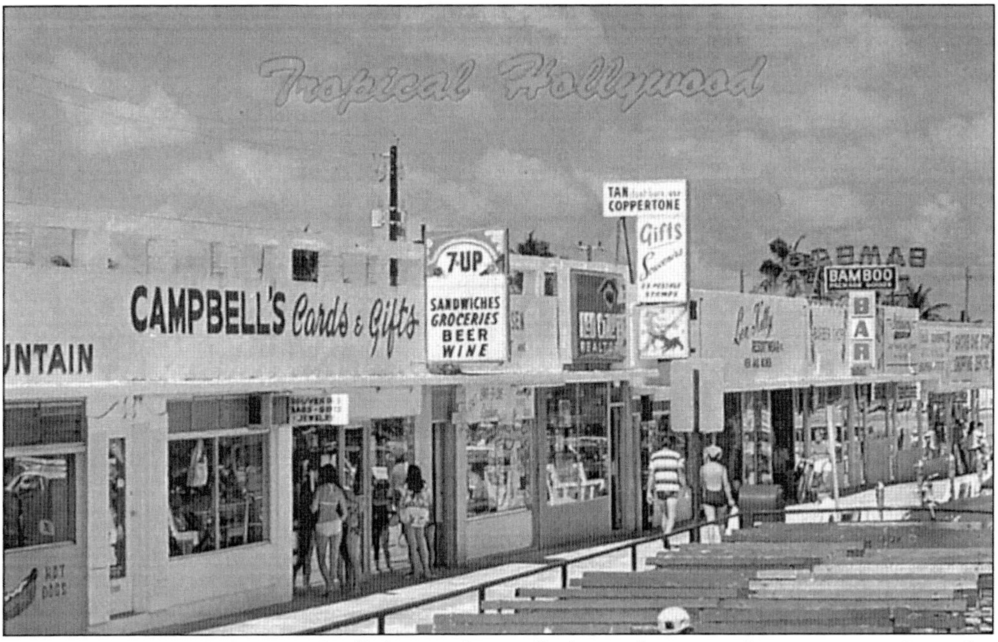

Johnson Street and the Broadwalk has traditionally been the main shopping area along the beach. Visitors have fond memories of Campbell's Cards and Gifts, the Bamboo Bar, and other shops. Today many stores are vacating to make room for city projects. The municipal pool now stands to the left of this scene.

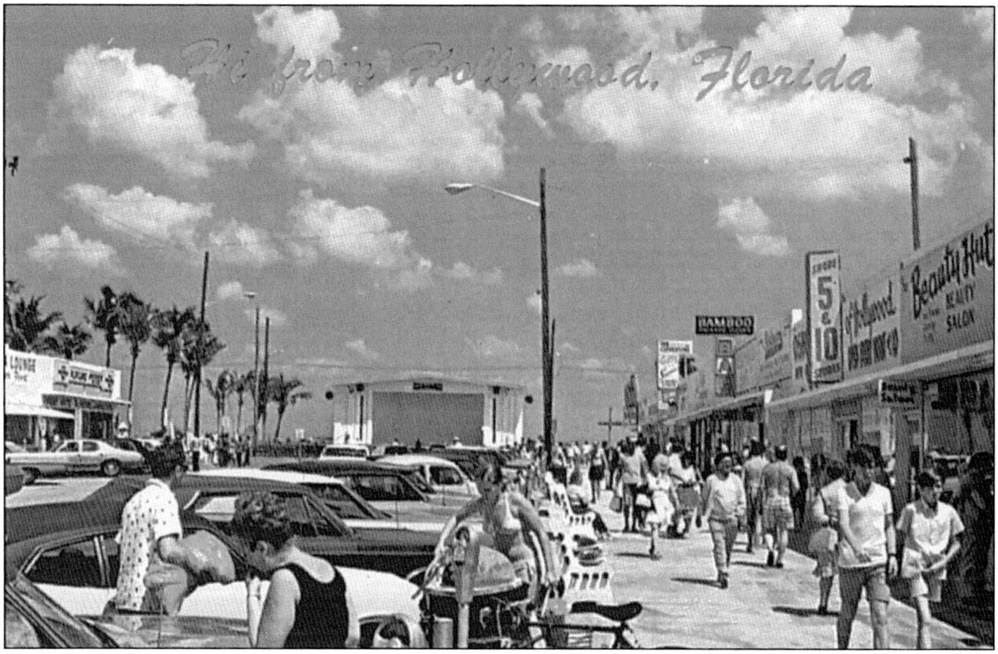

Local teenagers have always gathered along Johnson Street. Children with beach toys and shoppers in informal dress add to the relaxed vacation ambiance. The shops pictured on this early 1960s postcard include the Beauty Hut Beauty Salon and the Shore 5 & 10.

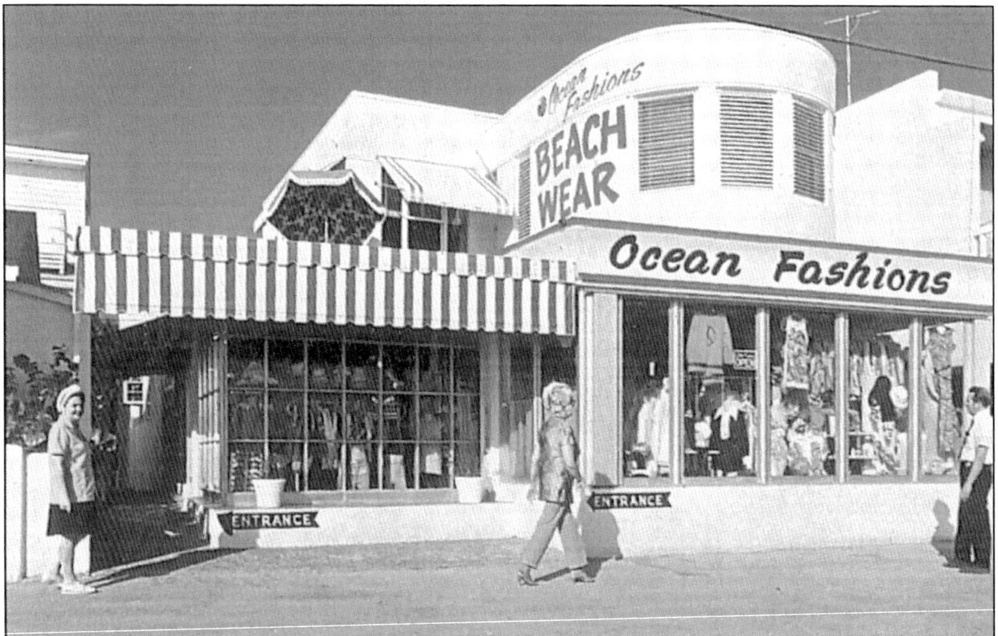

Ocean Fashions on the Broadwalk, located at 1504 North Surf Road just north of Johnson Street, was a popular, trendy shop. Brand-name beachwear, sportswear, swimsuits, and shoes, as well as hats and jewelry, were its specialties.

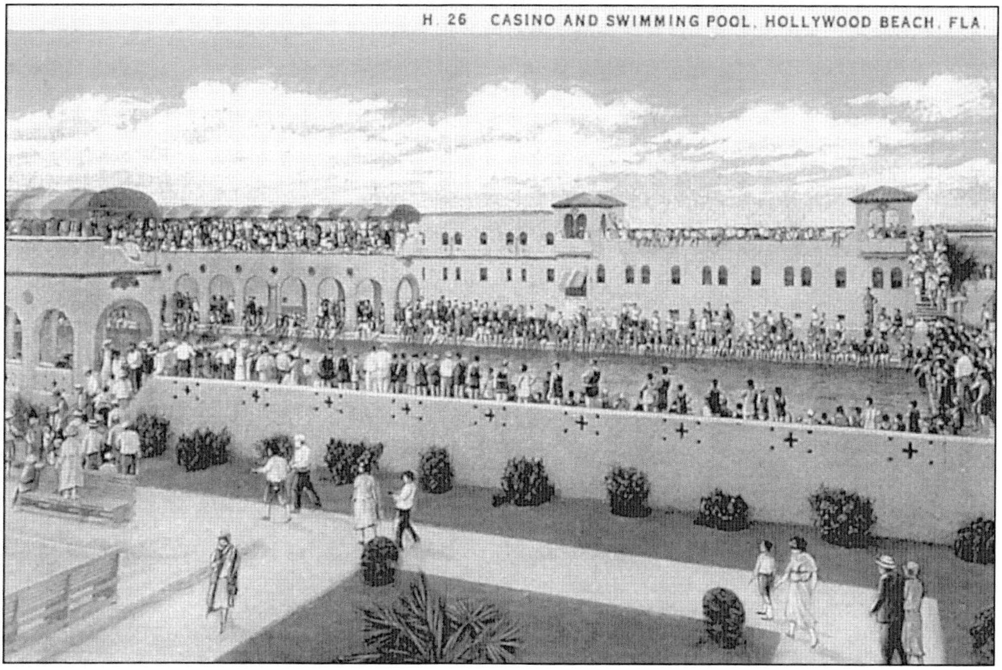

The Hollywood Casino and swimming pool was built in 1924 at a cost of $250,000. During the late 1920s and early 1930s, Katherine "Minnow" Rawls trained in this pool. She brought fame to Hollywood when she won national AAU titles in diving and swimming at the tender age of 14. She went on to win events in the 1932 Olympics.

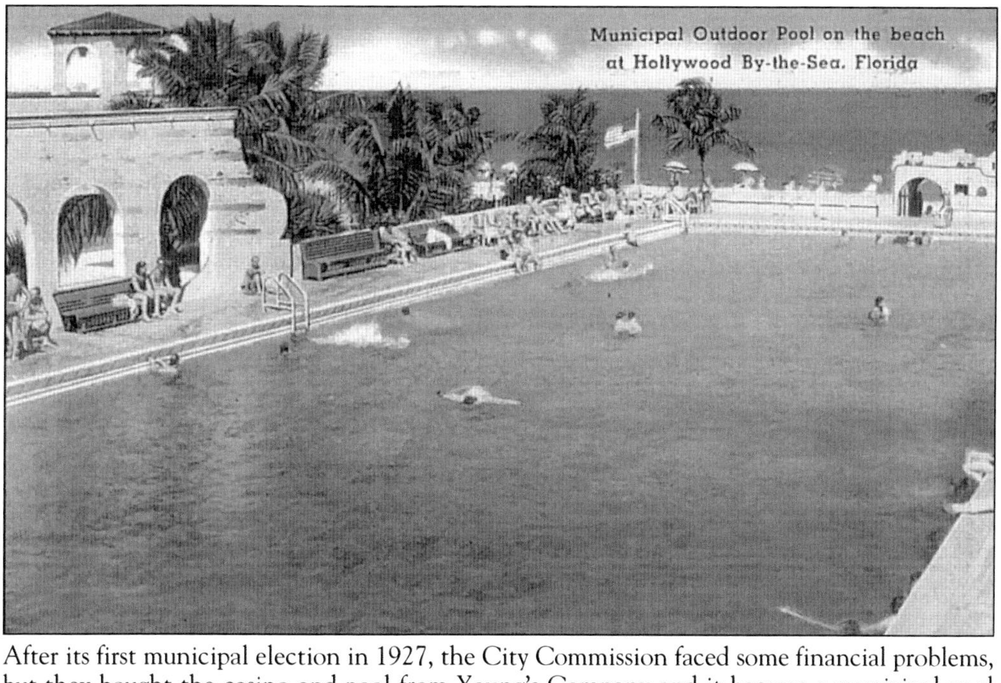

After its first municipal election in 1927, the City Commission faced some financial problems, but they bought the casino and pool from Young's Company and it became a municipal pool overlooking the beach. The distinctive, arched walls of the old casino can still be seen in this late 1940s view.

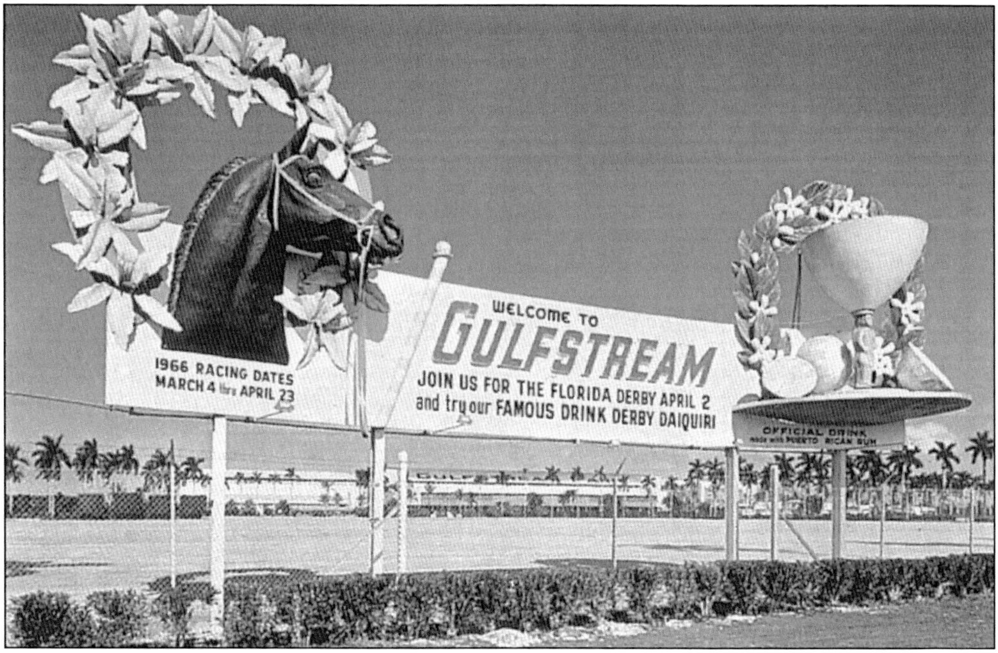

Just south of Hollywood in its sister city of Hallandale, Gulfstream Race Course Park has been a favorite entertainment spot for residents and tourists alike for over 50 years. This billboard lists the 1966 racing dates as March 4 through April 23, and Florida Derby Day as April 2. Doesn't the Derby Daiquiri look grand?

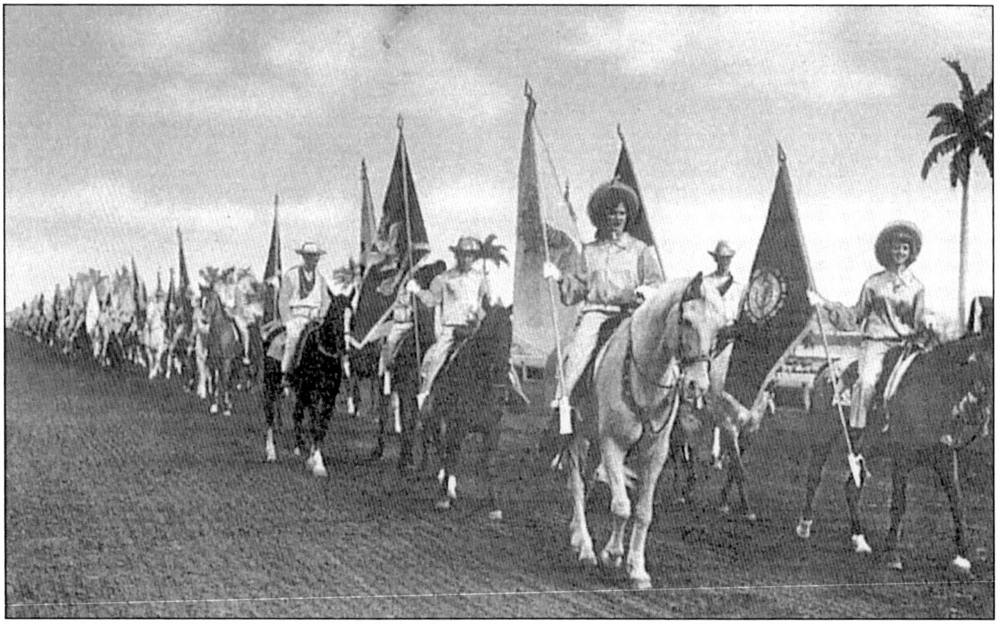

The Parade of States was an annual tradition. The extravaganza was held on Florida Derby Day at Gulfstream Park. Along with viewing a display of the flags of "all 48 states" borne by riders on horseback, the racetrack audience was serenaded by state songs.

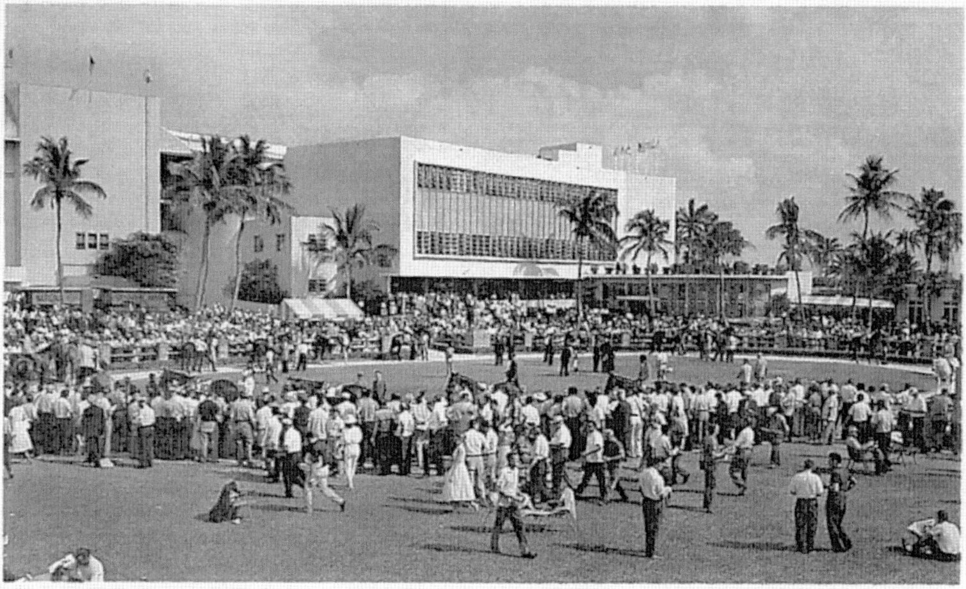

Gulfstream Park's Million Dollar Clubhouse, Paddock Area, Hallandale, Florida

In 1938 Jack Horning, owner of a Miami construction firm, brought thoroughbred horse racing to Gulfstream. Sonja Henie, a movie star and ice skating champion, cut the ribbon opening the track and 15,000 people attended the opening. But after three days, the track was declared bankrupt because there were more sight-seers than bettors and the take was very small.

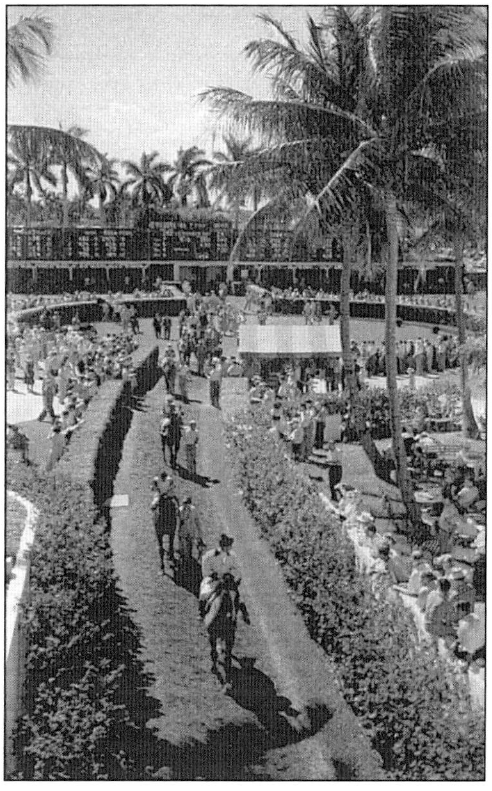

In December of 1944 the track reopened under the leadership of florist James Donn Senior, who became its president and principal stockholder. Gulfstream went on to become Florida's most successful racetrack. This view shows horses and jockeys leaving the paddock area, watched by a crowd of admirers.

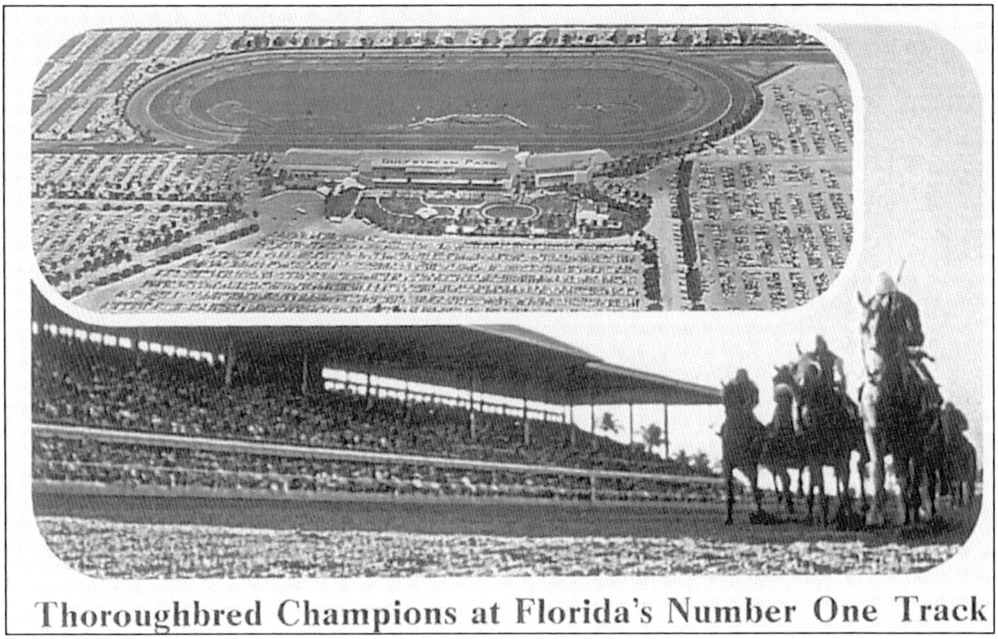

In the 1940s Miami's Tropical Park Racecourse was controlled by gangsters. When James Donn applied for Gulfstream's state racing license, approval was held up on "technicalities." A speech, deriding "racetrack politics," was made at the Hollywood Rotary Club and reported in the *Fort Lauderdale News*. Governor Holland ordered the red tape cut and Gulfstream opened on schedule.

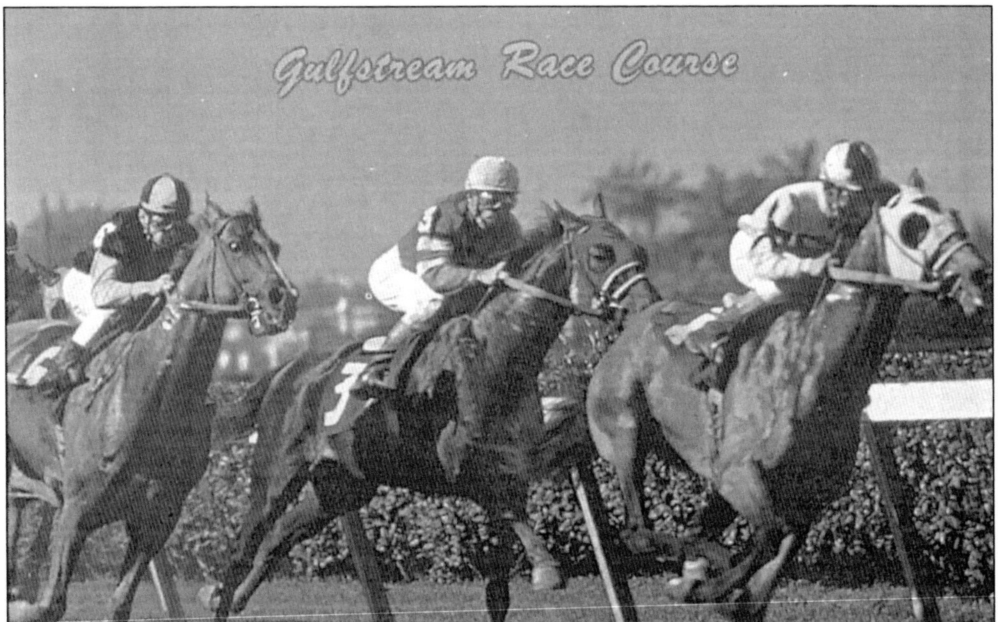

Gulfstream has long been home to the Florida Derby and the $125,000 Gulfstream Park Handicap. This grueling, 1.25-mile race is truly a test of champions. Its winner is crowned the national leader.

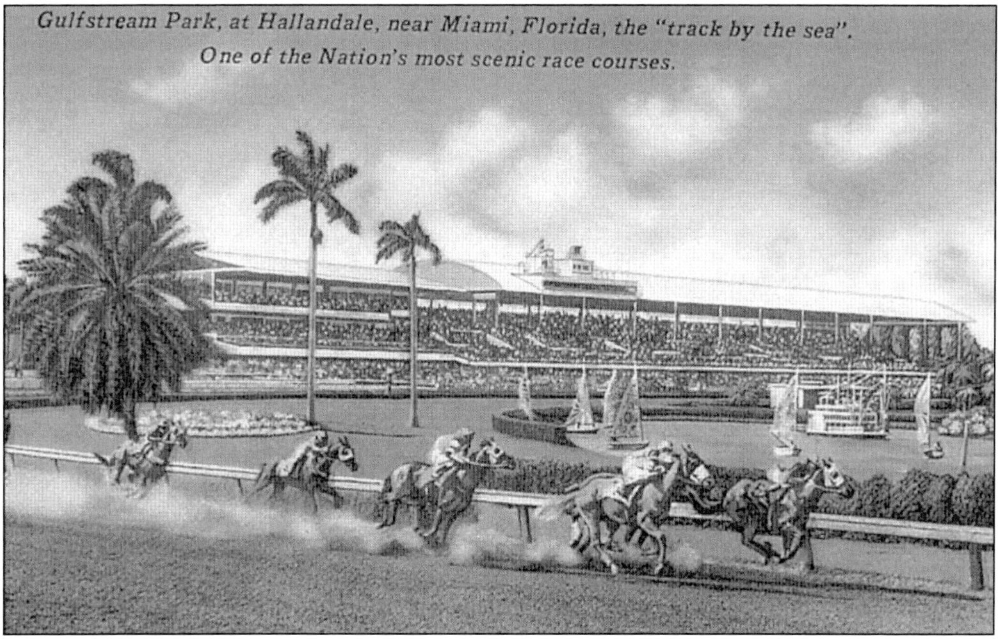

Gulfstream has always been known as a scenic racetrack. This 1940s postcard shows its unusual grandstand. The only cantilever stand in America, it had no posts to obstruct the view. Gulfstream boasted the greatest seating capacity of any track in Florida.

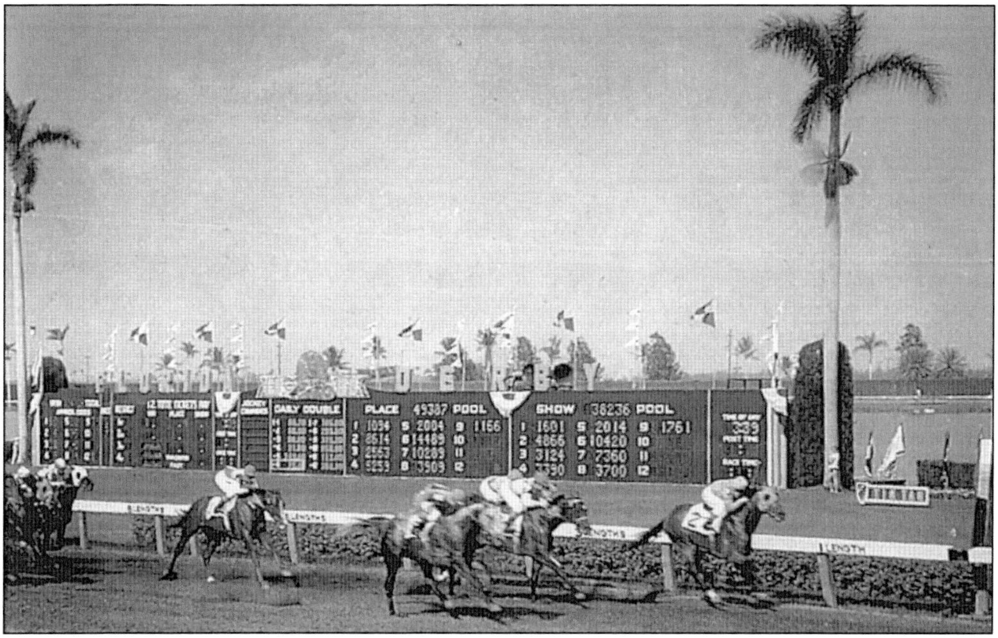

Horses cross the finish line at the Florida Derby during the early 1960s. The famous scoreboard kept track of each racehorse's standing during the event. Through the late 1980s a flea market used Gulfstream's grounds off season. Today racing is a family activity, with special events for children and rock concerts for teens.

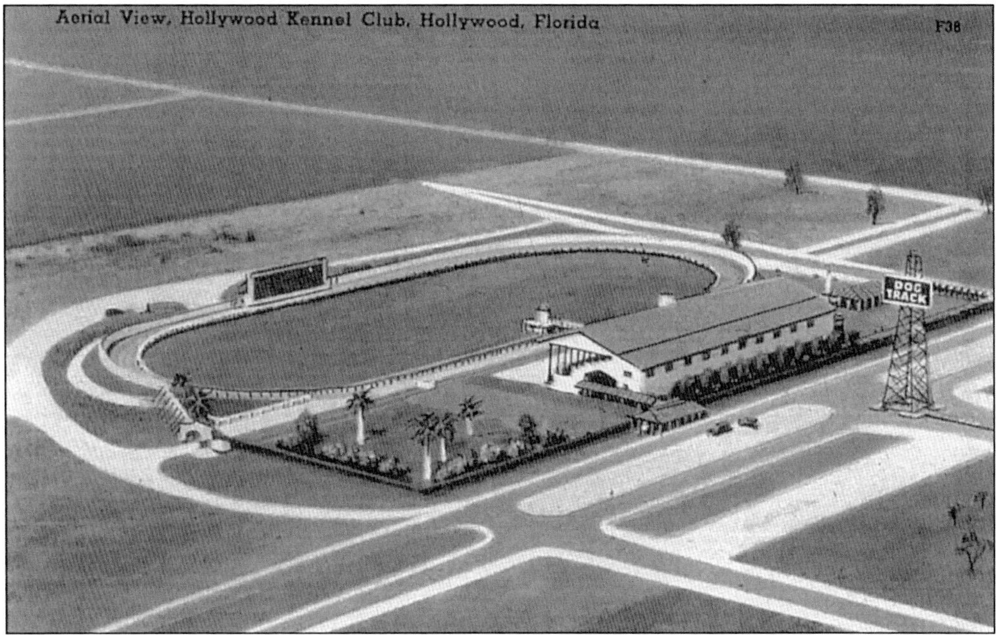

The Hollywood Kennel Club still occupies its original site, one mile south of Hollywood, on Federal Highway just over the Hallandale town line. In 1934 its voters approved the establishment of a dog track featuring pari-mutuel betting. Its opening day slogan was "The Aristocrat of Dog Tracks."

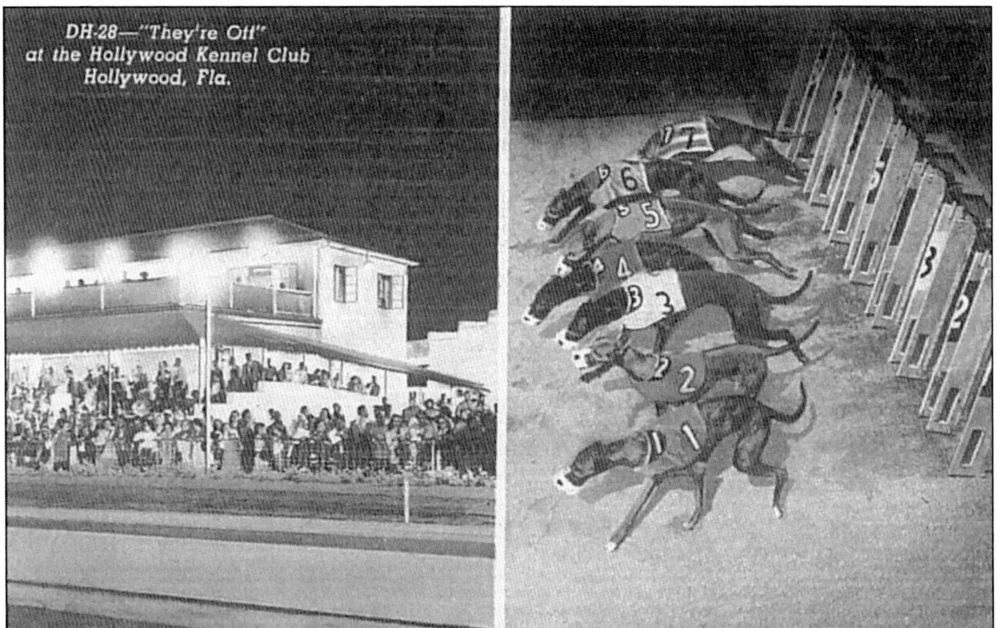

December 12, 1934, the Kennel Club's opening night, was one of the coldest in Hollywood's history, with near-freezing temperatures. Even so, 12,000 dedicated racing fans turned out and bet exactly $12,000. There was no guessing when it came to declaring the winner; the Electric Eye for photo finishes made the results official.

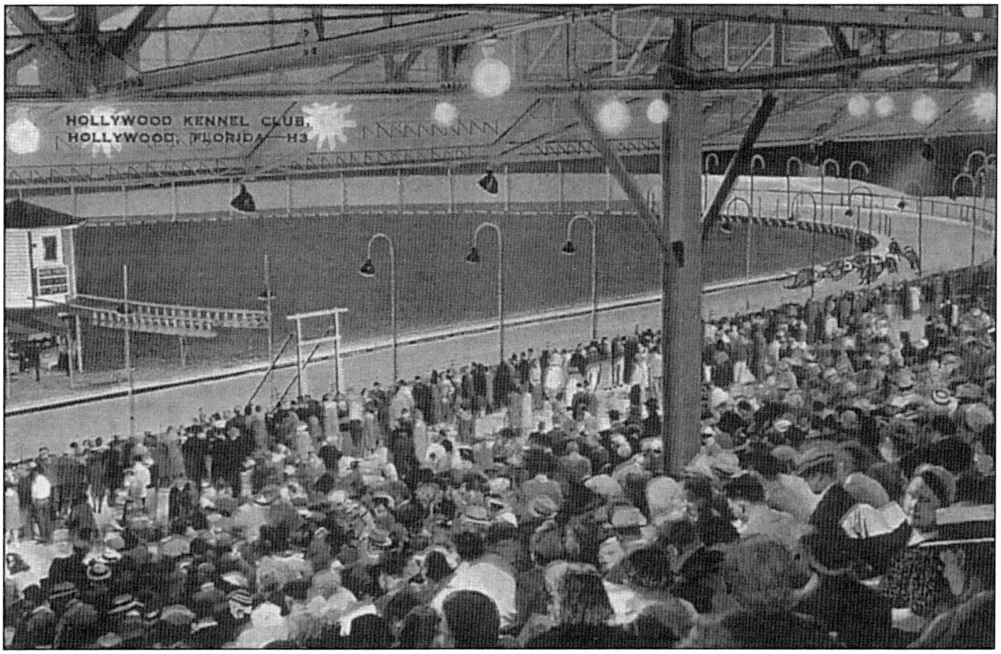

Traditionally a night sport, greyhound racing necessitated modern lighting during the 1940s. This postcard's inscription reads as follows: "Watching these graceful fleet greyhound thoroughbreds chasing their elusive rabbit, the smart set of this country is to be found at the kennels."

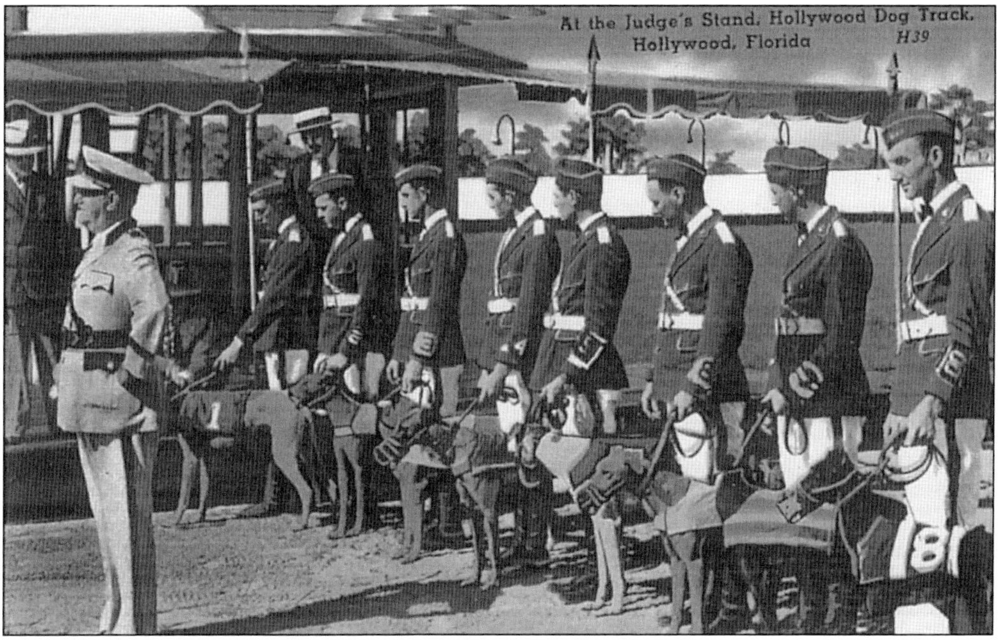

The greyhounds pose with their handlers at the Judge's Stand in this classic view at the Hollywood Kennel Club. Though the track closed temporarily during WW II, races continue to be held there today. The Kennel Club's Hollywood International Classic is still considered to be the superior bowl of dog racing events.

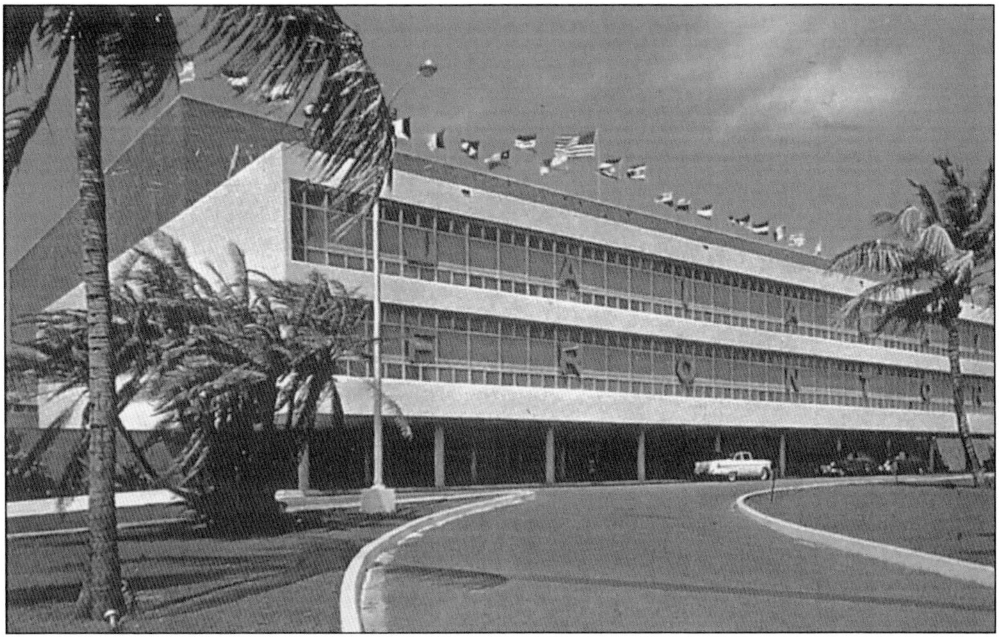

The Dania Jai Alai Fronton, located just north of Hollywood, was opened in 1953 by former circus owner Roy McAndrews. Jai-alai, meaning "merry festival" in the Basque language, is a traditional game using a cesta (woven basket) to catch the very hard pelota (ball) and throw it against the walls of the court. *Ripley's Believe it or Not* clocked the pelota at over 180 miles per hour, making jai-alai the fastest ball game in the world.

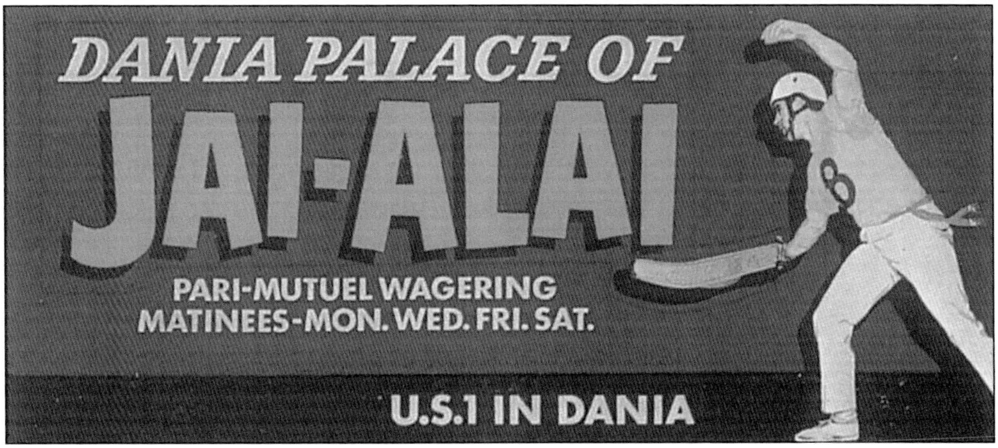

In 1970 new owners led by Steve Snyder, a former world-class sprinter, expanded the fronton to double its size, adding a luxurious clubhouse-restaurant and a bar overlooking the court. In 1980 fronton owners received a state license to operate year-round in Florida and over a million fans attended.

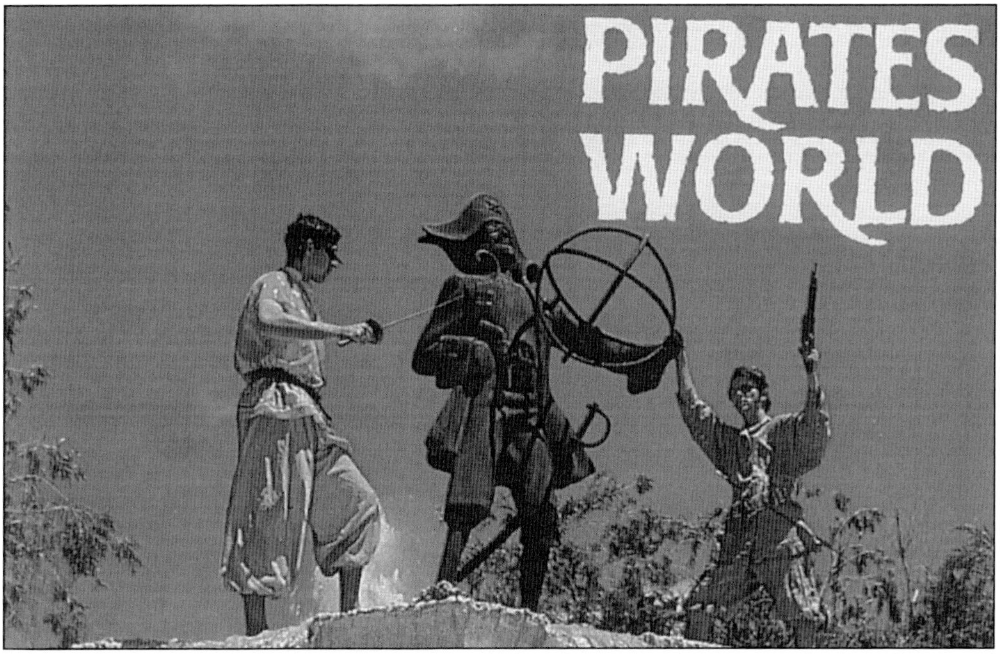

Pirates World was located on the north side of Sheridan Street, between Federal Highway and the Intracoastal Waterway. When it opened in the 1960s, it was touted as Florida's newest and most exciting amusement center.

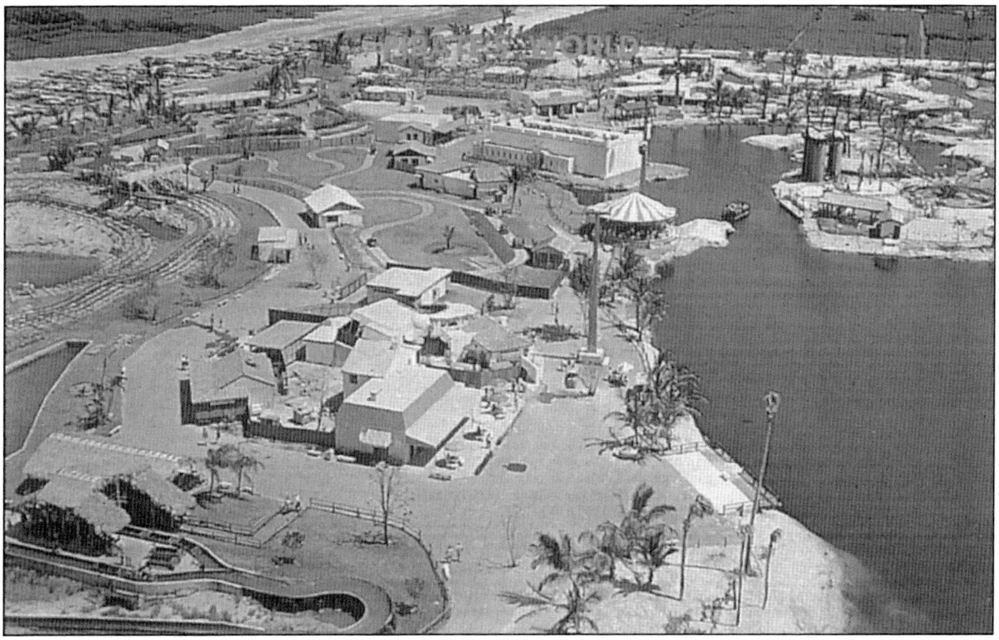

Millions of dollars went into this new park, which was built in Dania just north of the Hollywood line. This aerial view provides some geographic perspective and shows Hollywood in the background.

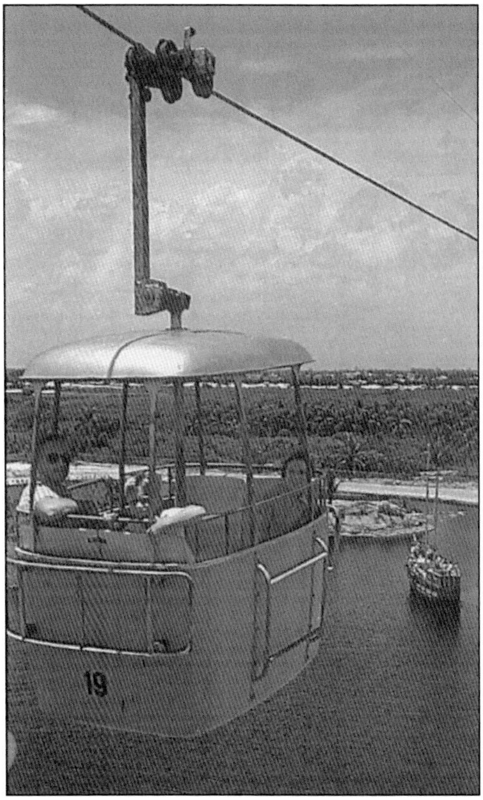

The Swiss Skytrail provided a cool and relaxing ride far above the lagoon. Many families in Hollywood have fond memories of visiting Pirates World with their children.

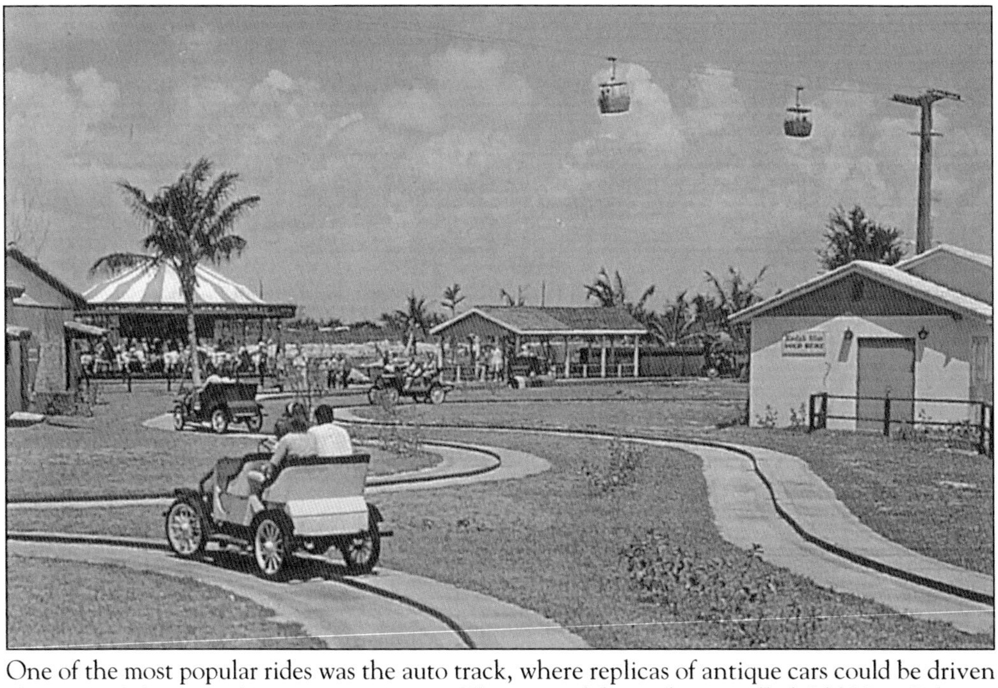

One of the most popular rides was the auto track, where replicas of antique cars could be driven along a path by even the youngest visitors. This area of the park was called Old New Orleans. The Swiss Skytrail can be seen in the background.

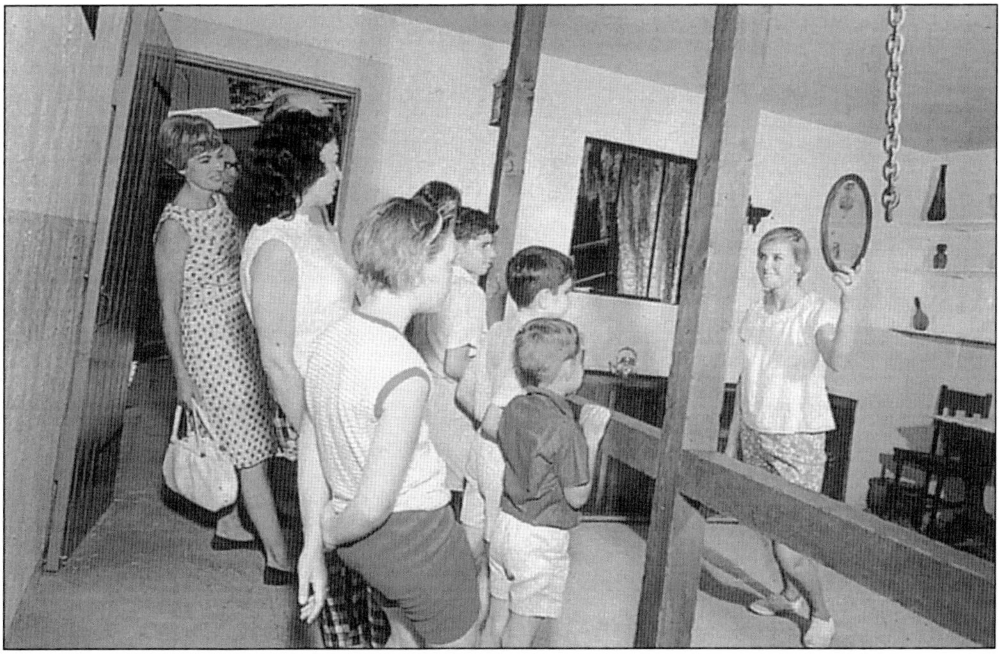

The "tilt-house," which mysteriously defied the laws of gravity, was located in the Jean Lafitte Hide Out. "It has to be seen to be believed," declares this postcard.

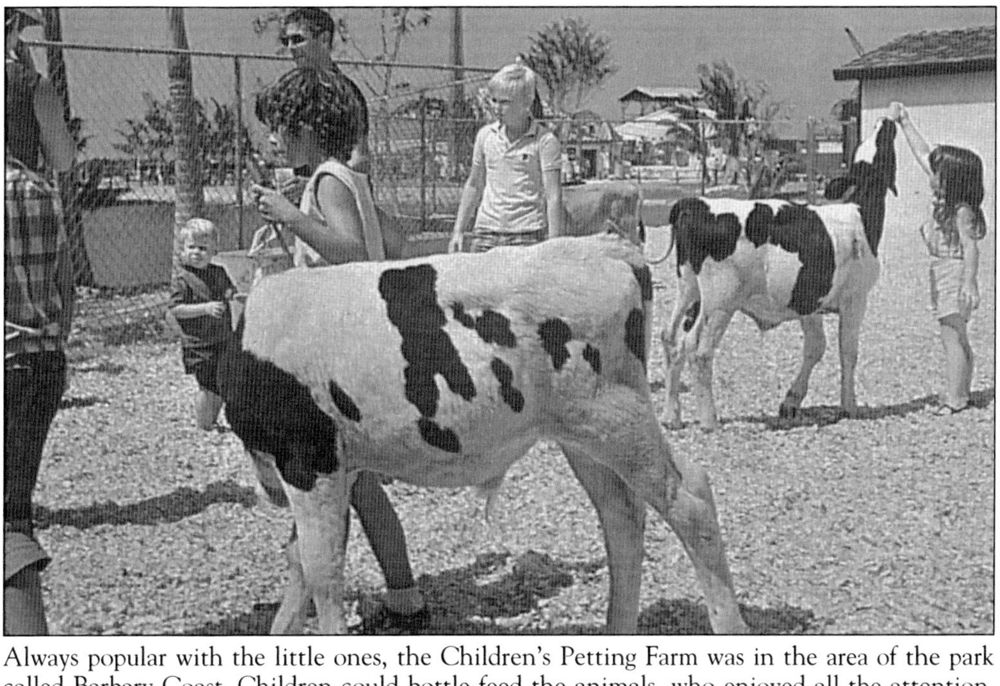

Always popular with the little ones, the Children's Petting Farm was in the area of the park called Barbary Coast. Children could bottle-feed the animals, who enjoyed all the attention. Pirates World was never a financial success and closed after only a few years. Today a housing development stands on the site.

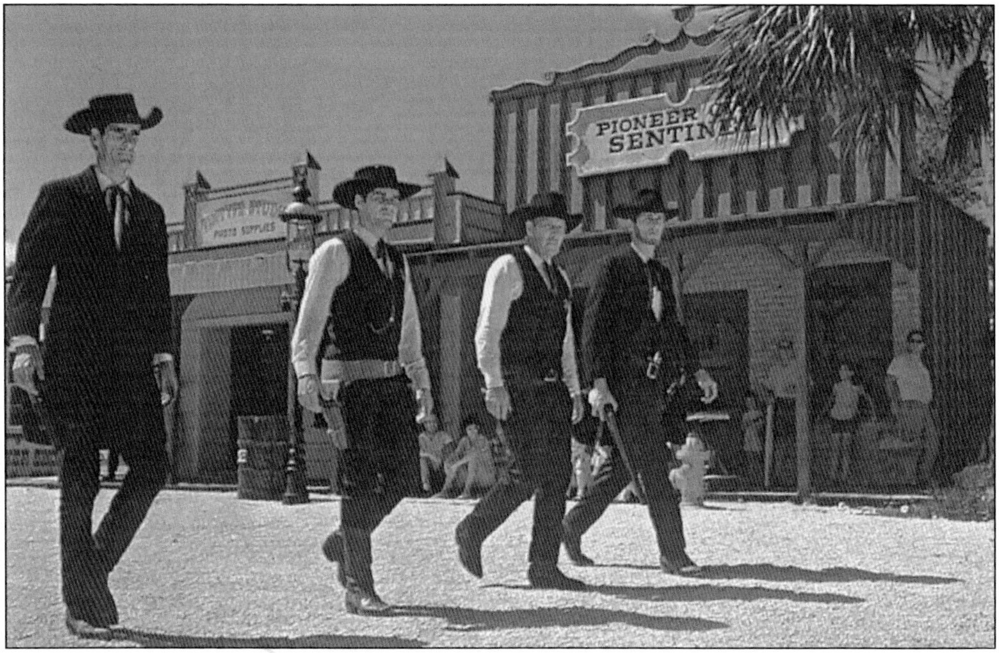

Another attempt at developing an amusement park was made in the 1960s, just 15 miles west of Hollywood. Pioneer City hoped to c¸apitalize on a cowboy theme by recreating its version of a town in the Old West.

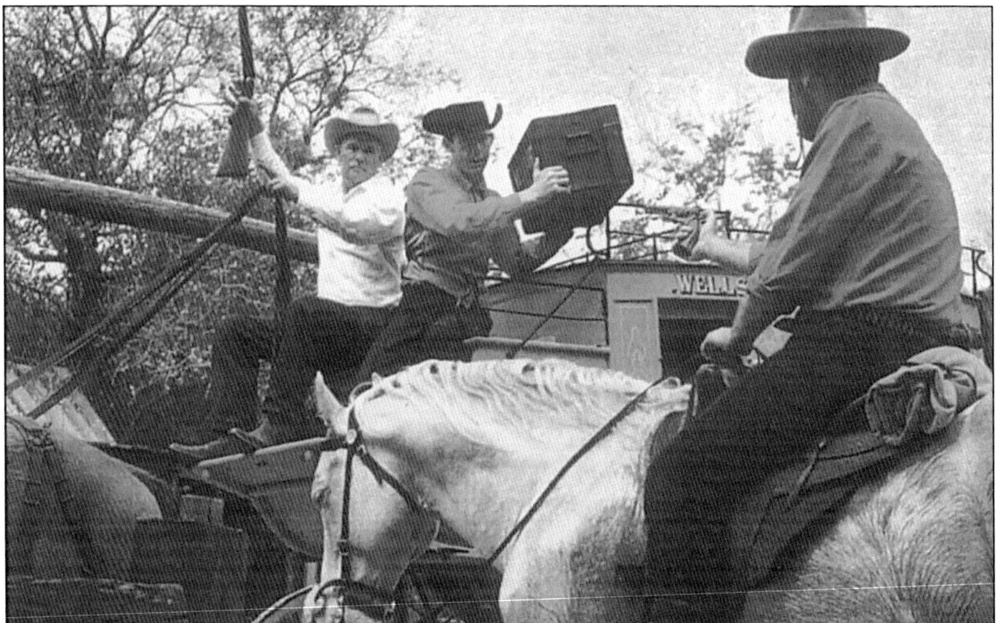

Fun-seekers could count on being caught in a "hold-up" during stagecoach rides at Pioneer City. This venture was also short-lived; it disappeared by the late 1960s.

In the natural wonder arena, the Famous Banyan Tree of Broward County was located just north of Hollywood, on the way to Fort Lauderdale. In spite of its ominous sign reading, "Danger! Do Not Touch The Tree," visitors often posed for photos next to its giant trunk.

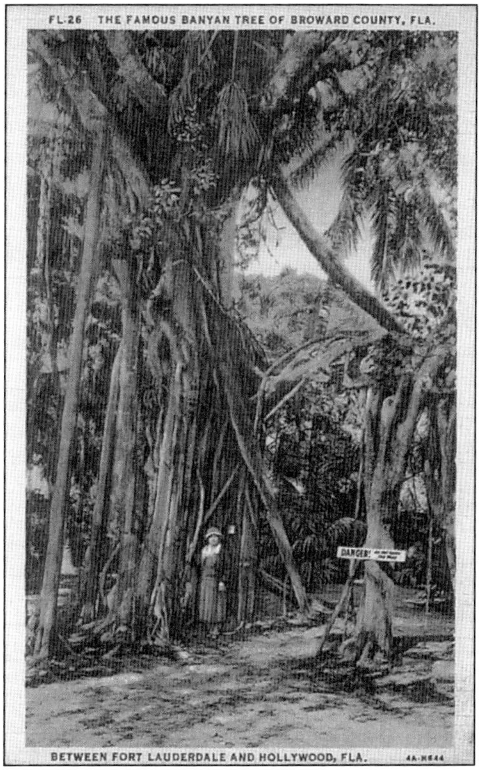

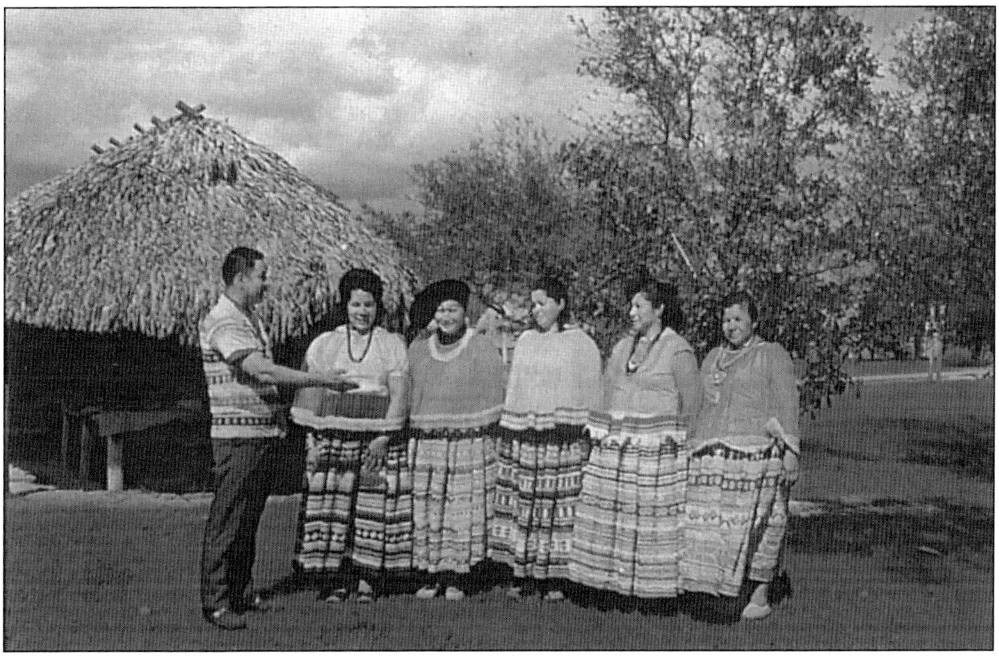

In 1926 the Seminole Reservation at Hollywood-Dania was opened. Tribe members resisted relocating from the Everglades area for many years. During the 1960s the Seminole Okalee Indian Village opened to tourists. By the 1980s Seminole Tribe Inc. was a successful enterprise, running a variety of businesses, from cigarette sales to bingo and land leases.

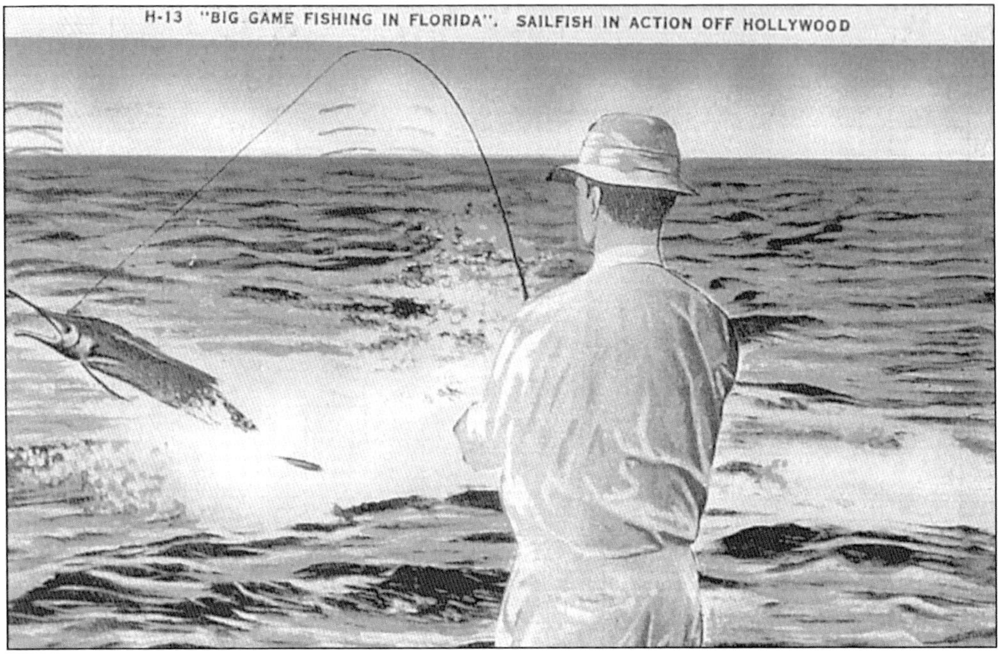

Amusement parks and tourist attractions may come and go, but the waters of the Atlantic Ocean have always provided a steady stream of recreational activities for residents and visitors alike. This 1930s postcard, produced by the Hollywood Chamber of Commerce, shows a sailfish in action.

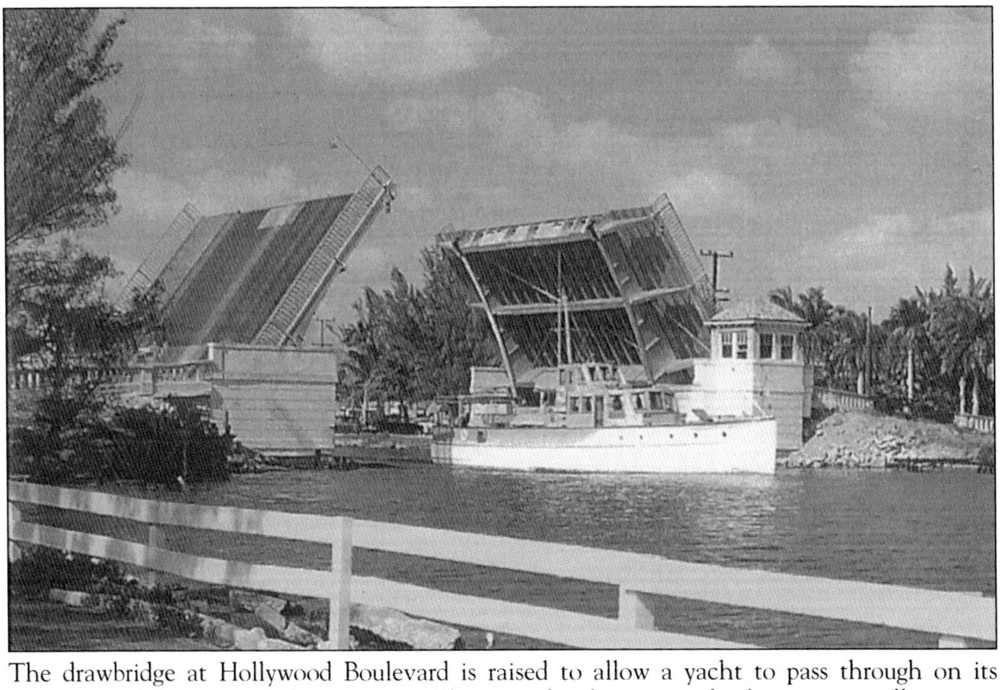

The drawbridge at Hollywood Boulevard is raised to allow a yacht to pass through on its way along the Intracoastal Waterway. This is a familiar scene for boaters as well as auto passengers traveling along the banks. The bridge serves as a friendly landmark to both arriving and departing visitors.